Word and Sacrament

Word and Sacrament

*Tracing the Theological
Movements of Reformed Worship*

Paul Galbreath

© 2024 Paul Galbreath
Foreword © 2024 Westminster John Knox Press

First edition
Published by Westminster John Knox Press
Louisville, Kentucky

24 25 26 27 28 29 30 31 32 33—10 9 8 7 6 5 4 3 2 1

All rights reserved. No part of this book may be reproduced or transmitted in any form or by any means, electronic or mechanical, including photocopying, recording, or by any information storage or retrieval system, without permission in writing from the publisher. For information, address Westminster John Knox Press, 100 Witherspoon Street, Louisville, Kentucky 40202-1396. Or contact us online at www.wjkbooks.com.

Unless otherwise indicated, Scripture quotations are taken from the New Revised Standard Version Updated Edition. Copyright © 2021 National Council of Churches of Christ in the United States of America. Used by permission. All rights reserved worldwide.

Book design by Sharon Adams
Cover design by designpointinc.com

Library of Congress Cataloging-in-Publication Data

Names: Galbreath, Paul, author.
Title: Word and sacrament : tracing the theological movements of reformed worship / Paul Galbreath.
Description: First edition. | Louisville, Kentucky : Westminster John Knox Press, [2024] | Includes bibliographical references. | Summary: "Liturgical scholar Paul Galbreath brings together key theological insights and historical analysis to offer a theological roadmap of where the Reformed tradition has traveled in order to propose directions for where it is heading"-- Provided by publisher.
Identifiers: LCCN 2024016332 (print) | LCCN 2024016333 (ebook) | ISBN 9780664268442 (paperback) | ISBN 9781646983858 (ebook)
Subjects: LCSH: Liturgics. | Liturgical reform. | Public worship--Reformed Church.
Classification: LCC BV176.3 .G34 2024 (print) | LCC BV176.3 (ebook) | DDC 264--dc23/eng/20240522
LC record available at https://lccn.loc.gov/2024016332
LC ebook record available at https://lccn.loc.gov/2024016333

Most Westminster John Knox Press books are available at special quantity discounts when purchased in bulk by corporations, organizations and special-interest groups. For more information, please e-mail SpecialSales @wjkbooks .com.

To Jan, companion on this journey called life

Contents

Foreword by Martha Moore-Keish	ix
Preface	xiii
Introduction	1

Part I: Calvin's Legacy

1. Scripture	7
2. The Lord's Supper	20
3. Baptism	32

Part II: Modern Influences: From Westminster to the *Book of Common Worship* (1993)

4. Scripture	47
5. The Lord's Supper	64
6. Baptism	82

Part III: The Future of Reformed Worship

7. Scripture	103
8. The Lord's Supper	123
9. Baptism	145
Conclusion	163
Notes	167
Bibliography	183

Foreword

Since the sixteenth century, leaders in the Reformed Protestant movement have affirmed that the visible church is recognized where the word is preached and heard and where the sacraments are rightly administered according to Christ's institution (as Calvin put it in the *Institutes*). As the early Reformers affirmed these central symbols of Word and sacrament, they looked to biblical and early church materials to critique existing sacramental theology and practice, to call the church to greater faithfulness to Scripture and relevance to the world around.

Four centuries later, the twentieth century witnessed a new spirit of ecumenical respect and shared learning, especially focused on biblical and early church scholarship. This led, by the second half of the century, to significant liturgical and sacramental reforms among Reformed Protestants, often using patterns common to Catholics as well as other Protestants. Church leaders began to critique older patterns of Word and sacrament that divided Christians from one another. Churches began to preach from a common lectionary, accompanied by increasing convergence in sacramental practice. Again, this emerged from a desire to reflect more fully the richness of Scripture and to speak a healing word to the world.

In this volume, Paul Galbreath continues and critiques both of these movements, embodying the spirit of Reformed Protestantism as *"reformed and ever being reformed according to the Word of God."* To this familiar adage, Galbreath implicitly adds an ethical purpose: *"for the sake of the earth and the poor."*

Shaped by his years of serving as a pastor, theologian, and seminary professor deeply engaged in liturgical and sacramental renewal, Galbreath argues that our theological presuppositions shape liturgical development. This was true for Calvin in the sixteenth century, for Barth in the early twentieth century, for the formation of the *Worshipbook* and the *Book of Common Worship* in the late twentieth century, and it remains true today. Given this reality, he argues, we need to make "conscious theological choices for the language and images that we use in worship."

This might sound like an obvious claim, but as Galbreath points out, this emphasis on the priority of theological presuppositions over liturgical practice challenges some interpretations of a key motto of liturgical renewal: the emphasis on *lex orandi, lex credendi*. This Latin phrase (most simply translated as "law of praying, law of believing") often attributed to the fifth-century theologian Prosper of Aquitaine has been much discussed in liturgical-theological circles, to underscore the way that worship practices (*orandi*) shape statements of belief (*credendi*) and that we therefore need to attend to the coherence between the two. On the one hand, Galbreath concurs—liturgical action can indeed shape people's commitments over time, and this is precisely what drives his critique of current practices that do not do this well. But he also argues forthrightly that Reformed liturgies have rarely begun with the priority of existing liturgical forms; instead, Reformers like Calvin have begun with theological commitments born of biblical interpretation, which has then shaped liturgical reform.

In focusing on biblical interpretation as shaping theology, which then shapes liturgical reform, Galbreath embodies a classical Reformed commitment to *scriptura* (though not *sola scriptura*) as the basis for liturgical revision. His confidence, like Karl Barth, in the possibility of the strange new world of the Bible to inspire our living in right relationship with God, one another, and the world reveals him as a Reformed pastor-theologian. And in the spirit of *semper reformanda*, Galbreath uses his close reading of Scripture to critique the liturgical decisions of earlier Reformers—as he does, for instance, with Calvin's interpretation of 1 Corinthians 11 in relation to the table, as well as Calvin's defense of infant baptism based on the analogy of circumcision. In this way, Galbreath honors the tradition of Calvin himself, even where he disagrees with Calvin's conclusions.

In this volume, we see a theologian and pastor deeply shaped by the mid-twentieth-century liturgical renewal movement who has both appreciation for and enough distance to be critical of some of the developments of that movement (including the Revised Common Lectionary, and the emphasis on salvation history and its focus on atonement theory that has shaped baptismal and eucharistic praying). This is his distinctive gift as an insider to the movement—and it may be possible only now, fifty years on.

We also encounter here a Presbyterian pastor-theologian who is both active leader in and active critic of the church he serves. For instance, Galbreath celebrates the 1993 *Book of Common Worship*, and he contributed to the 2018 revision of that denominational resource as well as the accompanying revision of the authoritative Directory for Worship in the *Book of Order*. His emphases on care of the earth and preferential option for the poor cohere with values articulated in the current Directory for Worship (see W-5.0304 and W-5.0305).

Even so, he longs for the church to do better, to turn increasingly to local communities to craft worship that is truly the work of the people, with stronger attention to care for the earth and people who are poor. He grows weary of congregations who are more concerned about decency and good order than about the crises that threaten our planet and vulnerable human lives.

In the face of the ecumenical developments in the twentieth century, Reformed theologians must ask: What are the distinctive insights of Reformed theology of Word and sacrament, and how do these relate to the wider ecumenical world? We no longer sharply define ourselves over against Roman Catholics, Lutherans, Methodists, Anabaptists, and others. What do we offer to the church catholic that is distinctive—and is distinctiveness the goal? Some scholars have focused on the role of the Holy Spirit in Word and sacrament as a particular gift of Reformed Protestantism. Galbreath agrees with this move, as evident in his discussion of Calvin's prayer for illumination, and in the work of twentieth-century French liturgical theologian Jean-Jacques von Allmen. He worries that such attention to the role of the Spirit has been lost, and in its place has come the emphasis on doctrine and rationality. He also worries that attention to the Spirit has been obscured by attention to printed words on a page. This focus on pneumatology needs to be retrieved among Reformed Christians, and it needs to be shared with others.

Other scholars raise concerns that the embrace of liturgical and sacramental renewal in concert with wider ecumenical trends has compromised distinctive insights of Reformed faith. This concern too is one that Galbreath shares, as evident especially in his discussion of how we read Scripture in worship. Though the embrace of the Revised Common Lectionary had the laudable goals of increasing ecumenical engagement and enhancing biblical literacy, we now live in an age when three readings and a psalm every week is more than many people can absorb. For the sake of actual transformation, we may need to engage in practices of Scripture reading and proclamation that enable worshipers to wrestle more deeply and directly with biblical passages, perhaps even learning from the *lectio continua* practices of Calvin himself.

This volume is the culmination of Paul Galbreath's lifetime of work as a scholar-practitioner who has always had particular interest in how, why, and whether liturgical practice makes a difference in the lives of people and for the future of our fragile planet. Here he continues the work that he began in his trilogy *Leading from the Table* (2008), *Leading through the Water* (2011), and *Leading into the World* (2014): nurturing sacramental practice that can move us from "ego to eco-centered lives" through closer attention to the natural elements of bread and wine, water and oil, bodies and soil, trees and light, and through closer attention to communities suffering economic and political oppression. As a good Reformed theologian, he refuses to be satisfied with the status quo.

He is possessed by an unrelenting (even Spirit-driven?) drive toward more just and life-giving practices that actually make a difference in the world. How do our theological presuppositions guide us in shaping worship practices at the local level, from the bottom up, in ways that reflect scriptural commitments to care for the earth and care for the poor? Paul rescues me—rescues many of us—from romanticism about the power of liturgical practice, pressing with clear-eyed realism the urgency of the world's needs.

Martha Moore-Keish
Columbia Theological Seminary

Preface

Not everyone lays awake at night and wonders why John Calvin's theology took peculiar turns when it came to the liturgies that he wrote and used in his congregations. Similarly, I hope that others avoid the nightmares that I have about why Calvin's theological breakthroughs often became stagnant and twisted in the hands of some of his followers. Perhaps even more troublesome is the existential crisis that so many congregations face as they try to imagine a future for the Reformed tradition in a world that is increasingly bewildered by the odd language and rituals that many of us take for granted and from which some of us find comfort. These are the conundrums that I attempt to unravel in the following pages.

While it may not initially appear this way, writing a book is a collaborative process that draws on the generosity and resources of a broad community. I am particularly grateful for a sabbatical from my teaching at Union Presbyterian Seminary that allowed me to focus on this project. The seminary's librarians, especially Lisa Janes, provided significant support for my research. This work draws especially on classroom conversations with students: for over a decade in classes on worship at our campus in Richmond and for the last seven years of teaching theology at our campus in Charlotte.

Along the way, I have been supported by colleagues and friends who read drafts, provided critical feedback, and encouraged me throughout the writing process. Special shout-outs are due to Thom and Cindy Nelson, Martha Moore-Keish, and Cláudio Carvalhaes. My work was strengthened by their questions, comments, and suggestions. Additionally, I am grateful to Max and the baristas at Farewell, who not only kept me well-caffeinated but also allowed me to camp out in the café while I toiled away on this manuscript. Finally, I owe deep gratitude to my family, Jan, Andi, Rena, and Taluli, whose patience and support throughout this process gave me the hope of bringing this work to a successful conclusion.

Introduction

Dear reader:

Thank you for picking up this book. It offers a series of theological reflections on my experiences as a church member, pastor, teacher, student, scholar, and curious reader/researcher. In these pages I am offering a set of guided reflections on particular periods of Reformed theology as a way to show how significant theological themes have influenced the ways that liturgical practices have been articulated and enacted. My main focus is on primary material, especially Reformed liturgies and confessions. Along the way I include key insights from significant Reformed theological figures (Schleiermacher, Barth, Moltmann) as well as recent literature, particularly in relationship to the role of Scripture and the sacraments in the Reformed tradition. The purpose of these reflections is to point to something that I believe is so obvious that we often take it for granted: namely, that our theological presuppositions and perspectives often provide the groundwork for liturgical developments and in many cases dictate the ways in which our liturgies are constructed and embodied. This is neither a surprising or radical thesis, but I aim to show ways that it has at times led to ritual confusion in our liturgical texts and practices. While this book is structured around the particularities of Reformed theology, I hope that ecumenical readers will see the ways in which their own liturgical traditions share similar tendencies.

In part 1, I examine the legacy of John Calvin, whose theological work and pastoral leadership provided the foundation for the emergence of Reformed theology as a distinct approach—theologically, ecclesiastically, and liturgically. My interest is to underscore the ways in which Calvin's theological distinctives dictated and controlled the radical liturgical practices that were central to the Reformed Church in Geneva and were exported and embodied in the development of the Reformed movement as it took root and grew in other parts of Europe. At the center of Calvin's intellectual, spiritual, and practical approach was a commitment to Word and sacrament. Calvin viewed this as a central component of restoration to the health and faithfulness of the church and as an authentic witness to the presentation of Jesus Christ in the Gospels. Reformed Christians have been quick to point with pride to this as a hallmark of Calvin's reformation of the church's practices. While Calvin argued, wrote, and worked tirelessly to push for liturgical practices that embodied the church's commitment to Word and sacrament, a closer look at the liturgical texts will show the difficult choices that Calvin faced in pushing the church toward the vision of communal life and spirituality that he desired. While Calvin viewed his work of church renewal primarily as a return to the practices of the early church, he faced the twofold task of dismantling established liturgical practices while creating and sustaining new ones at the same time. Further complicating this herculean effort was the fact that these different approaches to Word and sacrament shared the same vocabulary but relied on different theological arguments as a basis for their use in the life of the church.[1]

My aim here is to show how Calvin's interpretation of Word and sacrament is primarily the result of his reading of Scripture and the way in which he constructed theological arguments. By looking closely at the liturgical texts that were used in his congregations in Strasbourg and Geneva, we get a clearer picture of the ways in which the liturgical practices were designed and developed to support theological claims. We will see the pedagogical ways that Calvin used to provide explanations that rejected previous practices and offered biblical and theological rationales for alternative ways of celebrating Word and sacrament. These liturgical texts often include a critique of the previous practices (a kind of theology *via negativa*) while gesturing (mainly linguistically) toward other possibilities. For Calvin, this is understandably a work in progress, particularly given the enormity of the task of reformation. The surprising result for me is the way in which Calvin's bold initiative quickly became codified as his theological approach spread to other parts of the European continent (and over time was taken to the "new world"). I am suggesting that because this was first and foremost a theological vision it struggled to find ways to develop embodied liturgical practices that supported the commitment to Word and sacrament that inspired Calvin's approach. As a result, Reformed liturgies have often remained at the level of theological explanation that increasingly relied on forms of reasoning to make the case for their particular approach to spirituality. Throughout much of the history of the Reformed movement these approaches were also defined by their suspicion and rejection of any practices that were perceived as Roman Catholic.

I will begin my investigation of Calvin's contributions by looking at the positive contributions of recovering a commitment to Scripture as central to the life of the gathered assembly. This takes shape in particular ways, from the development of a distinctive prayer to a new approach to the public reading of Scripture and the role of proclamation as connected to this practice. In the next section, I will turn to look at the ways in which Calvin's rejection of the Mass led to the development of liturgical texts that supported his vision of recreating the Lord's Supper. Finally, I will explore the radical baptismal practices adopted in Geneva and especially the ways in which the liturgical texts stressed the claims of this theological vision.

In part 2, our study of the theological influences on Reformed worship focuses on those who followed Calvin's theological vision. We will examine the liturgies of John Knox and the Reformed church in Scotland as well as look at insights from early Reformed confessional statements. We will give special attention to the defining role of the Westminster Standards before turning our attention to the rise of new theological voices from the work of Friedrich Schleiermacher to Karl Barth and Jürgen Moltmann. We will examine how these voices eventually led to significant changes to the ways in which the Reformed tradition's commitment to the centrality of Word and sacrament took on new dimensions, both in descriptive terms in the adoption of new confessional statements and more particularly in terms of the development of new liturgies.

In part 3, the historical analysis will provide the basis for us to consider which common threads from Reformed history may provide significant guidance as well as what theological insights will resonate with those who seek to express and experience Christian faith in this postmodern and pluralistic time. Exploring these possibilities will include significant conversation with recent Reformed and ecumenical contributions around our explorations of the ongoing role of Word and sacrament in the lives of Reformed communities.

As I tell my students, the primary goal of reading theology is to nurture a critical and appreciative understanding of those who have explored dimensions of Christian faith. As a Reformed theologian and pastor, I remain inspired by the audacity and commitment of Calvin's theological vision. Furthermore, what he accomplished in the face of the perpetual reluctance to change as well as fierce hostility from some individuals in his community is mind-boggling. I know from my years as a pastor how difficult change is for congregations to embrace. Thus, the amount of dramatic change to liturgical practices that happened in a relatively short time is an area in which Calvin's contributions have often been underestimated.

At the same time, though, Calvin's struggle to find ways that fully develop embodied liturgical practices resulted in what I am suggesting is a commitment to spirituality that is largely defined by particular forms of rational argument. This can be seen both in the ways in which the Reformed church developed distinctive approaches to preaching, writing, and using creeds, and in the development of liturgical texts to support its approach to sacraments. The result is the popular portraits of Reformed Christians as the "frozen chosen." Oddly enough, while the Reformed tradition has vehemently defended its commitment to form and freedom versus any requirement of prescribed liturgical texts, by and large Reformed congregations remain rigidly defined by printed texts (bulletins) that offer prescribed responses by those who are participating in worship. Could this be the result of Calvin's attempt to prescribe proper theological reasons (along with a biblical rationale) for each component of the worship service? The rejection of form and the illusion of freedom have combined to leave Reformed congregations with types of spirituality that increasingly seem to be out of touch in an age that looks for visual and experiential ways to create communal identity.

In the hope of discovering what inspired Calvin (and for clues of what can inspire us today), we turn our attention to the dawn of the Protestant Reformation. Charting this movement is a way of tracing a family tree so that we can discover the accomplishment of our ancestors while learning more about the difficult choices they faced, the missteps they made, and the ways in which we resemble them.

PART I

Calvin's Legacy

1

Scripture

Long before Martin Luther tacked his list of items to debate on the Wittenberg door in 1517, a hunger to hear and read the Bible had emerged as a way to foster new forms of community across the European continent. The Protestant Reformation did not happen overnight. A variety of factors contributed to the long trajectory that prompted leaders to advocate for change. While one can point to different starting places, a helpful way to chart the course of transition is to start by noting the established method for theological discourse that held the day. Scholasticism, a theological method championed by Thomas Aquinas in the thirteenth century, became the standard way to present theological truths. In his classic work, *Summa Theologica*, Aquinas provided a pattern for theological arguments by showing the ways that philosophy, particularly Aristotle's writings (whose work had been preserved by Muslim scholars and recently rediscovered by Christians), could be used to present the doctrines of the church. This approach was developed as a way to make sense of Christian faith. In the hands of a genius like Aquinas, it provided an impressive attempt at summing up the teachings of the church. As a method that encouraged theological debate in order to refine and prove arguments, it could also devolve into purely speculative issues (e.g., Can God create a stone so heavy that even God cannot lift it?). Scholasticism remained the dominant method of theology that shaped leaders like Luther and Calvin even as they advocated for new approaches.

In contrast to scholasticism, the rise of humanism in northern Italy sought educational reform by pointing to the need for a return to primary sources. The emphasis on grammar and rhetoric was inspired by the reading of classic sources in their original languages (thus its rallying cry became *ad fontes* or "back to the sources"). Rather than pursue abstract ideas, humanism sought to identify a basis for truth claims. While the differences in these approaches were seen primarily as a matter of scholarly debate, at the cusp of the sixteenth-century reforms even some of the common folks attending mass in their local parish were increasingly aware of major issues: (1) that theology in the form of the teachings of the church was out of touch with daily life and (2) that certain practices of the church were increasingly corrupt, particularly the emphasis on raising money through the selling of indulgences and the attention given to relics.

Musicians and artists contributed to the sense of social unrest by fostering visions of new ways of life shared together.[1] Instead of the concentration of wealth held by a few, they steadily produced an imagined alternative way of communal life. Scripture emerged as a primary resource, especially with an emphasis on the prophetic tradition and the apocalyptic texts. The prophetic passages provided images of religion that advocated for change by drawing attention to the call for justice and the plight of the poor. In this era of social unrest, eschatological texts provided a basis for a liberative cry for release from the authoritarian systems that controlled society.

The closing decade of the fifteenth century carried with it a wide sense of apocalyptic change. Europe teetered on the brink of massive transformation as the process of expansion and control of the Americas emerged as a way to create new wealth for those in positions of power. The church legitimized these actions by providing the authority and rationalization for the expansion and plundering of the resources that would be discovered and captured. Pope Alexander VI (a member of the prominent Borgia family), one of the most colorful and corrupt leaders in the history of the papacy, wrote the papal bull, *Inter caetera*, that sanctioned the voyage to the "new world" as an act of expanding Christendom by taking the teachings of the church to the "heathens" who lived there in an involuntary exchange for the gold and spices in their territory. Alexander VI seized upon this opportunity as a financial basis for his ambitious building projects (including villas for his mistress and family). Similarly, the hunger for increased wealth by the royal and business elite provided the financial backing for Christopher Columbus and others who crossed the Atlantic in pursuit of resources to feed the growing appetite for expansion.

The result of these diverse processes was a growing divide between the haves and the have-nots. While the common people increasingly longed to hear voices that advocated for change, those in power leveraged practices that produced the income to support the vast ecclesial and secular empires that were working to expand their bases. In other words, a serious disconnect continued to grow between institutional concerns and the plight of common peasants. Into this cauldron, the work of pamphleteers and traveling preachers nurtured the sense of dissatisfaction, particularly of ecclesiastical leaders who seemed more interested in raising money and supporting the status quo than in addressing the concerns of those struggling to get by.

In this context, calls for change coalesced around a particular watchword: *sola scriptura*, Scripture alone. Scripture as the grounds for seeing the world in a new way grew out of the experience of those who led the charge for reform. In Germany, Martin Luther's study of the Bible prompted him to call for debate on a list of ecclesial malpractices that he identified as divergent from Scripture. For Luther, the issue was primarily an existential one. His reading of Romans challenged the way in which he had sought to achieve salvation. Luther sensed that in spite of his intense study and devotion, he still could not measure up to the demands of a wrathful God. It was in his exploration of Scripture (Psalms, Romans, Galatians, and Hebrews) that he discovered a liberative word that challenged the way in which he had constructed his life as an Augustinian monk. His meditation on Romans 1:17, "For in it the righteousness of God is revealed through faith for faith; as it is written, 'The one who is righteous will live by faith,'" provided the hermeneutical key that broke open his theological perspective. For Luther, it was no longer the good works that he accomplished that were instrumental, but instead the righteousness provided by God in Jesus Christ that was the source of faith.

Scripture provided the breakthrough moment for Luther (and other reformers), and it quickly became the benchmark to test the veracity and faithfulness of theological and ecclesial claims. Luther's attack on the selling of indulgences grew out of his recognition of grace as a free gift of God and a rejection of any attempts to earn or buy merit. Scripture alone was never intended as a rejection of tradition but as a corrective move that insisted on the priority of Scripture in theological debates. The Reformers shared a familiarity with the writings of the church fathers that drew on their education both in terms of scholasticism and humanism. The distinction that emerged in their work was an insistence on the priority of Scripture when debating teachings and practices of the church.[2]

CALVIN'S USE OF SCRIPTURE

While the study of Scripture produced significant theological insights, our interest here is around the use of Scripture as a distinctive component of worship. On the one hand, Calvin and other reformers shared a belief that hearing the Word in worship on a regular basis would produce similar insights to their own transformative moments. Thus, the focus on Scripture became a central hallmark across different streams of the Protestant Reformation. Distinct differences emerged, however, in the ways in which worship reflected on the role of Scripture. For Luther, the reading and preaching of the Word was a central component of Sunday worship. Luther's liturgical approach in the *Deutsche Messe* was primarily to preserve the mass but also to offer the service in the vernacular language of the people.

In contrast, the Reformed movement used its reading and interpretation of Scripture as the basis for distinguishing virtually all aspects of worship from Roman Catholic practices. Scripture served as the primary rationale for the ordering of worship and became the way in which Reformed congregations developed their liturgies. While Scripture was recognized as the source of liberation from the constraints of the authoritative teachings and the abuses of the church, the use of Scripture in worship was primarily intended as support for distinctive theological claims and as a pedagogical support for the emergence of this alternative theological movement.

An overview of one of Calvin's liturgies demonstrates the way in which Scripture is used to support the theological perspective of this nascent movement. The service begins with a citation from Psalm 124:8: "Our help is in the name of the LORD, who made heaven and earth. Amen."[3] The significance of this starting point is to assert Scripture as the initial word spoken to the assembly (in contrast to the mass, where the priest intones the Trinitarian formula as the initial theological and doctrinal assertion to the congregation). The choice of a psalm is noteworthy for a number of reasons. It reflects Calvin's deep affection for the Psalms as a primary source of spirituality. This devotion to the Psalms is reflected in Calvin's insistence on the congregation's singing of the Psalms as a distinctive feature of the Reformed tradition. The Psalms provided a key resource in the encouragement of household piety that was a distinctive aspect of Calvin's theology. Additionally, the use of the Psalms reinforces Calvin's commitment to the Hebrew Scriptures as a positive source of revelation that we will see in the third use of the law in the liturgy. Finally, a brief reference to Scripture provides a clear example of a biblical warrant—a way of using Scripture in the liturgy that continues to be an important part of Reformed worship today. (For example, note how the service for the Lord's Day in the most recent edition of the Presbyterian Church (U.S.A.)'s *Book of Common Worship* in 2018 still provides a scriptural citation in the right-hand column of each page as a way to show biblical support for each aspect of the service).

A second use of Scripture in Calvin's liturgy in Strasbourg occurs following the confession of sin where "the Minister delivers some word of Scripture to console the conscience."[4] The importance of this act is to ground the absolution of sin in the promise of Scripture (rather than solely in the declarative power of the priest on behalf of the church). Here Scripture provides the teaching that delivers the congregation from sin. Following this practice is Calvin's use of the decalogue as a source of instruction on how to live in community. Calvin understood this as the third and most important use of the law. Luther articulated that the (first) use of the law is to convict us of sin and a second use of the law (from Luther's colleague Phillipp Melanchthon) was to provide ethical norms for society. Calvin's emphasis on the third use of the law was in terms of its role in nurturing Christians in their life together in community. In Strasburg, the congregation sang the first table of the law immediately following the absolution. Then the minister offered a prayer that included thanksgiving for the gift of God's revelation that would "instruct them in the righteousness of thy law" and "that it may also be inscribed and impressed upon our hearts."[5] The congregation followed by singing together the second table of the decalogue as a declaration of the way in which they would share life together. In the Genevan liturgy, the congregational singing of a Psalm took priority over the singing of the decalogue. The emergence of these new practices reinforced Calvin's commitment to a liturgy that draws on the promises of Scripture.

We will look more closely at the practice of reading Scripture and the commitment to preaching on biblical texts in the next section of this chapter. Here we will simply note the attention that is given to the public reading of Scripture and the extended time dedicated to the explanation of biblical texts as a way of promoting theological literacy. The focus here is on a particular hermeneutical approach to Scripture: that is, it is more than reading Scripture for its own sake but is imbedded in a way of interpreting Scripture within a particular theological framework and perspective. The reading and interpretation of Scripture became the primary focal point for the service that Calvin referred to as "the incomparable treasure of the church."[6]

Calvin's reading of Scripture, alongside the influence of Luther, Zwingli, and other Reformation leaders, led to his acceptance of baptism and Communion as the two sacraments instituted by Christ. This came in stark contrast to the Roman Catholic emphasis on seven primary sacraments (baptism, confirmation, Communion, reconciliation/penance, marriage or ordination, anointing of the sick/last rites) as ways in which the church offered grace through the cycles of life. In its place, Calvin's emphasis on cultivating household piety provided an alternative pattern of spirituality that linked the witness of the church with that of daily life. Calvin's definition of sacraments and his reflection on the role of sacraments drew heavily from the writings of Augustine (as is often the case in Calvin's theology). Calvin describes sacraments as aids to our faith by which God offers us a visible word or sign (directly citing Augustine).[7] In this broad context, Calvin develops an understanding of sacrament that is linked to God's covenants as portrayed in Scripture. Calvin describes an array of signs that point to God's promises, for example the tree of life in the Garden of Eden or the rainbow following the flood.[8] For Calvin, though, it is still important to underscore the role of sacraments in the life of the church. While Calvin echoes Augustine's description of "Old Testament sacraments" (circumcision, purifications, sacrifices), their value is in the way that these signs point to Christ. While we will have more to say about the acceptance and appropriateness of the language of Old Testament sacraments in a later chapter, Calvin developed the notion in terms of the way in which sacraments as signs were fulfilled by Christ. This allows Calvin to acknowledge a limited role for Old Testament signs that pointed to Christ while also making the case for the ways in which baptism and the Lord's Supper show Christ "more richly and fully."[9]

While Calvin longed for a weekly celebration of the Lord's Supper, he never received approval for this change. Instead, the service of Word became the dominant form of gathering both on Sundays and in the weekday services, with the focus clearly on building biblical literacy within the community. Given the dramatic level of change to Communion practices advocated by Calvin, including the full participation by the congregation around the table, Calvin conceded that it would require substantial education in order for the congregation to grow into the new liturgical practices.

On Sundays when the Lord's Supper was celebrated, Scripture served as the primary way in which the actions at the Communion table were presented to the congregation. Calvin's liturgy used 1 Corinthians 11 as the theological framework during the service by beginning the celebration of the sacrament by reading verses 23–29. By selecting this text as the biblical warrant for the gathering at the table, Calvin reinforces two particular emphases that were central to this theological approach to the sacraments. First is to link the actions in the service with a biblical narrative that portrays Jesus as providing the rationale for these actions. Calvin spoke of this as the "dominical command" for the two sacraments (baptism and Communion) that he believed had sufficient biblical grounds to remain at the center of the congregation's life. The Pauline text provided the connection to the upper room tradition that would serve as a primary paradigm for the theological interpretation of the sacrament within the Reformed tradition. Second, the selection of this excerpt also clearly sets a tone that is perceived as central for the service. The emphasis on the Pauline words about worthiness provides a basis for an extended warning offered by the minister to those in the service. The minister uses this text as the basis for a lengthy declaration in which he declares that "in the name and authority of our Lord Jesus Christ" he is able to "excommunicate all idolaters, blasphemers and despisers of God."[10] In the next chapter on the Lord's Supper, we will look more closely at Calvin's understanding of Communion and its role within the community. Here, our primary interest remains on the role of Scripture within the weekly worship gathering.

Finally, the service closes with two additional biblical references: First, the congregation sings either a psalm or the Song of Simeon. Once again, the words of Scripture spoken by the congregation provide a way of teaching and forming their identity as members of the covenant community. Second, the minister offers a benediction from Scripture in the form of the blessing from Numbers 6. Once again, the use of a text from the Hebrew Scripture reinforces Calvin's conviction that all of Scripture is formative for Christian life.

A DISTINCTIVE REFORMED PRACTICE

Following this overview on the role of Scripture in Calvin's liturgy in his congregations in Strasbourg and Geneva, we are turning our attention to a distinctive feature of the Reformed approach to reading Scripture. My friend and colleague Stan Hall frequently labeled the Prayer for Illumination as the *only* significant liturgical contribution to the ecumenical church. As we will see, it offered a unique way in which Calvin's emphasis on the role of Scripture was grounded in a particular theological perspective. Calvin's development of this new form of prayer provides an important theological contrast to the Mass. In the Roman Mass, a collect for the day provided a prayer that offered a transition following the opening of the service while also announcing a particular focus for the service of the day.

Prior to Calvin, Reformed liturgies experimented with an alternative form of prayer to petition God that the "Sermon and the Word of God" may "be heard with profit."[11] This development already foreshadows a different understanding of the role of this prayer than that of the traditional collect. Rather than summing up the opening of the service, the prayer now draws attention to the actions to come in terms of the reading and interpretation of Scripture. In creating the Prayer for Illumination, Calvin seized on this possibility and used it to draw attention to a particular theological emphasis.

The primary role of this prayer in Calvin's liturgy is to highlight the pneumatological center of Calvin's theology. In contrast to Luther's emphasis on the perspicuity or clarity of Scripture, Calvin insists that the understanding of the Word is solely the result of the work of the Holy Spirit. In his debates with the Roman hierarchy, Luther had insisted that simply reading Scripture (in the same ways in which he read it!) would lead to a shared interpretation and theological agreement. As one who came later to the Reformation, Calvin was deeply aware (and pained) by the divisions between those who advocated for change. Thus, the Prayer for Illumination points to his theological conviction that clarity comes not from our ability to understand these texts but rests on the Spirit's presence among those who gather to hear the Word read and proclaimed.

In his description of Calvin's service, Bard Thompson describes the following action: the minister leaves the Communion table from where he led the opening of the service, moves to the pulpit (Calvin's church in Geneva, St. Pierre, had an elevated pulpit near the front of the congregation), and offers an extemporaneous prayer that the Holy Spirit will bring illumination that the word may be read and proclaimed. For Calvin, the reading, hearing, and proclamation of Scripture served as the mark of the true church along with the celebration of the sacraments according to the institutions of Christ. By locating this prayer in the pulpit, Calvin underscores its theological significance as decisive for this central act of worship. Calvin is under no illusion about our ability to understand Scripture on our own. While Scripture functions as the lens that provides correction to our flawed sight, the human condition of sin prevents us from being able to attain these insights from our own knowledge or intelligence.

As a humanist, Calvin was fully committed to the serious study of Scripture in its original language. Thus, the development of an academy in Geneva dedicated to rigorous training for ministers was a key part of Calvin's reform agenda. Yet, even with this commitment, it is ultimately the work of the Spirit that brings understanding to the congregation who gathers to hear the Word read and proclaimed. Calvin views this as an act of theological collaboration in which the Spirit's presence is the animating factor in breathing life into the community. Calvin draws on the Pentecost story in the book of Acts as the source of inspiration for this portrait of the church.[12] It is the Spirit's movement that leads to understanding and brings people together in a community that experiences growth and transformation.

The centrality of the Spirit in Calvin's theology has often been ignored or overlooked. This remains a largely underdeveloped aspect of Reformed theology even in contemporary works. To cite but one example, Daniel Migliore writes in *Faith Seeking Understanding* that "the doctrine of the Holy Spirit has seldom received the attention given to other doctrines of the faith."[13] Even as he calls attention to this claim and recognizes the need for closer ecumenical partnership with the Eastern Orthodox Church as well as Pentecostal and Charismatic communities, Migliore's own commitment to a christocentric theology restricts the focus on the Spirit's significance to Reformed theology in Calvin's theology.[14]

Pneumatology is a major component of Calvin's theology in the *Institutes of the Christian Religion*. In book 3 of the *Institutes*, Calvin develops the animating role of the Spirit as the key to his theological system.[15] Contemporary Reformed theologian Christopher Elwood describes the crucial role that the Spirit plays in Calvin's theology in terms of the role of power in providing the benefits of Christ to believers. "For Calvin it is the Spirt who . . . makes Christ present to believers, and Christ is made present by means of the Spirit's power."[16]

What happened within the Reformed movement that caused this primary emphasis in Calvin's theology to largely disappear? My sense is that the development of Calvinism in doctrinal directions led to a more stultified version of Calvin's theology that restricted the movement of the Spirit. While the numerous Reformed credal statements all share a basic commitment to a Trinitarian theology that reaffirms the classic Christian commitment to the Spirit, the emphasis on pure doctrine and an insistence on decency and order left little room for the Spirit to move in new directions. Over time, the characterization of Reformed congregations as the "frozen chosen" exemplifies the restrictive space for the Spirit to work within the boundaries of our theological expectations. One can see this development particularly in the historical and theological conflicts in the Dutch Reformed Church at the Synod of Dort in the seventeenth century. The articulation of strict forms of Calvinism with an emphasis on double predestination as a way to insist on the absolute sovereignty of God and salvation as solely God's action (in contrast to preserving room for human choice) led to the development of more rigid theological systems. This version, known as five-point Calvinism, was rearticulated in the twentieth century in English-speaking countries using the acronym of TULIP: Total Depravity, Unconditional Election, Limited Atonement, Irresistible Grace, and Perseverance of the Saints.[17] While the Westminster Standards softened some of the harsher claims of Dort, they maintained the overall doctrinal emphasis that became distinctive as Calvinism developed in different parts of the world.

By contrast, the Prayer for Illumination as a distinctive element of Calvin's pneumatology must be recognized within the context of the competing forces in the emergence of the Reformed movement in sixteenth-century Geneva. On the one hand, Calvin is forced to defend and distinguish his commitment to reforming the church in a highly contested space where the debate includes vastly different understandings from those who sought to reassert a vision of a unified Roman Catholic Church (see Cardinal Sadoleto's letter to the church at Geneva[18]) to Anabaptists who advocated that the Protestant Reformation should go further in its attempt to restore practices of the New Testament church. To navigate this conflict, Calvin was forced to articulate a theology with ecclesial practices that provided clear directions for the church. At the same time, Calvin's experience of the Spirit's vivifying movement in his life served as a source of inspiration for his vision of communal life together. The delicate dance of the emerging identity of the Reformed movement relied on the articulation of distinct aspects of this ecclesial movement as well as on a commitment to the Spirit as the source for the community to thrive amid both internal and external conflicts. Calvin brought these diverse experiences together to provide a theological vision for the central role of the Spirit in the life of the community.

The liturgical commitment to the centrality of this prayer underscores its role in Calvin's lived theology. Note that Calvin's liturgy presents this as an extemporaneous prayer. Here Calvin's recognition of the free movement of the Spirit is embodied in a particular practice, that of eschewing a prescribed text in favor of the minister exemplifying a reliance on the Spirit to provide the words of a prayer that embodies the community's dependence on the Spirit to bring life to the gathered assembly as the Word is read and proclaimed. Calvin did offer examples of this prayer as a way to model the central theological features. The example provided from his Strasbourg liturgy provides clues to the theological focus:

> Let us call upon our Heavenly Father, Father of all goodness and mercy, beseeching Him to cast the eye of His clemency upon us, His poor servants, neither impute to us the many faults and offenses which we have committed, provoking His wrath against us. But as we look into the face of the Son, Jesus Christ our Lord, whom He hath appointed Mediator between Himself and us, let us beseech Him, in whom is all fulness of wisdom and Light, to vouchsafe to guide us by His Holy Spirit into the true understanding of His holy doctrine, making it productive in us of all the fruits of righteousness: to the glory and exaltation of His name, and to the instruction and edification of His Church. And let us pray unto Him in the name and favor of His well-beloved Son, Jesus Christ, as He hath taught us to pray, saying: Our Father, which art in heaven, etc.[19]

The prayer is distinctly Trinitarian in form in naming and distinguishing each member of the Trinity. It begins with a focus on God the Father/Creator as the source "of all goodness and mercy" before turning to Christ as the Mediator between God and humanity. The prayer then names the Holy Spirit as the source of "wisdom and light" that guides the community "into the true understanding of His [God's] holy doctrine" in order that it may produce "the fruits of righteousness."[20] The prayer concludes with a collective recitation of the Lord's Prayer as a way for the congregation to affirm their desire for the Spirit to bring understanding to the reading and hearing of Scripture.

A second example of a Prayer for Illumination includes Calvin's adaption of a prayer written by Calvin's mentor, Martin Bucer. This briefer text shares the common feature of naming the members of the Trinity while asserting a distinctive role for the Holy Spirit. The prayer acknowledges that our salvation is dependent upon our knowledge of Scripture. This prayer closely resembles the opening of Calvin's *Institutes* with its emphasis on the knowledge of God and knowledge of ourselves, where the knowledge of ourselves leads to an awareness of our dependence on God for all of life and the knowledge of God comes solely from God's revelation known to us in Scripture. The prayer implores God to "strengthen us now by thy Holy Spirit that our hearts may be set free from all worldly thoughts and attachments of the flesh, so that we may hear and receive that same Word."[21] The purpose of this prayer, then, is articulated in terms of learning how to love and serve God with "earnest delight, praising and glorifying thee in Jesus Christ our Lord."[22]

The understanding that the Spirit brings through the reading and proclamation of the Scripture leads to active responses in the life of the community. The work of the Spirit in our lives provides for our growth in Christian piety in terms of sanctification. The result or fruit of the Spirit's work is our dependence on God and our care for our neighbor.[23] Here again there are traces of the description of the early Christian community from Acts 2 where the Spirit's descent on the followers of Jesus leads them to share their belongings with all who are in need. Calvin hints at this connection in the formula offered at the sharing of the bread and wine during Communion, where the gathering at the Table concludes with the words: "You are commended to have love among ourselves, and especially toward the poor."[24] Calvin envisions the Spirit's movement among us as leading to specific ethical actions. Faithfulness to the reading and hearing of Scripture that contains God's promises creates a distinct community that cares for one another and all those who are in need.[25]

As a liturgical innovation, the Prayer for Illumination provides a tangible practice rooted in the life of the worshiping community that signifies Calvin's commitment to a vibrant theology of the Holy Spirit. The prayer provided a place in which the commitment to and exploration of Scripture that was at the center of the Reformation was balanced by an openness to the Spirit to guide the community in its understanding and to inspire them to discover ways to live out the teachings of Scripture in community.[26]

SCRIPTURE: READ AND PROCLAIMED

At the center of Calvin's vision of the Christian community lies a hunger for Scripture as a guide for how to live as disciples of Jesus Christ. It is the regular exploration and study of God's revelation in the Bible that provides the knowledge for us to recognize our sin—the ways in which we deceive ourselves and fail to acknowledge our dependence on God. Scripture as the corrective lens that allows us to see ourselves and God in the proper light is a favorite metaphor of Calvin. To this end, the Reformed movement adopted new practices that highlighted their central commitment to Scripture.

At the time of the Reformation, the Roman Catholic lectionary was coordinated with the liturgical year and included readings from Scripture and the lives of the saints. In contrast, the Reformed approach developed the practice of *lectio continua*, which focused on the continuous reading of particular books of the Bible as a primary way to build biblical literacy in the lives of congregants. This historical approach, which is still followed in many Reformed congregations and more recently has been adapted to include semi-continuous readings of portions of Scripture, sees biblical pedagogy as a primary goal of worship. In the context of Calvin's time, where biblical literacy was minimal, this commitment to the regular public reading of Scripture was significant. The strength of the *lectio continua* method is that it preserves the connections within a particular text and over time provides a comprehensive sense of the way in which books were organized and written. In an era when access to Scripture had been primarily limited to the clergy, this central focus on the Word of God signified a radical shift in which the Reformation commitment to the priesthood of all believers took particular shape around the centrality of Scripture. Undergirded by an understanding of the Spirit's role in bringing understanding to communal hearing of Scripture, this method of reading Scripture emphasized a shared commitment to discovering ways that the text provides a place for us to encounter God.

This approach to reading Scripture presumes regular attendance in order for the listeners to maintain the continuity between portions of books. While attendance in Geneva was not mandatory, it was expected. In fact, periods of prolonged absence from worship resulted in summons to appear before the consistory. This attention to discipline was part of life in the Genevan community (and the role of discipline would emerge in the Church of Scotland as a third mark of the church in addition to preaching and the sacraments).[27] In Calvin's theology, all of Scripture was revelatory and pointed to the witness of Jesus Christ. Thus, the reading and preaching through the book of Deuteronomy was recognized as equally valid as the exploration of one of the Gospels. In Geneva, Calvin led four services each Sunday as well as preaching at services during the week.[28] Thus, there was a constant opportunity for people to gain regular exposure to Scripture.

The commitment to the reading of Scripture was connected to the explanation of Scripture in the form of "lively preaching" that points to "the promises of Christ."[29] The development of biblical literacy within the congregation is the primary task of the minister. The Reformed emphasis on the minister as a student of Scripture underscores the centrality of the proclamation of Scripture that leads to the formation of a distinct Christian community. Here the humanist roots of Calvin's training provided the basis for the attention given to the study of Scripture and the ways in which *sola scriptura* took shape in the life of congregations.

Finally, this commitment to Scripture carried with it distinct theological assumptions. While the study of Scripture may have prompted breakthrough moments in the lives of the Reformers (Luther's reading of Romans serves as a primary example), the development of a Reformed theological perspective provided the framework in which Scripture was explored. Calvin's own summary of Christian faith (in his initial edition of the *Institutes*, which he continued to revise throughout his life) provided a hermeneutical basis from which he explored Scripture and which guided the interpretations of texts that he offered in his sermons. There is nothing either surprising or nefarious about this; in fact, all of us approach biblical texts with particular expectations and commitments. The point to recognize here is how theology prescribes ways in which our liturgical practices and preaching take particular forms. As we have seen in this chapter, Scripture provided a way to make liturgical and theological claims that distinguished the Reformed movement from the alternative Christian perspectives of its day. While each approach claimed access to the true interpretation of the Bible (and usually accompanied this with a claim that all other interpretations were heretical), it was the use of Scripture to support the theological claims and liturgical practices of the Reformed church that distinguished its approach and development.

2

The Lord's Supper

In chapter 1, we noticed the way, in the sixteenth century, that Scripture served as the primary source to break open new visions and theological perspectives. Musicians, artists, and traveling preachers turned their attention particularly to prophetic and apocalyptic texts to advocate for change and to point toward the need for systemic transformation that addressed the needs of common people. The translations of Scripture into vernacular languages alongside the invention of the printing press suddenly provided access to Scripture for a vast new audience of readers. Access to the Bible and its interpretation would no longer solely be in the hands of the church.

While the study of Scripture served as a primary resource that grounded the movement leading to the Protestant Reformation, Scripture quickly became the tool used to critique malpractices in the church. Nowhere is this more evident than in the debate over the sacraments. In the twelfth century, the Roman Catholic scholastic theologian Peter Lombard provided a list of the seven primary sacraments that identified the church's offering: baptism, confirmation, Eucharist, penance, anointing of the sick, marriage, and ordination. These seven sacraments provided the church with ways to nurture faith and respond at critical junctures across the life cycle of its adherents. It was a unified way of embodying grace that sustained the lives of Christians for centuries. This approach to the sacraments had the advantage of extending a broad sense of sacramentality deeply connecting the material world to forms of spirituality and devotional practices that sustained Christian faith in the lives of believers.

The theological commitments that emerged during the Reformation era served as the basis for the critique of ecclesial practices that were identified as divergent from the clear teaching of Scriptures. At the forefront of the debates was the selling of indulgences that promised to provide a source of forgiveness in exchange for financial contributions to support the work of the Roman Catholic Church. The building of St. Peter's Basilica in Rome in the early sixteenth century is one example of a major construction project of the institutional church that required significant financial resources. Alongside the church's support for the ongoing work of colonization in the Americas, the process of institutional expansion (alongside the continued battles against Islam) consumed the attention of the church's hierarchy.

In contrast, the Protestant rallying cry of *sola gratia*, grace alone, grew out of the reading of Scripture and became a primary basis for the attack on practices of the church that pointed to any sources of grace that differed from the vision and experience of those advocating for church reform. This fault line opened up a radical critique on the sacramental practices of the church. It began with a response to the practice of private masses, which were usually offered on the basis of a donation, and grew to include wholesale rejections of the broader sacramental system of the Roman Church. At stake in these debates was the role of the church and in particular the priests as those who provided access to the grace that was available in the sacramental practices of the church.

Scripture served as the primary source of inspiration and an alternative vision of ways to address issues of justice for those with limited access to power. The growing awareness of other ways of interpreting Scripture prompted a desire to use biblical texts to address what were identified as malpractices in the life of the church. What started as a way to critique specific practices expanded to a widespread analysis of the sacramental system of the Roman Church. This scrutiny via Scripture led to an unraveling of the sacramental understanding that had guided the church for centuries. In place of the seven primary sacraments, reformers increasingly coalesced around the two sacraments of baptism and eucharist. The reading of Scripture to support these two sacraments opened up significant fault lines that produced division with Rome and between the Reformers themselves. In this chapter, we will examine Calvin's approach to the Lord's Supper before turning in the next chapter to his interpretation of baptism. At the outset of this reflection, it is important to recognize that Calvin's fundamental insistence on a dominical command as a biblical warrant for a sacrament led him to identify the two sacraments of the Lord's Supper and baptism as central to the life of the church. The challenge of this approach is twofold: First, the biblical warrants that Calvin uses to support these actions bring with them their own contested interpretations. For example, today we might wonder in what way Jesus's baptism by John the Baptist as an act of renewal within the Jewish community provides a precedence for Christian baptism. Second, other actions specifically commended by Jesus are overlooked, such as foot washing as a primary command to Jesus's disciples (see John 13:14–17). There are historical and theological reasons for how these arguments developed. We cannot examine all of these possibilities, so we will focus our attention on the ways in which Calvin's liturgies provide theological and biblical rationale for the actions of the church.

THE LORD'S SUPPER

For Calvin and other reformed leaders, the differentiation from the Roman Church began with the name of the sacrament itself; no longer was it referred to as the Mass, but as the Lord's Supper. Imbedded in this change of nomenclature is a fundamental shift in theological perspective. There is no polite way to describe the level of disgust and use of invectives that characterized Calvin's rejection of the Roman Catholic practices of his day. Christopher Elwood summarizes the Reformed opinion: "the Mass had come to symbolize everything that was wrong with the worship and devotional practice of the church."[1] Calvin shared this view; he abhorred the Mass and rejected it as completely inconsistent with his reading of Scripture. What he described as "the spectacle of the Mass" grew out of his concern that the role of the priests had become primary in terms of providing access to Christ's presence in the sacrament. As we will see, Calvin's reading of Scripture (and in particular the Pauline depiction of the practices of the church in Corinth) provides the primary basis for both his deconstruction of the Mass and his liturgical proposals for reconfiguring the actions of the congregation. On this point, the use of the language of the Lord's Supper serves as a hermeneutical key that points to central aspects of Calvin's new approach to this sacrament.

Calvin's caricature of the Mass as re-sacrificing Christ may significantly misrepresent the Roman Catholic understanding of the Mass as a re-presentation of Christ that both proclaimed and provided the benefits of Christ's death to those present. In contrast, Calvin's understanding of the Lord's Supper was guided by his attempt to recapture the practices of the early church portrayed in the New Testament. In this process, it is important to observe the selective way in which Calvin chooses and interprets particular texts that support his theological commitments.

Before he began serving as a pastor in Strasbourg, Calvin proposed a clear outline for his understanding of the Lord's Supper in his initial edition of the *Institutes* in 1536. His description focuses on what he sees as the essential elements: balancing a connection between the promises of regular participation in the Supper with the demand for careful introspection and discipline to ascertain appropriate worthiness to come to the Table and participate in the sacrament. It is important to note the consequences of these emphases. First, the understanding of regular participation marks a notable shift in ecclesial practice. Calvin's portrayal of participation at the Table expected (if not demanded!) the congregation to regularly partake of both Communion elements. This marked a significant shift in practice for congregational members who were accustomed (and required) to receive and consume the Communion bread only once a year. While Mass was celebrated frequently (often daily), full participation by the congregation was not expected. To see and experience the miracle of Christ's presence in the Mass was sufficient. For Calvin, a return to regular participation at the Lord's Table included receiving both the bread and wine.

Calvin's Communion liturgies in Strasbourg and Geneva were heavily influenced by the Protestant reformers Guillaume Farel and Martin Bucer. Together these central theological figures gravitated toward a portrayal of what they identified as the primitive aspects of the practices of the early church. They viewed this primarily in contrast to the Mass and in particular to the role and actions of the priest at the altar. At stake for these reformers was a theological commitment to the unique sacrifice of Christ on the cross. The proclamation of the cross alongside the visible word of the sacrament of the Lord's Supper were central to the Reformed agenda. In terms of ecclesial practices, there was a careful attempt to distinguish the gathering at the Table from the actions of the Mass.

The Reformed approach to the Lord's Supper is guided and grounded by the reading and interpretation of 1 Corinthians 11. Before we turn to examine Calvin's liturgical formulations, it is helpful for us to look for clues as to why this Pauline text held such a high degree of influence among the Reformers. For example, one might expect the Synoptic narratives of the Last Supper to provide the primary framework for the development of a liturgical alternative to the Mass, but it was the apostle Paul's use of the Synoptic tradition that would provide the interpretive keys to the emergence of Reformed practices. I will point to three key textual moves that provide its basis. First, the biblical text is presented in terms of an analysis of malpractice in the life of the early church. It is not surprising that the Reformers would have been attracted to a text that addressed an issue that they saw as similar to their own challenges, since Paul's argument in the text is that a primary role of the Lord's Supper is to foster unity. Note that this desire for unity represents a way that the Reformers can respond to the accusations that they are fostering division in the church.[2] The use of Scripture as the basis for a theological argument represents a classic Reformed approach. In this instance, the Pauline text provides a way to frame the attack on malpractices alongside a call for unity based upon the instructions that are provided in the text.

Second, the language of the Lord's Supper in the biblical text provides the distinctive nomenclature that associates the practice with the actions of Jesus at table. It is easy to overlook the significance this vocabulary had for the reformers. What the Reformed church seeks to reclaim is a regular participation in the Lord's Supper, which is understood as distinct from the priestly actions at the altar in Mass. Instead, it is the remembering of Christ's sacrifice that provides the hermeneutical key in this rendering of the Pauline text. Paul's instructions to the church in Corinth reframe the Synoptic tradition in a way that links the actions of Jesus with the actions of the congregation around the table. For Calvin, this form of a biblical warrant is compelling because it provides the logical argument that the church's actions should mirror those that are depicted as Jesus's actions—in this instance, the breaking of the bread and sharing of the cup as a form of proclamation.

Third, the Pauline text further connects this practice with the need for ethical examination. For the reformers, the language of worthiness became central in terms of their approach to the sacrament. The emphasis on examination, judgment, and discipline became a central component in Reformed congregational practices.[3] For Calvin, the process of self-examination was key because it reflected his own theological starting place. In the opening sentences of the *Institutes*, Calvin describes the correlation between knowledge of self and knowledge of God. Knowledge of self prompts one to see our own limitations and sin and to turn to God as the source of all life whereas knowledge of God comes to us from the hearing of Scripture as the witness to God's faithfulness in Jesus Christ. The reading of 1 Corinthians 11 captures this movement as it presents the promise of the Lord's Supper by linking these actions with the narrative of Jesus Christ, while the importance of self-examination makes clear that worthiness is solely dependent on God's grace that meets us at the Table.

It is interesting to note the aspects of the Corinthians text that Calvin and other Reformers chose to highlight as well as those that they chose to ignore, particularly given their stated desire to emulate the practices of the early church. While they quickly latched onto the name as the Lord's Supper (v. 20) and to the sharing of the bread and cup as authorized by Jesus, they showed no interest in the broader meal tradition that represents the communal practice in Corinth. Paul's critique of this practice is not an objection to a full meal (which seems was standard in the early church) but the inequitable sharing of the food between the rich and the poor. For Paul, the exhortation on self-examination is based on the command to care for the poor. As we will see in Calvin's liturgies, remnants of this ethical encouragement show up at the conclusion of the liturgy of the Lord's Supper, but the stress on self-examination in Paul is reappropriated in Calvin for the theological purpose of stressing the theme of worthiness, underscoring the need to depend on God's grace.

CALVIN'S COMMUNION LITURGIES

Before we turn to look at the specific language of the liturgies in Strasbourg and Geneva, it is important to see the broader context in which these services occurred. Ministers provided instructions to the congregation that emphasized the need for preparation so that one is worthy to participate in the service the week before the celebration of the Lord's Supper. The practice of fencing the table from those who were deemed unworthy (i.e., banned from participating for moral reasons) is grounded in this practice. Over time, Calvin's interest in cultivating piety by stressing the relationship between self-examination as a discipline for communal belonging (where worthiness is determined by awareness of dependence on God's grace) in Scottish and Dutch congregations became a focus on the need for a moral, personal inventory. The instructions include a warning against participation by children who have not been adequately prepared as well as strangers who "may still be untaught and ignorant" and who are in need of further instruction.[4] These instructions point to the historical context in terms of the attempt to distinguish the celebration of the Lord's Supper from Mass.

Following the singing of the Apostles' Creed, the Strasbourg liturgy provides a prayer that points toward the movement to the table. The text of the prayer provides a clear theological orientation for the celebration of the Lord's Supper. The theological context offers insights into the way in which the Reformers understood the link between atonement theory and the ritual observance of Communion. A primary distinction for Calvin and other Reformers was to emphasize the unique sacrifice of Jesus Christ that was remembered in the gathering at the table. They understood this as distinct from the practices of the sixteenth-century Mass where the presence of Christ in the bread and wine was often perceived in (hyper) literal ways by the participants in spite of the sophisticated explanations offered by Roman Catholic theologians. The miracle of the Mass in terms of the transubstantiation of the bread and wine into the body and blood of Christ portrayed the salvific effects of Christ's death. A primary concern for Calvin was a fear of idolatry, and Calvin's rejection of the Mass is driven by his fear of the objectification of the elements. In contrast, Calvin's liturgy attempts to draw a clear contrast between the Reformed and Roman Catholic understandings and practices.

As we look closely at Calvin's liturgies, we will discover that rather than providing a poetic quality, they prescribe theological explanations for the liturgical movements. The pre-Communion prayer in the Strasbourg liturgy provides a clear example of these tendencies. The emphasis in this prayer is to clearly articulate theological doctrine while pointing out its connection to the gathering at the table. Thus, the prayer begins with an acknowledgment that "our

Lord Jesus Christ has not only offered His body and blood once on the Cross for the remission of our sins, but also desires to impart them to us as our nourishment unto everlasting life."[5] For our purposes, it is important to notice the ways in which the theological claims frame the liturgical actions and language. Notice the insistence on the past offering of Christ (once) as a clear historical marker that highlights the Reformed insistence on the memorial nature of the gathering while providing a contrast to the sacrifice of the Mass. On the one hand, Calvin and other reformers assumed the traditional approach of their day toward atonement theology, which is generally described as a version of Anselm's theory of substitutionary atonement.[6] The difference is that they seek to highlight the efficacy of Christ's death primarily in terms of an exhortation of the theological and historical account rather than through a form of ritual enactment that sought to embody the narratives in a way that captured the attention of the participants.[7] The Zurich Agreement (*Consensus Tigurinus*) in 1549, a Reformed confessional agreement on the Lord's Supper, provides descriptive language of this approach to the Eucharist where Calvin insisted on including the commentary that "eating Christ's body and drinking his blood" signifies "that we draw life from the flesh once offered in sacrifice and the blood shed in expiation."[8]

Similarly, the Strasbourg prayer begins with a theological explanation of the past event of Christ's death and its importance for persons of faith. The prayer then stresses the significance of proper participation in the sacrament in order that the "covenant of grace" that is remembered at the Table will "provide for us . . . all our needs of soul and body."[9] The prayer concludes by naming "the blessed memorial and remembrance of thy dear Son" that it may "proclaim the benefit of His death."[10] This rearticulation of the theological premise of celebrating the Lord's Supper attempts to make clear the distinctively Reformed approach to this sacrament. Perhaps it is obvious, but we should also note that in contrast to the Latin language of the Mass, which was understood by only some of the more highly educated members of the congregation, the Reformed liturgies were always done in the vernacular language of the people (in this instance in French) and provided key pedagogical moments for educating the congregation. Calvin's liturgy in Geneva did not include the pre-Communion prayer that was a part of the Strasbourg service. Perhaps this is because there was less need for a theological explanation of the Lord's Supper in Geneva at this time as the Reformed practices began to take root within particular communities.

As we previously noted, the Reformed movement drew on 1 Corinthians 11 as the primary biblical source to define its service. Thus, this part of the service begins with a reading of the text (vv. 23–29) to provide the biblical warrant that was used as a justification for the gathering at the table. This is followed by an interpretation of the text that begins by proclaiming "how our Lord observed His Supper with His disciples."[11] What is interesting to note is the shift that takes place in terms of relocating the Pauline description of the appropriate way to celebrate the Lord's Supper so that it portrays Jesus's actions with his disciples. It is a subtle move in terms of following the way in which Paul has framed his own historical argument (notice that Paul claims "to have received this from the Lord" rather than having learned it as a teaching shared in the church). Notice as well how Paul adds to the portrait the warning about examining one's self so that one is eating and drinking worthily (vv. 28–29). Calvin's liturgies immediately expand upon these verses by denying a place for "strangers and those who do not belong to the company of His faithful people."[12] This provides the justification for the minister to declare the right to excommunicate individuals who are viewed as a danger to the integrity of the community. This list begins by naming idolaters (a primary theological issue for Calvin) before describing other forms of heresy that were intended to deny participation at the Table.[13] This includes those who "break the unity of the Church" before naming other sins. There are two important aspects to this declaration: (1) Calvin, who was accused of creating schism, reverses the charges of dividing the church by casting the blame on those who (in his mind) are not properly following the teaching of Scripture, in this instance the description of the Lord's Supper in 1 Corinthians 11; and (2) the catalog of sin named in the Communion liturgy provides a basis for a growing tendency within the Reformed movement to judge participation in the liturgy in light of moral categories.[14] Calvin's list includes those who promote disorder, whether in civil circles or within the home (e.g., those who rebel against their parents), adulterers, thieves, greedy people, drunkards, and others whose lives are not marked by moderation. All of these receive a warning "to abstain from this Holy Table lest they defile and contaminate the holy food which our Lord Jesus Christ gives to none except they [who] belong to His household of faith."[15]

It is challenging to make sense of this portion of the liturgy. One wonders how the bread and cup could be defiled and contaminated if the Lord only provides to those who are recognized as part of the covenant community. Is the concern actually primarily about the need for examination so that individuals do not damage themselves by unworthy participation (already a distortion of the communal exhortation in the Pauline text) or is there a risk to the community if the wrong people participate in the actions at the Table? There is an unresolved tension that runs through this portion of the liturgical text that reflects the perilous times in which the Reformed church sought to clarify its identity (primarily in contrast to the Roman Catholic Church) while also trying to maintain discipline within its own ranks. Christopher Elwood interprets this as a commitment to protecting the gathering at the Table so that it served "as a faithful and genuine reflection of the mystical body [of Christ] that was actually constituted through the instrument of the sacrament."[16] As we will see in chapter 5, this concern with restricting access to the Table by excommunicating those who violated moral codes would lead to the practice of fencing the table in some Reformed congregations.

After this stern warning, Calvin adds additional instructions for the need for introspection before participating in the Lord's Supper. The liturgy circles back to the biblical warrant in order to make a case for the importance of proper examination to determine if individuals had truly repented of their faults and grievances from their sins and whether they desired to live a "holy life according to God."[17] The congregation is encouraged to place their trust in the mercy of God and seek salvation in Jesus Christ alone. The liturgy then points to the ethical goal of living in peace with one's neighbors.

Finally, the liturgy turns toward the promises that accompany participation at the Table. The purpose of repentance is to rest assured that God claims us as God's children and invites us to the Table to partake in the holy sacrament that Jesus gave to his disciples. Here the liturgy moves to connect the ritual actions of the congregation with the description of Jesus's breaking bread and sharing the cup as a source of comfort that God provides for us as part of this covenant community.

This brief word of hope (one sentence in a lengthy prayer[18]) precedes a lengthy reminder that the grace that we receive is solely dependent on God's goodness and in no way should be mistaken as the result of our actions. Here, Calvin positions himself against any charges of works righteousness. The risk for Calvin is that the heavy emphasis on self-examination and preparation may lead to an understanding that one makes oneself worthy to participate at the Table through acts of penitence. This is a major part of the critique of the Mass that Calvin and other Reformers had rejected through their portrayal of the role of the sacraments within the practices of the Roman Catholic Church.

Calvin seeks to provide a theological contrast by offering another explanation of the distinctive Reformed approach. The liturgy offers this theological explanation by insisting that the work of self-examination is not directed toward perfecting our faith since we as humans are inclined toward sin (Calvin's acceptance of the total depravity of humans is apparent here). Instead, Calvin develops the argument of our need "to fight daily against the lusts of our flesh."[19] The need for dependence on God's grace as the only source of faith is characteristic of Calvin's theology. In the Communion liturgy, Calvin outlines the sources that God provides us as (1) the gospel engraved on our hearts and (2) grace given to us so that we will renounce our own urges in order that we may follow God's commandments. The implications of this language draw from Calvin's understanding of the baptismal covenant where

God's grace is imparted to us as we find ourselves welcomed into this household of faith as God's beloved children. We will see in the coming chapter the ways in which Calvin's portrayal of the sacrament of baptism draws directly on the Old Testament images of circumcision. This Communion prayer uses nuanced language that parallels this emphasis in terms of its reference to engraving on our hearts and the role of the commandments (as the third and primary use of the Law, which serves as a guide for our life as a community). The language reinforces the central role of covenant in Calvin's understanding of the sacraments. This shared dependence on God's grace provides the basis for participation at the Lord's Table, where we understand that we come based not upon our accomplishments but upon the goodness of God to welcome us in spite of our sin and imperfections.

Two additional distinctives can be highlighted in the Communion prayer. First, Calvin inserts into the liturgy an important description by noting that we are participating in "this spiritual Table."[20] While Calvin uses the language of God's accommodation as a way to affirm Christ's presence in the bread and wine, the stress remains firmly on a spiritual presence. Calvin will develop this emphasis as a way to express his disdain for the materiality of the Roman Mass, which he viewed as coming suspiciously close to the ultimate sin of idolatry. By naming the Table as primarily spiritual, Calvin augments the process of distinguishing his understanding of the sacrament from Roman Catholic practice.[21] Secondly, Calvin draws on the language of the early church fathers by naming the sacrament as a "medicine for the poor sick souls." The tangible imagery of the Table as a source of healing where we consume the elements contrasts with the emphasis on the spiritual properties of the Table. It seems to me that Calvin is trying to find a way to encourage full participation in the Table as a practical way of experiencing grace through the gift of the sacrament (which would have been a familiar theme for those in his congregation) while at the same time guarding against what he feared were objective actions that could be misconstrued as material sources or human accomplishments.

Calvin's liturgy then turns toward a more forceful explanation of the promises that are provided by participating in the Lord's Supper. These promises are provided by Jesus Christ since they draw on the words that he spoke (*ipsissima verba*) in the institution of this holy meal with his disciples. The promise is that through partaking of "His body and blood ... that we may possess Him wholly and in such ways that He may live in us and we in Him."[22] With this statement, we have Calvin's strongest affirmation of the significance of the elements and of the congregation's full participation at the Table. This has been described by some as Calvin's commitment to a mystical union with Christ that occurs in Communion.[23] However, Calvin immediately backtracks by qualifying this bold claim by insisting that "we see but bread and wine" as a way to differentiate the Reformed understanding of the elements from the transubstantiation of the Mass (or Luther's description of consubstantiation). Calvin's miracle at the Table is an accomplishment by God that happens "spiritually in our souls" where these "outward visible signs" show and nourish us.[24] The blessing of participation in this sacrament is tied to the "virtue of His death and passion" that provides the source for righteousness to be imputed to us.[25] This claim reinforces the theological connection between Calvin's theory of atonement and the ritual/liturgical gathering at the Table. In the end, the question of worthiness is resolved in terms of Christ's worthiness that is truly given to us and provides a model for us to imitate that we may "present ourselves with ardent zeal, that He may make us capable of receiving it [the gift of Christ's life]."[26] Once again, we encounter this curious logic in which it appears that the reception of grace at the Table seems dependent upon our commitment to show up in a way ("with ardent zeal") by making sure that we have repented of all sin. Perhaps Calvin approached this language more in terms of encouragement rather than reciprocity, but nevertheless it is easily open to misunderstanding.[27]

The Communion prayer finally closes by turning to a classic articulation of the Reformed era: the *Sursum Corda*. The congregation is urged to "lift our spirits and hearts on high where Jesus Christ is in the glory of His Father."[28] With these words, Calvin designates the primary sphere of the ritual's actions as occurring in the heavenly realm. With this rhetorical move Calvin is able to avoid the controversies of his day in terms of where and how the Communion elements are transformed. However, in doing so, Calvin creates a different theological problem by discounting the ritual actions and projecting them into an alternative space. If this sounds harsh, then simply note that Calvin's liturgy explicitly instructs participants to "not be fascinated by these earthly and corruptible elements" in order that our souls can "be nourished and vivified by His substance when they are lifted up above all earthly things."[29] Thus, for Calvin, the spiritual realm is designated as distinct and separate from the physical world where the actions at Table take place. The connection between these spaces is provided by the "bread and wine as signs and witnesses" that point to spiritual truths.[30]

Following this prayer, the Minister invites the people to come forward reverently to receive the elements of bread and wine. The actions at the Table are accompanied by words that reinforce the primary emphasis on the passion of Jesus and Calvin's commitment to the centrality of Christ's atonement. Alongside the sharing of the bread the following words are spoken: "Take, eat, the body of Jesus which has been delivered unto death for you."[31] It is important to note that these words are a theological extension that grows out of the Pauline text in 1 Corinthians 11 (which similarly relies on the Synoptic depictions of the Last Supper). Similarly, the sharing of the cup includes the theological declaration: "This is the cup of the new testament in the blood of Jesus which has been shed for you."[32] In the Strasbourg liturgy, Calvin prescribes that Psalm 138 is sung while people come to the Table. This psalm stresses thanksgiving and praise as central acts, which is surely what attracted Calvin to it. Two quick notes, however, on the choice of this psalm: (1) the psalm itself is in praise of embodied actions in the temple ("I bow down towards your holy temple"[33]). Calvin's spiritualization of the sacrament stands in contrast to the physicality pictured in the language of this psalm; and (2) It is likely that Calvin was attracted to this psalm as one that was used at the conclusion of a Passover meal and could be interpreted as in keeping with the note in John 17 that the gathering in the upper room concluded with the singing of a psalm.

The service closes with a prayer after Communion, the singing of the Canticle of Simeon, and a benediction. The prayer stresses the theological claims that we have previously noted that are central to Calvin's liturgy, namely the connection between the Lord's Supper and Christ's passion. Then the prayer turns toward ethical exhortation for the growth of faith for all who have come to the Table. The choice of the Canticle of Simeon draws on the language that "our eyes have seen your salvation," which gestures toward the understanding of Christ's presence through the work of the Holy Spirit. Finally, the biblical recitation of a benediction uses the words of Numbers 6:24–26 as a biblical text to accompany the congregation as they leave the sanctuary.

3

Baptism

In the opening chapter, we witnessed the ways in which Calvin's theological presuppositions shaped how he read, interpreted, and used Scripture in worship. In the last chapter, we saw how this played out in terms of his understanding of the Lord's Supper and especially how it provided him with a particular approach to using Scripture in the Communion liturgies that he wrote for the congregations in Strasbourg and Geneva where he served as pastor. In this chapter, we will explore the similar ways in which these theological commitments shaped his approach to baptism.

Calvin's approach was to use Scripture to critique what he viewed as the malpractices of the Roman Catholic Church. Similar to his critique of the Mass, Calvin strongly objected to the complex rituals that surrounded the baptismal practices of his time. He sought a simpler baptismal ceremony in which the promises of Scripture would be clearly heard and understood by all in the congregation. As we will see, though, Calvin's own liturgies underscore the complicated theological choices that he made to advance the baptismal practices and theology of the Reformed tradition. The starting place for Calvin and the Reformers was to show the biblical association between a sacrament and Scripture and, in particular, to point toward a way in which the church's practice was linked with a command of Christ.

Alongside the Lord's Supper, Calvin accepted baptism as one of two sacraments that were instituted by Christ. For Calvin, the role of baptism was primarily to serve as a rite of initiation in which one was received into the body of Christ and named as a child of God. In this way, Calvin stands in agreement with the other theological options of his day—be they Roman Catholic,

Lutheran, or Anabaptist. However, Calvin's emphatic stress on the sovereignty of God, especially in terms of his doctrine of election (that God chooses those who are part of the covenant community), presented him with a quandary. How does one affirm the significance of the act of baptism without placing emphasis on either the ritual and presider (in this instance, the words of the priest as efficacious) or the decision and action of the individual being baptized (the profession of faith by the one who is receiving "believer's baptism" as was stressed by the Anabaptists)? Calvin solved this theological conundrum in a creative and radical way by insisting that baptism was not essential for salvation. There were significant theological and pastoral consequences connected to this position, and it required a delicate balancing act for Calvin to navigate a way to hold on to a central role for the baptismal rite while also unlinking it from its place as a salvific act provided by the church or chosen by the individual.

A primary connection was to link the act of baptism with the repentance of sin. For Calvin, the baptismal service underscored the role of God's promise of forgiveness to all those who were chosen to participate in the new community that was made possible by Christ. This emphasis allowed Calvin to stress the primary role of the Word as that which contains the promises of Scripture that then can be seen in the sacramental acts (the visible word). As with the Lord's Supper, the promise of salvation is inextricably connected to Calvin's interpretation of atonement in which the sacrificial death of Christ on the cross provides the means by which God forgives our sin and receives us into the body of Christ. Calvin underscores the relationship between baptism and forgiveness by referring to baptism as the sacrament of repentance. In the *Institutes*, Calvin notes that "through baptism, believers are assured that this condemnation has been removed and withdrawn from them, since . . . the Lord promises us by this sign that full and complete remission has been made."[1]

From the very beginning of our exploration of baptism, we are faced with the complexity of the ways in which Calvin's reading of Scripture provides the theological justification for his liturgical decisions. For example, notice Calvin's declaration about the role of water in the baptismal rite. Calvin finds the biblical warrant for baptism and its role in cleansing us of sin by drawing on 1 Peter 3:21, which pictures baptism as an appeal to God rather than as a "removal of dirt from the body." The text allows Calvin to develop a tension that exists in the New Testament around the tendency to view the cleansing metaphor in baptism in a hyper-literal way. This becomes even more important in terms of the historical association of baptism as a cleansing from original sin (a particularly unfortunate aspect of the Augustinian tradition). Calvin draws on the text from 1 Peter to downplay the role of water in baptism by insisting that "baptism promises us no other purification than through the sprinkling of Christ's blood, which is represented by means of water from the resemblance to cleansing and washing."[2] The stress on Christ's salvific act provides Calvin with the opportunity to locate forgiveness in the one-time event of Christ's death on the cross. This move is parallel to Calvin's approach to the Lord's Supper, which insists that the sacramental actions in the sanctuary provide a way to actively remember (which is closely akin to the meaning of the Greek word *anamnēsis*) the passion of Christ. An advantage of this theological approach is that it provides a rationale for the way in which the act of baptism pictures God's forgiveness of sins throughout one's life. This allows Calvin to avoid several controversial issues: (1) it reinforces his theological insistence that baptism is not salvific in itself by locating salvation within God's action in the historical event of the cross; (2) it provides a way for Calvin to recognize the fallenness of humanity and to affirm his understanding of the total depravity of humanity, which again places the stress on God's grace rather than on human agency; (3) it secures an emphasis on election as God's action independent of human response (which becomes particularly significant in terms of Calvin's defense of infant baptism); and (4) it provides an important contrast to the concern that one's salvation could be jeopardized by sin after one's baptism.

Calvin employs the Pauline language in Romans of engrafting to discuss how the act of baptism unites us with Christ.[3] The text provides a significant parallel to Calvin's understanding of participating in the Lord's Supper as providing mystical union with Christ. Calvin still needs to show a dominical command that provides the basis for recognizing baptism as a sacrament. In the *Institutes*, he cites the narrative of the baptism of Jesus in Matthew 3 as the biblical warrant for the theological claim of "baptism as token of our union with Christ."[4] The Scripture also provides him a link to Jesus's own mystical experience portrayed as the heavens opening, a dove descending, and a divine voice proclaiming, "This is my beloved Son, in whom I am well pleased"[5] and offers important themes that Calvin will explore in his baptismal theology: (1) God as the primary actor in the event of baptism; (2) the dove as the sign of the Holy Spirit, which connects with Calvin's pneumatological emphasis throughout his theology; and (3) the declaration of divine kinship signified by baptism. By using the Gospel narrative in this way (not as the primary biblical warrant for the actions of baptism, but for the claims that are central to his theological position), Calvin is forced to wrestle with the apparent differences between Jesus's baptism by John the Baptist in the Jordan River and the ceremonial aspects of baptism in the sixteenth-century church (all while insisting on a return to the primitive church). Calvin insists that John's baptism for the forgiveness of sins represents exactly the same doctrine as that of the apostles even though they are administered in different ways.[6] Calvin turns away from the actions of both the biblical text and the rituals in the sanctuary to insist on a true spiritual meaning that connects disparate actions.

The hermeneutical key is found in Calvin's use of circumcision as the primary biblical metaphor for Christian baptism. Calvin refers to the Old Testament ritual as a prototype of baptism, particularly in terms of the relationship of this ritual act as a sign of inclusion in a covenant community. This figurative interpretation of Old Testament texts is prevalent among early reformed writers. Theodore Beza develops this line of reasoning in reflecting on the proper way to interpret the Words of Institution in the Lord's Supper: "Thus also it is said that circumcision is the covenant, that is, the true sign and ratification of the covenant."[7] While we will explore the rich ways in which Calvin uses biblical text to buttress this claim, his presentation of this point is filled with metaphorical confusion. For example, note the convoluted route that Calvin explores in order to show a way that circumcision functions as a "symbol of cleansing." Calvin uses the image of the cloud that accompanies the children of Israel as a sign of cleansing and protection to the covenant people (marked by circumcision) as an analogy to the way in which "in baptism we are covered and protected by Christ's blood."[8] It is important to note the way in which Calvin utilizes Old Testament texts to develop his claim about the continuity between the covenants in the two testaments. His approach contrasts with Luther's emphasis on law and gospel by developing ways to show how the relationship of the promises in the Hebrew Scripture align with those in the New Testament. As we have previously noted, this hermeneutical approach provides an important rationale for Calvin's practice of regularly preaching through Old Testament books of the Bible. It is Calvin's theology that guides his use of Scripture and provides the interpretive keys through which he presents the liturgical framework that supports his understanding of the sacraments.

In placing the primary emphases in baptism on welcoming and the forgiveness of sin, Calvin is able to locate God as the primary actor in the baptismal rite. It is not the confession of sin from the initiate that is efficacious, but the celebration of God's bountiful mercy that is portrayed in this sacrament. This allows Calvin the opportunity to provide a rigorous theological defense of the practice of infant baptism even though it lacks the kind of biblical warrant that he normally requires. Here Calvin turns to circumcision as the primary biblical action that prefigures infant baptism. The topic is so important to Calvin that he devotes an entire chapter (with thirty-two sections!) to present his defense of infant baptism as the normative practice of the church.

Calvin's defensive posture is warranted given the attacks on the practice made by the Anabaptists. Their rejection of infant baptism due to the lack of any clear description in the New Testament provided both Zwingli and Calvin with significant challenges. On the one hand, Calvin's approach to baptism faced significant challenges from parents who were concerned about the fate of their children's salvation. Calvin's denial of the salvific significance of baptism (as a guarantee of eternal life) presented pastoral conflicts particularly in responding to concerns from parents of infants with critical illnesses.[9] At the same time, Anabaptists insisted that Calvin's acceptance of infant baptism demonstrated his lack of commitment to the true reformation of the church via the pure teachings of Scripture.

Calvin is determined to defend the practice of infant baptism by using biblical texts to show the ways in which this sacrament is based on Scripture and founded on revelation and the authority of God. As Calvin notes, "For a sacrament, unless it rests upon the sure foundation of God's word, hangs by a thread."[10] As with his analysis of the Lord's Supper, Calvin separates the spiritual meaning from the ritual actions as a way to point toward the "inner mysteries" that are presented in the sacrament of baptism. As we have seen, the promise of baptism is dependent on its theological connection to the analogy of cleansing that Calvin connects to Christ's death on the cross. Since this primary meaning of the sacraments is grounded in the way in which Calvin develops his theological understanding of God's covenant with humanity, Calvin quickly turns to the relationship between circumcision and the Abrahamic covenant as analogous to Christian baptism. For Calvin, the spiritual meaning of these two distinct practices points toward a shared truth that is derived from Calvin's interpretation of these signs. To make this case, Calvin draws on the biblical image that the circumcision of the heart is the true meaning of baptism. The citation of Deuteronomy 30:6 ("Moreover, the LORD your God will circumcise your heart and the heart of your descendants, so that you will love the LORD your God with all your heart and with all your soul, in order that you may live.") establishes the logic of the primary point that supports Calvin's argument. First, it locates the meaning of the event in God's action rather than a human act performed by a priest or minister. Second, it underscores the commitment to an inner spiritual meaning as primary and in many ways distinct from the visible acts. Third, it provides the biblical warrant that is so important to Calvin in justifying the theological and liturgical actions of the church. Fourth, it shows a way to develop the logic that supports the practice of infant baptism by linking it with the adoption of the descendants in the context of a covenant community. The use of these motifs in the prophetic tradition provides Calvin with additional biblical warrants to present his case. He concludes: "We have, therefore a spiritual promise given to the patriarchs in circumcision such as is given us in baptism, since it represented for them forgiveness of sins and mortification of flesh."[11] This broad, associative way of reading Scripture serves as the primary logic in the creative and correlative way that Calvin develops the analogy between circumcision and baptism. Both signs point to the grace extended by God in the covenant that God makes with humanity.

Just in case we have missed this point, Calvin titles his next section: "The difference is in externals only."[12] Here Calvin contends that the promise of circumcision and baptism is the same: namely, that God provides forgiveness and salvation. Any differences between these acts (and let's be clear, there are some pretty significant ones!) is in Calvin's words "a very slight factor."[13] This theological sleight of hand provides the launching pad for the expansive claims that Calvin develops in terms of his defense of infant baptism. Since circumcision for the Jews "assured adoption as the people and household of God," so too baptism functions in this way for Christians. With this theological method, Calvin is able to defend his liturgical practices while relying on the traditional way he develops the relationship between Hebrew Scriptures and the New Testament. What we see here became a distinctive theological signature of the Reformed tradition, in which the theological use of Scripture is marshalled to present an argument to defend the liturgical practices of congregations. This theological defense seeks to avoid acknowledging the decision of continuing the practice of infant baptism as a way to provide for social order (a point made by historian Karen Spierling[14]). In a time of significant unrest, when Calvin and other reformers were already responsible for dramatic upheaval in terms of the regular worship practices of congregational life, it is worth paying attention to the ways in which Calvin searches for theological and biblical grounds to defend his commitment to support the normative practice of infant baptism.

By defining the rituals of circumcision and baptism in terms of their primary role as initiation rites that welcome children into the life of a community of faith, Calvin develops a second way to link to a biblical warrant to support infant baptism. As we will see in the coming section, this becomes particularly important in terms of the baptismal liturgy that he writes for the church in Geneva. In the *Institutes*, Calvin offers his initial justification by arguing that Jesus's welcoming of the children in Matthew 19:13–15 provides the christological example of welcoming modeled by the church in the practice of infant baptism. While Calvin quickly acknowledges that this is not a baptismal text in terms of the practice itself, Jesus's words to the disciples about the importance of embracing children provide the hermeneutical link that connects the text with the sacrament. "Let the children come to me, and do not stop them, for it is to such as these that the kingdom of heaven belongs" in verse 14 persuades Calvin that the portrait of Jesus welcoming children as part of God's reign provides the theological basis that then is symbolized in the rite of baptism. "If the Kingdom of Heaven belongs to them, why is the sign denied which . . .

opens to them a door into the church. . . ."[15] Note that Calvin's argument here once again develops a point of separation between the meaning of baptism and the act of it, with the external sign of baptism functioning as a form of witness to the real, spiritual event that is perceived as God's act that is independent from the actions of a minister or the rites of a church.

Calvin develops this point while also noting that Scripture is silent on the subject of infant baptism, which, ironically, affirms the lack of a clear biblical warrant for the practice. However, for Calvin this silence serves as a way to push aside the objection of the Anabaptists and to signal the theological rationale in terms of affirming God's action in establishing the covenant and welcoming members of the family into the community. This logic leads Calvin back to circumcision as the primary grounds for accepting the practice of infant baptism. From this basis, Calvin struggles to defend the apparent differences between these ritual practices, including the obvious fact that circumcision applies to only male infants whereas baptism is for all children. Because these rites function to point to a broader spiritual claim, Calvin sweeps aside any differences between them by affirming "the resemblance between baptism and circumcision, which we see most completely in accord with respect to the inner mystery, the promises, the use, and efficacy."[16]

Only following an extensive exploration of the commonalities between circumcision and baptism does Calvin finally turn to the Gospels and the baptismal language both in Jesus's baptism by John the Baptist and in Jesus's instruction to his disciples to baptize and teach (in the Great Commission in Matthew 28). Calvin quickly rejects the Anabaptist argument that these texts provide the biblical rationale for adult baptism by insisting that the order of baptizing and teaching provides the pattern for baptism preceding the instruction of children in the Christian faith. Similarly, he alludes to the pattern in John 3 of being born of water and the Spirit to support the act of baptism that then is followed by teaching and growth in the Spirit. In this instance, Calvin emphasizes the initiatory experience of baptism that is followed by the Spirit's work in our lives in contrast to his previous emphasis that stressed God's action that leads to baptism.

In the end, Calvin is content to make a theological argument that is grounded in prioritizing the role of baptism as an initiation rite that supports the emphasis on a distinctive role of the covenant community. At its best, this allows Calvin to affirm a primary place of gratitude as the appropriate response for humans in responding to God's initiative. He concludes the section on baptism with the following exhortation: "unless we wish spitefully to obscure God's goodness, let us offer our infants to him, for he gives them a place among those of his family and household, that is, the members of the church."[17] We will see how this theology takes shape in the church's liturgy in Geneva.

REARRANGING THE BAPTISMAL SERVICE

In our overview of the Lord's Supper, we noted the ways in which Calvin distinguished Reformed practice from Roman Catholic patterns. The dramatic differentiation in the form of ritual action and participation were clear points of demarcation between the theological interpretations. This can be seen in the moving of the altar (and insisting on referring to it as a table), the use of the vernacular language, full and regular participation in terms of both eating and drinking at the Table, and the development of a new liturgy (with the words of institution as the one remaining textual link). When it came to baptism, Calvin's decision to continue the normative practice of infant baptism placed him in a less radical position than the Anabaptists.

There is one dramatic area of ritual change that grew out of Calvin's theological presuppositions. Calvin's affirmation of baptism as an initiation ritual that welcomes infants into the covenant community led him to insist on the significance of the baptismal rite taking place as part of a regular worship service in the congregation (either on Sunday or one of the daily services). This change represents a major transition to the normal baptismal practices that were understood as private services held either in the church or at home. Godparents were usually the primary ones to present the child (often the mother was recovering from the birthing process and the father was in charge of the celebration of this significant rite of passage). Calvin's clarity on baptism as incorporation into the household of faith prompted him to locate this rite in the regular life of the congregation. For him, this turned the emphasis in baptism away from a private affair designed to ensure salvation for the infant to a shared event that bound together the community to live into the promises offered in the sacrament. This vision of baptism prompted Calvin to simplify the ritual so that the primary claim of baptism (in terms of God's initiative in choosing us in spite of our sin) was not overshadowed by the design and celebration of the ritual. The result was a dramatic reorientation of the baptismal rite that focused the action within the context of the life of the community. The insistence on baptism occurring during a regular worship service marks the first sign of this change and is accompanied with the expectation that the parents will be present at the baptism. Prioritizing the claims of the church over the social expectations of the society and at times health needs of the mother and child presented an enormous shift in the accepted practices. Calvin's liturgy simplified the baptismal rite by removing aspects that he viewed as unnecessary accretions that lacked biblical support and failed to affirm the central theological claims of baptism.

We can observe changes in baptismal practices that in many ways are analogous to Calvin's revision of the Lord's Supper. The removal of major elements of the Mass was designed to highlight the promises of the Table, where the spiritual truth of the sacrament was celebrated as a visible word to sustain the life of the community. Similarly, the removal of what Calvin deemed as extraneous elements (his language on these acts was much more colorful) centered the rite on primary theological claims that he outlined in the *Institutes*. This included a host of rituals that surrounded the act of baptism itself, including rites of exorcism that had become a central component of the baptismal rite and portrayed an understanding of baptism that dramatized the movement of baptism as cleansing and release from evil and sin to the assurance of salvation through participation in the church's proclamation of grace.

Calvin's first move, then, is to deconstruct the Roman rituals in order to realign them with his theological commitments that were informed by his reading and interpretation of Scripture. The result was the rejection of a series of associated rituals, including actions outside the door of the church building as well as the use of oil, salt, candles, and spit along with other gestures that for Calvin decentered the sacrament's focus on the font. The shift in making the font central is parallel to the way in which Calvin's moving of the table into the congregation provided a place of communal gathering focused on the bread and cup. Similarly, the simplification of the baptismal rite is designed to highlight the communal promises that are shared around the baptismal font. The demand of parental presence and participation in the rite aligns with Calvin's commitment to promoting household piety and the role of education as key to spiritual formation and development.

THE BAPTISMAL LITURGY IN GENEVA

The rubrics for Calvin's liturgy begin by stressing the importance of the congregation's participation in the service since "baptism is a kind of formal adoption into the Church."[18] This understanding provides the basis for Calvin's insistence that baptism occurs as part of the regular worship services of the church. The baptismal liturgy begins with a citation from Psalm 124:8: "Our help is the Lord who made heaven and earth." The role of Scripture here is to assert our dependence on God who is the source of hope. This serves as a kind of broad biblical warrant for the theological claims of baptism as God's initiative. The citation is followed by the minister asking the parents, "Do you offer this infant for baptism?"[19] Note the assumptions here (1) that baptism is for infants, which was the normative practice in Calvin's day, and (2) that baptism acts as a form of offering in giving back to God the blessing of new life in the form of an infant.

The minister then offers an extended explanation of the theological rationale for baptism. For our purposes, it is fascinating to note the arc of this argument in terms of the primary ways that baptism is presented. Two preliminary observations seem salient: (1) While we see that there is a christological argument that is central to this rite, it is not connected to the Gospel stories of Jesus's own baptism by John the Baptist. Calvin's liturgy makes no attempt to provide this biblical link or to present the act of baptism in any way as a mimetic form of Jesus's life (which could easily be done either by referencing Jesus's baptism, which is a narrative shared by all four of the Gospels, or in terms of the Pauline interpretation of baptism in Romans 6:4 as participation in Christ's death and resurrection—"We were buried with him [Christ] by baptism into death, so that, just as Christ was raised from the dead by the Father, so we also might walk in newness of life"); and (2) the liturgy creates an extended arc that connects baptism to the life-long journey of discipleship. This is a remarkable accomplishment that has often been overlooked in Calvin's liturgy. Against the theological tradition of Rome, with the church offering the sacrament of baptism to respond to our need for salvation and the claims of the Anabaptist of baptism as a sign of the regeneration that is the result of our decision to follow Christ, Calvin charts a theological course in which the gift of baptism is a response to the human condition but is in many ways dependent upon our growth in the community of faith that provides us with the educational resources to assist us in the goal of maturing in the life of faith as a way of living into the promises of baptism.

Calvin's liturgy provides a vision of renewed life in which baptism is offered as a way to participate in the contours of this broader theological trajectory. The liturgy begins by pointing toward human finitude and our need for grace by noting that we are born in "poverty and wretchedness."[20] The christological link comes by affirming Christ's incarnation as an act of solidarity with the purpose of pointing us toward our inability to rely on our own abilities while opening up for us the opportunity of new birth as a gift of God (interestingly the word "sin" is not mentioned in this opening paragraph).[21] The liturgy rehearses the opening claims of the *Institutes* in terms of the relationship between the knowledge of self and our limitations and the knowledge of God, who is the only source of life. Similarly, the baptismal rite begins by stressing that an awareness of our finitude can serve to help us recognize our dependence on God.

Next, the liturgy develops a key pneumatological theme that animates Calvin's theology. The possibility of new life comes via the Holy Spirit. Calvin stresses this throughout the liturgy that regeneration comes to us by the Holy Spirit and that it is the Spirit that "conducts and governs us, to produce in us works that are agreeable."[22] The renunciation of our dependence on ourselves parallels the christological move. While the liturgy does not explicitly reference Philippians 2, it follows the logic of the text where the incarnation and Jesus's humility and obedience led to his death on the cross. Calvin's liturgy nods in this direction by linking the Spirit's work as dependent upon the "accomplishment" of "our Lord Jesus Christ, whose death and passion have such virtue, that in participating in it we are as it were buried to sin . . . [and] by virtue of his resurrection, we rise again to new life."[23] To summarize, this section of the baptismal liturgy develops a christological foundation of the rite in terms of the passion of Christ that identifies the Spirit's work as prompting us to turn to God as the sole source of grace.

The prayer then turns to reassert the role of baptism as confirmation of God's work of incorporating us into the church. Calvin identifies the purpose of the sacrament as a way that "attests to the remission of our sins."[24] This is an additional way in which Calvin points out a form of separation between the experience of forgiveness and grace and the act of baptism, which serves as a sign of God's action. For Calvin, the water is a symbolic gesture of our need for spiritual cleansing that points to our need for God to cleanse us. Calvin presents this interpretation as a "twofold grace": first, that God is willing to look beyond our sin and grant us new life; and second, that in baptism we receive the Holy Spirit who works within us to contest the forces of evil and temptation. For Calvin, this twofold grace provides the basis for this discussion of the relationship between justification and sanctification. These actions are grounded in the work of Jesus Christ, whose death and resurrection provide the source of our cleansing ("we have no other laver than his blood").[25]

These actions provide the basis for the covenant that God extends to us. Here Calvin doubles back to connect to the sign of circumcision, which remains the primary source for his baptismal theology. This again gives Calvin a way to extend the promises of baptism to the children of believers who are adopted into the covenant. Calvin even cites Genesis 17:12 as a warrant for the action that links the Abrahamic covenant with the church—an argument that is dependent upon Calvin's conviction that the signs of circumcision and baptism are identical. The christological turn provides Calvin with a way for God "to extend the covenant of salvation over all the world, instead of confining it as formerly to the Jews."[26] This provides the grounds for the liturgical move to cite Jesus's welcoming of the children in Matthew 19:14 as a biblical warrant for the baptism of infants. Jesus's actions provide the rule for us to follow in our practice of welcoming children into the life of the community.[27]

Following this lengthy prayer by the minister, the liturgy turns to three unison elements: (1) a collective prayer that summarizes the logic of the minister's prayer. The role of this is to offer a petition to God that the baptism will be efficacious, which is connected in the prayer to the proper understanding of the role of baptism and in this way provides a form of catechesis; (2) the recitation of the Lord's Prayer, which serves as a way to participate in a kind of christological mimesis that provides a parallel to the use of the so-called words of institution (*ipsissima verba*) in the Lord's Supper; here the congregation recites the words of Jesus as a way to provide dominical support for the actions at the font; and (3) the recitation of the Apostles' Creed as a summation of the doctrine of the church that is to be passed on to the one receiving baptism. In the use of the Apostles' Creed, Calvin follows the tradition of the Roman Catholic Church and the historical role of the creed in the baptismal liturgy.

These three shared pieces of the liturgy are essential in terms of Calvin's emphasis on congregational participation and to the importance of continued growth as essential to the formation of faith. Following these elements, the minister asserts the significance of education in order for us to live into the promises of baptism. The emphasis here is on the shared commitment to instruct the baptized in the truth of Christian faith. Calvin offers one more theological turn in the liturgy by using his broad understanding of the third use of the law as the goal of Christian life. Calvin cites Jesus's summation of the law as the *telos* of Christian life: "to love God with heart, mind, strength, and our neighbor as ourselves."[28]

Finally, the naming of the child is linked to the act of baptism using the traditional Trinitarian formula. The rubrics of the liturgy stress the importance of the liturgy in the vernacular language so that people will understand the meaning of baptism and experience it as a form of renewal of their own baptism. The rubrics end with a forceful rejection of the use of any additional ritual elements that are "not of the ordination of God, but have been added by men."[29] For Calvin, these additional actions are not part of the form of baptism that was instituted by Jesus Christ. As we have seen both in Calvin's theological explanation of baptism as well as his liturgy, Calvin prefers to draw on circumcision and covenant language rather than centering the rite on the narrative of Jesus's baptism.

Our analysis of Calvin's liturgies shows how Calvin's theological commitments directed his reading and interpretation of Scripture. The liturgies Calvin developed for the Reformed communities in Strasbourg and Geneva develop the theological ideas that undergird Calvin's understanding of the central role of Word and sacrament. In the following section, we will explore ways in which the Reformed tradition drew on Calvin's insights as well as the ways in which they codified particular aspects of Calvin's theology. We can track these developments in early Reformed confessional statements as well as in liturgies that were used in Reformed communities.

PART II

Modern Influences
From Westminster to the *Book of Common Worship* (1993)

4

Scripture

SCRIPTURE IN THE EARLY REFORMED CONFESSIONS

Scripture served as the central ingredient in the direction that Calvin and other early reformers led their communities. Their approach to reading Scripture was guided by their commitment to humanistic approaches that emphasized the need to study texts in their original languages as a way to free the text from dogmatic interpretations and claims in order to recover the Word of God as the source that served as the foundation for the covenant community. The commitment to read and study the Bible required several critical steps. First, the study of Scripture prompted Calvin (and others) to recognize a striking disparity between the teachings and practices of the Roman Catholic Church of their time and their vision of worship in early Christian communities. Thus, Scripture was read to differentiate these new movements from other approaches (Roman Catholic or Anabaptist). Among the wider reformation efforts, the rallying cry of *sola scriptura* provided a basis for insisting on particular interpretations of Scripture as the source to guide the theological visions and claims for diverse Protestant communities. The Augsburg Confession in 1530 marks an important milestone in summarizing the theological claims that distinguished the Lutheran movement in Germany. The goal of this and subsequent confessions was to provide additional clarity to the distinctive biblical and theological claims beyond the shared basis of the Nicene and Apostles' Creeds. The Augsburg Confession includes scriptural citations to support the theological claims set forth in the articles. A decade later, Phillipp Melanchthon set forth a revised version of the Augsburg Confession (1540), known as the *Variata*, in an effort to broaden cooperation between Protestant communities. While Calvin and other reformed leaders participated in the meeting and signed the document, the revisions, particularly around the statement on Christ's presence in the Lord's Supper, proved to be divisive among Lutherans.[1]

These confessional statements served as a primary method by which communities articulated and clarified their theological positions. The Augsburg Confession provided a pattern by which communities positively stated their theological commitments while also underscoring their differences from the Roman Catholic Church. In making this case, the statement relied on biblical citations to support the theological claims articulated in the confession.

Reformed communities across the European continent developed confessional statements to guide congregations in their geographical areas: the French Confession in 1559 (which was written by Calvin), the Scots Confession in 1560, the Belgic Confession in 1561, and the Heidelberg Catechism in 1563 are examples of confessional statements that articulate a Reformed theological perspective for the context of congregations in particular geographical areas. In fact, more than sixty statements of faith were written and adopted by Reformed communities during the latter half of the sixteenth century. In terms of their approach to Scripture, there are two key characteristics that mark these confessional documents. First, each statement provides a theological declaration of the centrality of Scripture to the faith of their communities. While there is a wide variance in terms of the length and placement of the articles on the authority of Scripture in the confessional documents, Reformed communities across geographic areas were united in affirming the significance of Scripture through their theological declarations and communal practices. The French Confession of 1559 includes four articles early in the confessional document (3 through 6) that strongly assert the Bible as the "sure rule of our faith, not so much by the common accord and consent of the church, as by the testimony and inward illumination of the Holy Spirit."[2] By contrast the Scots Confession, written only one year later, provides one brief paragraph on the authority of Scripture (19). The Second Helvetic Confession, written in 1562, begins with two lengthy opening chapters on Scripture as the true Word of God. While there are interesting distinctions between these statements on Scripture, they all share a common commitment to asserting the theological significance of Scripture in their communities.

There is a second equally important common practice in these early Reformed confessional statements, namely the use of biblical citations in order to show that the theological claims are supported by the interpretation of particular scriptural texts. This use of biblical warrants was prominent in Calvin's writings and, as we saw in chapter 1, became a key aspect of the development of Reformed liturgies. The Heidelberg Catechism particularly illustrates this method by offering theological summaries and key excerpts from Scripture in the Ten Commandments and the Lord's Prayer. This summary of belief in the form of question and answer is deeply rooted in the language of Scripture and carefully documented with references to particular texts.

SCRIPTURE AND THE WESTMINSTER STANDARDS

The Westminster Standards mark an important transitional moment in terms of the role of confessional statements for Reformed congregations, particularly in the English-speaking world. Like earlier confessional documents, the Westminster divines understood their role as providing a clear outline of Reformed theological teachings. However, in England in the mid-seventeenth century, there was less of a need to clarify the opposition to Roman Catholic doctrine than to articulate a Reformed theology for their own particular context. Their work included a confessional statement (with a list of scriptural citations), shorter and larger catechisms, a directory for worship, and a form of church government. While the documents emphasized primary theological commitments of earlier Reformed confessions, they pulled back on certain theological claims, for example in naming the doctrine of predestination as a "high mystery" that "is to be handled with special attendance and care."[3] The confession is noteworthy in its attempt to soften harsher versions of Calvinism that emerged, particularly the strict interpretation of election and (double) predestination offered by the Dutch Reformed Church at the Synod of Dort in 1618–19.

In its description of the purpose of Scripture, the Westminster Confession provides a clear articulation in its opening chapter by offering a list of the canonical books and asserting the authority of Scripture as derived from God. Westminster offers a strong summary of Scripture's authority that stands directly in line with Calvin and other Reformed confessions. In starting with a statement on the Bible, it seeks to show Scripture as the source from which all theological claims are made. Both the confession and the Shorter and Larger Catechism rely heavily on scriptural language and images, but it is interesting to note that the list of biblical citations (warrants) was added later at the request of the House of Commons. As a whole, the Westminster Standards provide a summary of the Reformed movement as it developed over its first century. In this regard, the documents are essential reading for those who study the early theological commitments of diverse Reformed congregations. Equally important, though, is the role that Westminster played over the course of the next three centuries, particularly among English-speaking communities. Even when there were disagreements about the extent to which the doctrinal outlines required subscription, Westminster provided the terms of the debate.

THE RISE OF MODERNITY AND THE
ROLE OF BIBLICAL CRITICISM

One can interpret the rise of modernity in different ways. The humanistic roots that spurred Protestant reform movements certainly provided impetus for new forms of inquiry to emerge. This is particularly the case in terms of a commitment to study Scripture as a way to question the dogmatic teachings of the church. The early Reformed confessions all use Scripture as the primary source in constructing new theological teachings. In doing so, they model important elements that became central in theological and philosophical circles. Even before Westminster provided a theological summation, philosophers like Descartes, Spinoza, and Leibniz were providing the basis for what became known as the age of reason. Looking back at Westminster from a twentieth-century perspective, theologian Edward A. Dowey Jr. observed that its language and style were no longer intelligible. "While Westminster is thus a post-Reformation statement, it is by no means a modern one. It derives from an age of scholastic theology, of pre-occupation with authority and law, of churchly and political absolutism."[4] The new focus on reason that became a central component in the emergence of modernity began to turn its attention to new methods for reading Scripture in order to contest dogmatic claims now coming from both Roman Catholic and Protestant churches.

The development of historical-critical methodologies challenged the hermeneutical approaches that had previously dominated the reading and preaching of biblical texts. The goal of this methodology was to free the reading of Scripture from the dogmatic constraints that controlled its interpretation. The strength of the quest for the historical Jesus (in all of its iterations) was in its attempt to break through the ecclesial and dogmatic assumptions that often restricted the reading of the texts in order for the readers of the gospel to encounter the witness of Scripture to Jesus Christ. While Albert Schweitzer later exposed the naive cultural assumptions that at times guided these efforts (e.g., the rejection of eschatological language or stories of miracles as contrary to the expectations and needs of modern people), the critical study of biblical texts established its roots within the academy and trained clergy in particular methodologies of reading Scripture.

For our purposes, we will note the way in which this shift in reading Scripture challenges the normative ways that we described Calvin's commitment to Word and sacrament. On the one hand, the rise of source and textual critical tools to study the biblical canon can be seen as reinforcing Calvin's commitment to the value of reading and preaching on texts from both of the testaments. On the other hand, the dominance of the historical-critical method led increasingly to the sense that the reading and interpretation of Scripture belonged in the hands of experts who were properly trained to make sense of these strange texts. As we will see in the coming chapters on the Lord's Supper and baptism, Calvin's typological and associative ways of reading Scripture are increasingly labeled as eisegetical explorations of biblical texts that violate the historical settings and meaning(s) of a particular passage. By contrast, the use of historical-critical tools seeks to determine the original meaning(s) of a text in its particular historical context in order that the readers/hearers will discover ways that the text addresses them. This approach to Scripture places a renewed emphasis on an educated clergy who can interpret the biblical texts in an increasingly secular world. It is interesting to note how this development can be read parallel to the rise of humanism and its role in the Reformation, alongside the accompanying need to find ways to address the biblical literacy of those within congregations.

SCHLEIERMACHER AND MODERN THEOLOGY

Alongside the rise of critical methodologies for reading Scripture, new theological methods brought an emphasis on the role of reason in articulating theological statements. For Schleiermacher, often referred to as the father of modern theology, the shift is marked by a turn to the self through which talk of God is closely connected to one's own existence.[5] The result is an understanding of theology that views doctrine less as a primary summary that requires intellectual agreement than as a secondhand articulation of the feelings of the heart. "Christian doctrines are accounts of the Christian religious affections set forth in speech."[6] Rather than identifying Scripture as the external ground from which one makes a case for the significance of the sacraments, Schleiermacher begins by acknowledging the gift of faith as the grounds by which one comes to Scripture in order to grow in Christian piety. To this end, Scripture plays a different role: rather than providing the primary historical data, Schleiermacher describes Scripture as that which continues to provide a powerful witness to the presence of the Infinite, which for Christians is named as God in Christ. Scripture serves as a testimony that moves us to apprehend God through the feeling of utter dependence on the divine. Schleiermacher concludes that "just as the Apostles already had faith before they arrived at that condition of mind . . . in our case too faith must pre-exist before . . ."[7] The testimony of Scripture serves as a confirmation of the gift of faith.

This alternative approach to reading and interpreting Scripture shifts away from the use of biblical warrants and typological readings that supported theological presuppositions and liturgical practices. This includes a significant critique of the language of the sacraments given the absence of the word "sacrament" in Scripture. On this point, Schleiermacher followed up on an insight from the sixteenth-century reformer Huldrych Zwingli, who decried the use of the word "sacrament" since it seemed to imply "something great and holy which by its own power can free the conscience from sin."[8] Schleiermacher's concerns go beyond the connotations of the term and focus on the role of baptism and the Lord's Supper as ordinances of Christ for the maintenance of the community of the church. On this basis, we will discover how Schleiermacher's approach to baptism and the Lord's Supper breaks new ground within the Reformed tradition. Here we will simply note the way in which he links baptism and the Lord's Supper to Christ's priestly activity because "they are continued workings of Christ wrapped in and most closely bound to observances of the church."[9] This critical shift allows Schleiermacher to dismiss attempts to connect baptism and the Lord's Supper to the "Old Testament institutions" of "circumcision and the Passover Feast" as "frequently quite badly misconceived."[10]

KARL BARTH AND SCRIPTURE AS THE WORD OF GOD

The emphasis on the primacy of Scripture received new attention in theological developments within the Reformed tradition during the twentieth century. The primary work of liberal Protestantism in the nineteenth century was to shed the dogmatic restrictions imposed by the church. This can be seen most clearly in the extensive literature of the quest for the historical Jesus, which sought to mine the biblical texts with the emerging tools of the historical-critical method. The goal was that this pursuit of the historical data would free the portrayal of Jesus developed and defended by the church in order that the life of Jesus would address the needs and questions of people in the modern world. This work focused on removing the obstacles of a first-century worldview so that the teachings of Jesus could speak to the lives of people in a scientific and industrial age. The efforts were framed in the optimism of a changing world through the lens of a progressive view of history and a growing confidence in humanity. These assumptions would come to a crashing halt with the outbreak of World War I.

Albert Schweitzer's brilliant overview in *The Quest of the Historical Jesus* charted the futility and elusiveness of the efforts of biblical and theological scholars to capture the message of the Gospels. While we will turn our attention shortly to positive insights and contributions that biblical critical tools continue to offer us, Schweitzer's analysis laid bare the ways in which the theological presuppositions dictated the biographical sketches of the historical Jesus. To cite but one important example from Schweitzer, the rejection of

Jesus's eschatological teachings as inconsistent with modern understandings of human progress displays a dismissive approach to ways Scripture may confront us with a message beyond our expectations. It is precisely this point that serves as a primary starting place in the work of Karl Barth, who became the dominant voice in Reformed theology in the twentieth century.

While Barth had been educated in the theological approaches of classic liberal Protestantism (with Adolf Harnack in Berlin among others), his work as a pastor in a working-class congregation in Safenwil, Switzerland, pushed him to reexamine his theological presuppositions. As he watched the horrors of WWI wreak havoc across the European continent, Barth could no longer accept the assumption of human progress that accompanied his theological training. His study of Scripture culminated in the publication of his groundbreaking commentary on the Epistle to the Romans that shook the theological world when the first edition appeared in Germany in 1918. Even before its publication, we can chart the new direction that Barth's theology is heading in his 1917 address to pastors titled "The New World in the Bible."

Barth begins this essay by noting three common misconceptions about the Bible. Barth dismisses the ways that the Bible has been used as a primary resource for history, morality, and piety. While one can find these elements in Scripture, Barth is keenly aware of how both popular and academic theology have used these categories in order to find biblical support for their own views. Instead, Barth recognizes Scripture as *the* source of revelation and the place we encounter the God who invites us into a "strange new world."[11] Barth signals here that his theology is moving in a new direction, one that will insist that theology must be done from above rather than below. In making this move, Barth takes his cues from Calvin's description of the knowledge of God and self as the source of theology in the opening of the *Institutes*. Barth's development of a neo-orthodox alternative to the prevailing liberal theological alternative of his day can be read as a christocentric reworking of Calvin's *Institutes*.

Barth plays a central role in our study of the place of Scripture in the Reformed tradition. As the dominant voice for the Reformed tradition in the twentieth century, his work reestablished a theological agenda that focused on the central place of Scripture: "the Bible leads us out of the stale atmosphere of humanity and into the open doors of a *new* world, the world of God."[12] For Barth, the Bible serves as the place to encounter the Word of God—a dynamic place in which we find ourselves addressed by God. This provides the sole source of knowledge of God, a point that led to Barth's infamous break with Emil Brunner over the possibility of natural theology. Barth's denial of any role for natural theology is found in his searing essay titled "No! An Answer to Emil Brunner."

Barth's theology reasserts a focus for the theological priorities of Reformed worship by insisting on the centrality of reading and proclaiming Scripture as the place to encounter the Word of God. In an era when questions of biblical relevance were increasingly prominent and where preaching became preoccupied with questions of self-development and a renewed sense of human optimism (which one can chart from the social gospel movement to the later emergence of the prosperity gospel), Barth challenged preachers to take the Bible seriously as the record of God's revelation in Jesus Christ. This commitment to preaching as the place of witness to Christ reflects Barth's priorities, which were pictured by his desk in the form of a copy of Matthias Grünewald's painting of the Isenheim altarpiece portraying John the Baptist pointing to Christ on the cross (painted between 1512 and 1516 on the eve of the Reformation). For Barth, the painting reflected his own primary commitment to developing a theology that pointed to Jesus Christ. This image reflected Barth's understanding of preaching as the place to encounter the Word of God that breaks into our lives. Any other approach runs the risk of idolatry, of creating a god that reflects our own interests and priorities.

We can see Barth's theological and liturgical emphasis on the primacy of Scripture in two important confessional documents that reflect his language and priorities, the Barmen Declaration and the Confession of 1967. Barth served as the primary author of the Barmen Declaration, which articulated the urgent need for the church to oppose Hitler's demand that the German Evangelical Church support the Nazi agenda. There are several important aspects of the confession to note in terms of its theological orientation and the role of Scripture. Barth's christocentrism runs throughout the statement with its emphasis on Jesus Christ as the "one Word of God" and the only object of our obedience in every area of life.[13] For Barth, the centrality of Jesus Christ is clearly connected to the witness of Scripture. Barth emphasizes this point both explicitly and implicitly. Barmen declares that "Jesus Christ, as he is attested for us in Holy Scripture, is the one Word of God which we have to hear and which we have to trust and obey in life and in death."[14] Even beyond this direct assertion, the confession uses biblical citations in a strikingly similar way to what we noted in our sketch of Calvin's theology. Each of the six statements that are identified as evangelical truths begins with a scriptural citation, a form of biblical warrant that was a traditional approach of the Reformed tradition. In this sense, Barmen provides an important model and witness to a distinctly Reformed way to frame a theological position. The use of the confession in worship reinforces this way of reading and citing Scripture to make theological claims.

A second sign of Barth's significant influence can be seen in the Confession of 1967 (C-67). The purpose of this confession was to provide a contemporary statement of faith in light of growing concerns about the relevance of the Westminster Confession of Faith. The decision was not to replace Westminster but to bring together a collection of confessions that represented the church's response at particular times in its history. C-67 channels Barth's theological emphases with the confession framing God's work of reconciliation in Jesus Christ at the center of the document with its opening words: "In Jesus Christ, God was reconciling the world to himself."[15] This theological assertion is connected to Scripture in Section C on the Holy Spirit, which describes the Bible in terms of its witness to Jesus Christ: "The Bible is to be interpreted in the light of its witness to God's work of reconciliation in Christ."[16] It marks an important shift in starting point compared to other confessional statements; C-67 starts with a focus on Jesus Christ in section A, whereas the Scots Confession began with a section on God (the Father/Creator) and Westminster started with Scripture. By placing Scripture in the section on the Holy Spirit, C-67 reinforces the pneumatological emphasis that we noted in Calvin, particularly around the emergence of the Prayer for Illumination in Calvin's liturgy. Here the confession asserts the unique witness of Scripture to Jesus Christ as the Word of God and states that "the Bible is to be interpreted in the light of its witness to God's work of reconciliation in Christ."[17] While affirming the value of both the Old and New Testament and the importance of the historical-critical study of Scripture in order to understand its cultural context, C-67 draws on the covenantal themes in Calvin and Barth to point toward the central theological theme of reconciliation that it stresses throughout the confession.

Barth's influence on the rise of neo-orthodoxy was particularly significant within the Reformed tradition. His insistence on the Bible as the source of revelation where we encounter the Word of God reset the critical conversation on the role of Scripture and preaching in worship. This focus grew out of Barth's own existential struggle to proclaim the gospel in the context of his congregation in the midst of the struggle and loss experienced in WWI. The call for serious engagement with Scripture was not at the expense of the historical-critical method. Instead, the critical study of biblical texts was recognized as a way to open up space so that readers/hearers could encounter God's word. As we saw, Barth's own conviction in his address to pastoral colleagues was to remove the restrictions that readers bring to the text. For Barth, the assumptions of liberal theology ran the risk of idolatry by creating a god who conformed to our own assumptions and expectations. Scripture as God's revelation breaks into our world to offer us "a *new world* ... God, God's lordship! God's honor! God's inconceivable love! Not the history of humanity, but the history of God."[18] In Barth's version of dialectical theology, with its stress on the otherness of God, the reading and proclamation of Scripture point to the one true sacrament, Jesus Christ. Barth underscores this Christocentric approach to Scripture in his description of the three forms of the Word of God (preaching, Scripture, and Jesus Christ) which all serve as witnesses to Christ.

Before we move on to examine other influences on the role of Scripture in worship, it is important to consider the change in the approach to sacraments by significant Reformed theologians. We have seen how Barth shifts the focus of the sacraments from the event of baptism and the Lord's Supper to the meaning of the sacraments, which is Jesus Christ. Barth develops this notion in a way that is analogous to his understanding of the Bible as the place we encounter the Word of God in Jesus Christ. For Barth, Scripture and sacrament provide places where, through the work of the Spirit, we encounter God.

SALVATION HISTORY AS A THEME OF LITURGICAL RENEWAL

As concerns in some circles rose that critical methods were breaking apart any way to hold together a unitive reading of Scripture, two diverse theological movements, one focusing on salvation history and one on liturgical renewal, found common ground in identifying a way to highlight the reading of Scripture in worship for a shared theological goal. A group of biblical theologians began to advocate for salvation history as a unifying way of holding together diverse biblical texts. In Germany, theologians had previously pointed out a linguistic distinction between two German words for history: *Historie* as the basic historical data and *Geschichte* as the interpretation of these events. These distinctions rippled through the historical Jesus research to the extent that some scholars were accused of separating the Jesus of history from the Christ of faith. At stake in these conversations was the attempt to determine verifiable historical data through a critical reading of the Gospels as distinct from dogmatic and theological assertions intended to sustain the teachings of the church.

Proponents of *Heilsgeschichte* (salvation history) sought to solve the tension between historical fact and interpretation by stressing that the primary purpose of Scripture was to present the story of salvation as a theological account of God's action in human history. It was a thoroughly modernist approach that provided a single focal point as a way to deal with the diverse perspectives in the biblical canon. Additionally, the approach avoided the growing concerns about whether biblical literature met the historical standards of modern interpreters. Instead, biblical theologians focused on the ways that passages could be linked to a shared theological theme.

The importance of this for our study is the way in which this theological movement coincided with the emerging influence of the liturgical renewal movement. Beginning in the late nineteenth century among Roman Catholic liturgical scholars, advocates for change to the Mass drew on the recovery of ancient texts that brought new light to liturgical practices in the early centuries of the church. The movement became increasingly influential with its call for reform within the Roman Catholic Church as well as attracting dialogue partners from among Protestants in an era in which ecumenical cooperation emerged as a major area of concern (e.g., note the founding of the World Council of Churches in 1948).

Since the primary focus of our attention in this chapter is on the role of Scripture in worship, we are paying attention to the ways in which these diverse movements come together to produce tangible results in the life of the church. Thus far we have noted Barth's leadership in the emergence of a neo-orthodox theological movement that insisted on the primacy of Scripture. Alongside Barth's theological challenge to the dominance of nineteenth-century liberal Protestantism, the rise of historical-critical methodology provided a way for biblical scholars to approach texts with a new set of tools that sought to determine the meaning(s) of text by focusing on their historical contexts.

DEVELOPING A NEW LECTIONARY

The fruits of these diverse streams of biblical theology and liturgical renewal can be seen in the development of a new common lectionary for Sunday worship that would mark an era of cooperation between diverse ecumenical communities. The significance of a new lectionary reflects the goal of biblical literacy and the theological-pedagogical priorities that we noted in our study of Calvin's approach to the public reading of Scripture in chapter 1. However, unlike the shift to *lectio continua* as a way to distinguish the Reformed approach from the prevailing Roman Catholic practices, the creation of a new lectionary that was accepted by many Reformed congregations was spearheaded by Roman Catholics in the liturgical renewal movement whose monumental effort to reform the Roman Catholic Church culminated in the work of the Second Vatican Council (1962–65). The documents of Vatican II included a call that "The treasures of the Bible are to be opened up more lavishly so that a richer fare may be provided for the faithful at the table of God's word. In this way the more significant parts of sacred Scripture will be read to the people over a fixed number of years."[19] For Roman Catholics, this included shifting to a regular reading of Old Testament texts each Sunday. We can recognize in this brief overview the significance of this practice in mirroring Calvin's priorities of promoting biblical literacy in the regular worship life of the congregation as well as underscoring the value of Hebrew Scripture as a central part of God's revelation to humanity.

The major aspect of this lectionary that distinguishes it from Calvin's approach is the effort to coordinate the Old Testament and Epistle lessons with the reading of the Gospel rather than to focus on a continuous reading from one particular book of the Bible. There are three interesting components to this approach for us to note. First, while the selection of texts that loosely coordinate to the Gospel reading and are roughly coordinated to the liturgical year as it follows the life of Jesus diverges in significant ways from the *lectio continua* method, it shares a hermeneutical commitment to a christocentric reading of Scripture that we recognized as central in the theological methods of both Calvin and Barth. Second, the new lectionary provided a weekly singing/reading of the Psalms which we highlighted as an integral component of Calvin's liturgies. Third, the adoption of a new common lectionary (and subsequently a revised common lectionary) among diverse Christian denominations was led by the work of the ecumenical committee known as the Consultation on Common Texts (CCT) which formed in 1969. This group reviewed the initial set of readings developed for the Mass and revised them in ways that reflected particular priorities from Protestant and Anglican members of the committee (one example of this is the development of alternative readings to those that had been selected from the Apocrypha). From a Reformed perspective, the most interesting debate was the decision for a semicontinuous set of readings during ordinary time that provided an alternative track of the lectionary that was designed to appeal primarily to the historical practice of reading Scripture in Reformed congregations.[20]

In a fascinating survey of the development and reception of the lectionary among Presbyterians, Roman Catholic pastor Harry Winter notes that, "Even before American Catholics were using the Sunday Lectionary of Vatican II, the United Presbyterian Church in U.S.A. (UPCUSA) had obtained and published it."[21] Winter's keen analysis of the development and adoption of a common lectionary for use in 1970 by Presbyterians highlights the way in which the reading of Scripture in worship points to a place of theological convergence with a shared commitment to balance the role of Word and sacrament in the worship life of congregations.

ARTICULATING A REFORMED LITURGICAL THEOLOGY

These diverse threads come together in the work of the Swiss theological scholar Jean-Jacques von Allmen, whose work *Worship: Its Theology and Practice* provided the Reformed church with a distinctive vision of liturgical theology that drew deeply on its historical roots even while it incorporated and responded to emerging ecumenical and theological influences. From the opening sentences of this important work, von Allmen signals his allegiance to a Barthian framework. After noting the urgent need for a Reformed theology of worship, von Allmen cites Barth: "Christian worship is the most momentous, the most urgent, the most glorious action that can take place in human life."[22] From the onset, then, von Allmen notes the ironic tension that exists within the Reformed approach that defines Christianity as the result of divine revelation while noting that the actions of worship are distinctly rooted in human experience. As we saw in part 1 of the book, Calvin sought to solve this problem by reorienting worship alongside his reading of the primitive practices of the early church. For Calvin, the temptation to idolatry represented the most significant threat to Christian faith. Thus, aligning worship with the perceived practices of the early church provided a way for Calvin to draw on Scripture as the only reliable source of revelation to guide the lives of Christians. Looking back, it is easy to wonder what the sixteenth-century customs of the Reformed Church in Geneva actually had in common with the early gatherings of the followers of Jesus in Jerusalem, Corinth, or Rome. For Calvin, it was convenient to point to the glaring inconsistencies between the biblical depictions of early Christian worship and the Roman Catholic practices of his day (we noticed this particularly in his critique of sacramental practices), but much more difficult to ascertain the ways in which his own theological and ritual preferences diverged from the complex portraits of the diverse Christian communities in the first century. To be fair, liturgical scholars have only in recent years gained an appreciation of the diversity of liturgical practices within the early church. My point is not to raise unfair and unrealistic expectations of Calvin given the limited access to historical documents in his time, but to note the challenge facing von Allmen and other Reformed scholars in developing a liturgical theology for their times and contexts.

By drawing on the work of Barth and biblical theological trends of his day, von Allmen develops two fundamental insights that support his vision of liturgical theology. From Barth, von Allmen insists on a "Christological basis of Christian worship"[23] that recognizes worship as an "event" or a place of "encounter between the Lord . . . and His people."[24] By building on the dynamic nature of the Word of God as a place of witness to encounter Jesus Christ, von Allmen avoids the dangers of either a naive reading of Scripture or of outright bibliolatry. Instead, this approach draws on Calvin's commitment to the role of the Spirit as that which brings life and meaning to the text as we gather to hear it read and proclaimed. Like Barth, von Allmen's focus on a christological center of worship draws on Calvin's own theological and homiletical practices and prepares the way for the acceptance of an ecumenical lectionary that, as we have seen, also maintains a Christocentric hermeneutical framework.

Secondly, von Allmen's approach to liturgical theology defines Christian worship "as the recapitulation of salvation history."[25] This definition draws on the insights of biblical theologians of the time as a way to provide a unitive, thematic reading of the Bible. Their attempts to carve out a special role for salvation history as an interpretive, theological account of God's participation in human history allows the biblical text an escape route from the demands of those who are seeking historical verification and certainty. For von Allmen, this move creates space so that the practices of worship are presented in light of their development from within the witness of Scripture to the history of salvation, rather than following Calvin's attempt to return to the primitive practices of the church. It also provides a basis for the church's role in continuing to present the story of God's salvation in human history. As we will see in the next two chapters, this approach will have significant consequences in terms of understanding the Lord's Supper and baptism.

Von Allmen contends that the act of reading the Bible in worship offers an enlivening possibility for the Scripture's witness to Jesus Christ to come alive: "It is forgotten that the Gospel is enclosed in the letter of the Bible and must be freed, that to read scripture is to experience the paschal joy; the Lord reappears . . . to summon us and give us life."[26] Such a claim follows Barth's lead on the revelatory role of Scripture in pointing us toward the strange new world in Scripture where we encounter God. Therefore, the reading of Scripture and the proclamation move beyond the initial goal of biblical literacy in the expectation that the Spirit will bring life to those who gather to hear the word read and proclaimed and the sacraments administered according to the institutions of Christ (Calvin's marks of the true church). This Reformed vision of worship reaffirms the primary role of Scripture as that which defines the church and provides the basis on which the church stands. Von Allmen notes the significance of bodily responses to the reading of Scripture by referencing the historic options of the procession of the Gospel in the Orthodox Church or the practice of the reader kissing the Gospel that was common in Zwingli's church in Zurich before he settled on the option of standing for the reading of the Gospel.[27]

In von Allmen, we can detect the ways in which a Reformed liturgical theology draws on the insights of biblical and theological priorities of the twentieth century in order to preserve Calvin's vision of the role of Word and sacrament while re-orienting these priorities in light of the development of the historical-critical reading of Scripture and a new emphasis on liturgical renewal as part of the desire for ecumenical cooperation.

LITURGICAL RENEWAL: RE-ARRANGING THE ELEMENTS OF WORSHIP

The development of an ecumenically shared lectionary provided a new emphasis for the Reformed commitment to the primary role of Scripture in worship. Its inclusion (with minor alterations) as part of *The Worshipbook*—a Presbyterian hymnal—in 1970 marks a significant shift in the way texts from diverse parts of the biblical canon are brought together to provide both context and content for preaching. The preface to *The Worshipbook* includes a brief commentary on the new lectionary that concludes with the note that the members of the committee "discovered that the new Roman Catholic selections, and manner of their organization, were remarkably in harmony with the teachings of the Reformation."[28]

For Reformed congregations, the use of the lectionary remained optional based upon the minister's preferred method of selecting texts for worship. The practices varied dramatically from church to church. Some congregations followed the lectionary closely by using all three readings and the appointed psalm. Other pastors opted to limit the number of readings each week. In some settings, the historical approach of *lectio continua* remained the primary way of selecting texts. Thematic approaches to sermon topics grew in popularity. The result was an emerging diversity in how Scripture was chosen and read in Sunday worship within Reformed congregations.

In the midst of this diversity, the work of publishers provided an enormous boost to the use of an ecumenical lectionary. From lectionary-based commentaries and sermon preparation materials to musical settings of lectionary texts to Sunday School materials based on the lectionary texts, a vast range of products supported the adoption of a common lectionary. In many ways, the common lectionary (and the later Revised Common Lectionary) advanced the ecumenical hopes that grew out of Vatican II and led to the historic document *Baptism, Eucharist and Ministry (BEM)* that was adopted by the members of the World Council of Churches at its meeting in Lima, Peru, in 1982. As we have seen, the common lectionary drew on a theological script driven by an unlikely coalition of theological forces that included a neo-orthodox Protestant insistence on the primacy of Scripture, the emergence of an ecumenical movement that worked to soften the theological divisions between ecclesial bodies, a predominantly Roman Catholic movement for liturgical renewal, and a coalition of biblical scholars who articulated a case for salvation history as the hermeneutical principle for reading Scripture. In part 3, we will explore some of the limitations to reading Scripture that grew out of this approach, but for the present moment it is enough to note the historic contributions and the significant results that grew out of this hermeneutical experiment.

There are two other significant contributions that emerged from this period that reshaped the reading of Scripture in the worship life of Reformed congregations. The first of these shifts involves the renewed effort for regular Sunday worship to provide parity between Word and sacrament (with a specific focus on the frequency of celebrating the Lord's Supper). Karl Barth once again reprises the theological insistence of Calvin in making the case for weekly celebration of Communion. Von Allmen summarizes Barth's claim in *Church Dogmatics* by noting that for Barth "the Eucharist is the point, the spearhead of the cult . . . when he says that worship without the Eucharist is a theological impossibility."[29] A survey of Reformed worship books from the twentieth century shows a deliberate movement toward weekly eucharist as the normative expression of worship. This model becomes clear in the dramatic shift in the liturgy for the Service for the Lord's Day in *The Worshipbook* (1970) and *The Book of Common Worship* (1993). In contrast to previous Reformed worship books, the primary liturgy for the Sunday service includes the celebration of the Lord's Supper rather than presenting the Communion service as a separate liturgy.[30]

Once again, the work of the liturgical renewal movement is significant in pressing for change. For Roman Catholics the agenda included renewed attention to the Word in terms of both a new lectionary and a renewed emphasis on preaching. In contrast, mainline Protestants shared a commitment to an increasing frequency of Communion. The common lectionary that developed out of the work of Vatican II further prompted this movement by the way the selection of texts assumed and supported regular Sunday worship that included both Word and Table.

There is one more important shift to the role of Scripture in worship that is critical for us to note. The work of reclaiming the regular connection between word and sacrament shifted the sermon from its place at the end of the service and linked it more closely to the reading of Scripture. This shift reflects the priorities of Calvin's liturgy in Geneva, where the pastoral prayer follows the sermon in contrast to the pattern outlined in the Directory for the Public Worship of God (adopted by the Church of Scotland in 1645) that was written as part of the Westminster Standards. Similarly, the 1946 *Book of Common Worship* (UPCUSA) follows the pattern of Westminster by providing a liturgy for morning worship that places the sermon at the end of the service. The Scripture readings are followed by a creed, pastoral prayer, and the offering. Finally, the sermon proceeds as a culmination of the service through reflection on a biblical text(s). The service concludes with a hymn and benediction. By contrast, The Service for the Lord's Day in both *The Worshipbook* (1970) and the *Book of Common Worship* (1993) locates the sermon following the reading of Scripture in the middle of the worship service. The Word, read and proclaimed, is held more closely together in its liturgical rhythm.

SUMMARY THOUGHTS

We have noted some dramatic shifts in the ways in which Scripture was read in Reformed congregations during the last century. These changes grew out of movements that included a return to key insights from Calvin's own work as a theologian and pastor as well as the influence of biblical, theological, and ecumenical scholars who drew on particular theological and hermeneutical approaches as ways to advocate for renewal. The liturgical fruits of this work among Reformed Christians provided a way for churches to navigate rapidly changing cultural patterns that challenged the role and influence of the church in an increasingly secular society. For many of us who lived, worshiped, and led congregations through the tumultuous times of the late twentieth century, these theological and liturgical patterns made sense. Personally, I remain grateful for the ways in which I experienced this part of the Reformed tradition. However, in part 3 we will turn to a closer critical examination of the theological assumptions imbedded in these liturgical moves while asking the question to what extent they still make sense in a postmodern and post-Christian world.

5

The Lord's Supper

In the preceding chapter, we explored the way Barth's theology and the rise of neo-orthodoxy provided Reformed congregations with new ways of appropriating Calvin's theology, particularly with its focus on the Word of God. The renewed attention to Scripture alongside the work of historical-critical scholarship prompted a theological renaissance in which many biblical theologians turned to salvation history as a unitary theme as a way to hold the diverse voices of Scripture together. The development of a common, ecumenical lectionary consolidated these efforts by providing a christological framework that placed the Gospel readings in the primary hermeneutical role by coordinating Old Testament and Epistle readings with the assigned Gospel lesson each week. As we turn our attention to the role of the sacraments, it is important to highlight the way in which the common lectionary assumed a weekly eucharistic service as normative and selected texts that resonated with these liturgical assumptions.[1]

During the mid-nineteenth century, the Mercersburg theological movement spearheaded the effort to heighten the role of the sacraments within Reformed congregations. John Williamson Nevin's work, *The Mystical Presence*, provided a significant impetus for reappraising the Reformed celebration of the Lord's Supper and argued for the need for a new liturgy. An important contribution of the movement was in its reclaiming Calvin's emphasis on Communion as union with Christ and in its advocacy for increased frequency of celebration of the Lord's Supper as part of a richer sacramental theology within the Reformed church.[2]

In the last chapter, we noted that at the outset of the twentieth century, Barth and other Reformed theologians were advocating for Calvin's vision of regular

Sunday celebration of Word and Table. In this chapter, we will examine the theological influences that charted a pathway for this development as well as the liturgical resources that offered new patterns for a more frequent gathering around the Table. While Calvin's eucharistic liturgy placed the primary focus on the Words of Institution as the dominical warrant for the celebration of the Lord's Supper, twentieth-century Reformed eucharistic liturgies were increasingly influenced by the ecumenical movement and in particular the calls for liturgical renewal that led to Vatican II. Thus, while one can still note the primary role of the Words of Institution (which remain required in the Presbyterian Church (U.S.A.) Directory for Worship), Reformed eucharistic liturgies increasingly located the *ipsissima verba* within the context of a broader prayer that pointed to the role of God's work in salvation history. In contrast to Calvin's heavily didactic explanations that differentiated a Reformed approach to the Lord's Supper from the Roman Catholic Mass, the twentieth century has witnessed Reformed liturgies that articulated Reformed theological commitments while also becoming increasingly influenced by liturgical scholarship that led to the revisions of the Roman Mass that developed out of Vatican II.

THEOLOGICAL DEVELOPMENTS TO THE COMMUNION LITURGY

In chapter 2, we highlighted major theological themes that Calvin used in developing a new Reformed liturgy for the celebration of the Lord's Supper. First and foremost was the desire to distinguish the actions around the Table from the sacrifice at the altar in the Roman Catholic Mass. Calvin believed that he could accomplish this by returning to Scripture as the basis for the liturgy. His Communion liturgies in Strasbourg and Geneva drew almost exclusively from a particular interpretation of 1 Corinthians 11, which led him to dismantle all of the Mass except for the Words of Institution that, for him, provided the necessary connection to Jesus's actions. For Calvin, the primary theological message of the sacrament as a visible word was to provide an active remembering of the atoning work accomplished in the death of Christ on the cross. This emphasis reinforced his understanding of salvation as God's work on our behalf, which we receive with grateful and penitent hearts. Calvin's fear of idolatry prompted him to avoid drawing attention to the material elements of the meal in favor of a spiritual Communion that was shared by the covenant community as a way to encourage the development of spiritual piety and to foster a keen awareness of our dependence on God for every aspect of our lives.

Subsequent versions of Calvinism underscored and heightened the theological tendencies within Calvin's work, particularly in terms of the link between the Communion liturgy and a theology of atonement. For example, John Knox's liturgy that was received by the Church of Scotland in 1564 follows closely upon the lines drawn out in Calvin's liturgy. The liturgy for the Lord's Supper begins with a reading of the biblical warrant from 1 Corinthians 11. It is followed by a lengthy prayer of exhortation by the minister on the benefits and risks of participating in the service. Once again, the issue of worthiness is named prominently and the 1 Corinthians text is used to justify the excommunication of "all blasphemers of God, all idolaters, all murtherers, all adulterers, all that be in malice or envie, all disobedient persons . . . all theves and disceivers of their neighbours; and finally, all suche as lyve a lyfe directly fighting against the wil of God."[3] Only those who are truly penitent of their sins and sufficiently aware of their "frailtie and wretchedness" are "worthie to come to his spirituall Table."[4]

After this lengthy warning, there are two noteworthy aspects included in the extended pastoral exhortation. First, the sacrament is named as "a singuler medicine for all poore sicke creatures."[5] Our worthy participation in the sacrament enables us to not be distracted by the material elements of bread and wine (Knox contrasts the Reformed approach to the Roman understanding of transubstantiation of the elements). Second, the effectiveness of our worthy participation is connected to the action to "lift up our mindes by fayth above all thinges worldlye and sensible, and therby to entre into heaven, that we may finde and receive Christ."[6] It is important to note the shift that Knox makes in terms of Calvin's use of the *Sursum Corda*: namely, the change from lifting up our hearts to lifting up our minds. For Knox, it seems that the proper cognitive understanding is requisite in order that the benefits of the sacrament may be fully received by the participants.

Knox's liturgy includes a prayer that provides a primary theological interpretation for the sacrament. Knox pictures the sacrament taking place in the midst of the struggle between God and Satan. Here, Knox develops a broader narrative where the sacrament offers participants the opportunity for repentance, redemption, and reception of God's grace that delivers us from the "everlasting death damnation, into which Satan drew mankinde by the meane of synne."[7] It is only through the redemptive work of Christ's death on the cross that God's justice is satisfied so that we may be restored to the fullness of life that God envisioned for us when we were created in the image of God. Finally, Knox's liturgy recommends that a reading of Scriptures about the death of Christ occur while congregants are receiving the elements of bread and wine. Knox's theology draws explicitly from Anselm's model of penal substitutionary atonement in a way that exceeds Calvin's more nuanced approach. In the rubrics following the liturgy, Knox contrasts the Reformed approach with that of the Roman Catholics and maintains that the goal of the service is "to teach us how to behave ourselves" in order that we may benefit from participating in this sacrament instituted by Christ.[8]

Since Knox was also one of the authors of the Scots Confession, it is not surprising that it includes similar themes to Knox's liturgy. Especially noteworthy is the theological stress on the Lord's Supper as the commemoration of the atoning death of Jesus. While distinguishing a Reformed understanding from the Roman doctrine of transubstantiation (which is denounced as "perniciously taught and wrongly believed"), the Scots Confession affirms that the Holy Spirit lifts the recipients up to heaven and "makes us feed upon the body and blood of Christ Jesus, once broken and shed for us but now in heaven, and appearing for us in the presence of his Father."[9] Ironically, the confession avoids a literal and graphic description of cannibalism only to propose a different form of literal and graphic depiction that "the faithful . . . do so eat the body and drink the blood of the Lord Jesus that he remains in them and they in him; they are so made flesh of his flesh and bone of his bone. . . ."[10] The Confession follows Calvin in terms of portraying the goal of the sacrament as union with Christ, but in naming Christ's presence as at the right hand of the Father, it is forced to shift the focus from the table to heaven. The Confession concludes by declaring that "if anyone slanders us by saying that we affirm or believe the sacraments to be symbols and nothing more, they are libelous and speak against the plain facts."[11]

By comparison, other early Reformed confessions avoid the most blatant imagery of Knox and the Scots Confession even while primarily articulating the meaning of the Lord's Supper in terms of a doctrine of atonement. The Heidelberg Catechism frames its presentation on the Lord's Supper as a way to "share in Christ's one sacrifice on the cross and in all his benefits."[12] Here, though, the understanding of the actions at the Table are portrayed in terms of accepting "with a believing heart the entire suffering and death of Christ."[13] Furthermore, Heidelberg repeatedly uses the language of sign in keeping with "the nature and language of sacraments."[14]

Similarly, the Second Helvetic Confession describes the sacraments as "mystical signs of sacred things" whose value "depends upon faith and upon the truthfulness and pure goodness of God."[15] The Lord's Supper is presented as a memorial to the benefits that God provides through the death of Christ that is the basis for the forgiveness of sin and our redemption from "eternal death and the power of the devil."[16] These benefits are provided for us because of Christ's blood that was shed for us. Participation in the Lord's Supper is described as a spiritual eating of Christ's body, which is not imaginary but a form of "higher spiritual eating" or "sacramental eating of the body of the Lord" that is considered as necessary for salvation.[17] The Confession affirms the language of Christ's presence in heaven where the hearts of the faithful are lifted up to participate in "an unbloody and mystical Supper, as it was universally called by antiquity."[18]

Others who followed Calvin's trajectory tended to both highlight and harden the edges of these theological claims. We observed this in terms of the rejection of any form of human agency in the Synod of Dort, which developed a form of five-point Calvinism that provided rigid definitions for subsequent generations. One can note this in Dort's emphasis on the limited atonement of Christ (the third point of what became known as TULIP) which stressed that the benefit of Christ's redemptive death was only available for those whom God elected. In Dort, atonement theology was interwoven with a firm commitment to double predestination with its emphasis on God's sovereignty and foreknowledge of both the elect and the "damned." This connection is clearly articulated in Article 8: "it was God's will that Christ through the blood of the cross (by which he confirmed the new covenant) should effectively redeem from every people, tribe, nation, and language all those and only those who were chosen from eternity to salvation and given to him by the Father."[19] While elements of these connections between doctrinal claims, atonement theory, and eucharistic reflection remain in the Westminster Standards, the threads between them are loosened. The harsher claims of the language of Dort are removed even while presenting a stricter version of Reformed theology than Calvin's less systematic view.

Similarly, some of the harshness of Knox's liturgy is curtailed by the time of the writing of the Westminster Standards a century later. Still, we can see how Calvin's theological commitments continued to be heightened. For example, chapter 31 of the Westminster Confession titled "Of the Lord's Supper" begins by noting the biblical warrant for the celebration of this sacrament by linking it with Jesus's actions "in the night wherein he was betrayed" (a reference to 1 Corinthians 11:23 that provided the basis for the sacrament which is immediately identified as the Lord's Supper in contrast to the language of the Mass). The purpose of this "perpetual remembrance" is to recall "the sacrifice of himself in his death" which provides the "spiritual nourishment" for those who participate "as members of his mystical body."[20]

Westminster follows this opening statement by reasserting the Reformed understanding that the actions in the service are not in any way a "real sacrifice made at all for the remission of sins," but a "commemoration" of the one-time sacrifice of Jesus on the cross (which is explicitly contrasted to the "so-called sacrifice of the mass.")[21] Like Calvin's liturgy, this Reformed articulation of the Lord's Supper begins by providing a stark contrast to the actions of the Mass.

Westminster follows by insisting on the claim that the sacrament is appointed by Jesus and by emphasizing the role of the ministers in articulating the Words of Institution (as the biblical warrant), to offer prayer, bless the bread and wine, and thereby to "set them apart from a common to an holy use," to take and break the bread and share the cup with those in the congregation.[22] What is interesting for us to note here is the specific and limited role for the minister in this service and the way in which his actions are particularly dependent on the christological basis that is laid out as the rationale for the Lord's Supper. The Confession follows up with a series of statements that further contrast Reformed from Roman Catholic practices. There is a rejection of private masses, of adoration of the element, or of any actions associated with a reserved host. While Westminster recognizes that the language of the liturgy references the bread and wine as the body and blood of Christ, it rejects any transformation of the elements and labels the doctrine of transubstantiation as "superstitious" and supporting "gross idolatries."[23] Here the Reformed understanding of the elements is clearly articulated: that the elements remain bread and wine but are for holy and not for common use. Those who are worthy recipients of the elements (note again the particular reliance on an interpretation of 1 Cor. 11 that we highlighted in chapter 2) participate "inwardly and spiritually" (rather than "carnally and corporally") and thereby receive the benefits of Christ's death on the cross. Finally, any who participate unworthily or ignorantly "bring judgment on themselves."[24]

Similarly, the Directory for the Publick Worship of God that was included in the Westminster Standards provides a snapshot of the expectations and the emotive framework that surrounded the celebration of the Lord's Supper. Once again, the primary lens is cast in terms of worthiness and the dangers of participation in the service for any who are "ignorant, scandalous, profane, or that live in any sin."[25] Following an extensive list of the dangers of unworthy participation, the directory turns to outline the proper way to set up the table so that the service will be conducted in a decent and orderly manner. The liturgy itself begins with the Words of Institution and is followed by a prayer of thanksgiving. This prayer names as the central aspect of the sacrament "the sufferings and merits of the Lord Jesus Christ" in order that they may be "applied and sealed up unto us." The sacrament then offers participants the opportunity to transfer the work of Christ's death in order that we receive God's mercy in spite of our unworthiness.[26] One other noteworthy aspect is the way the Directory follows Calvin's guidance in collecting resources for the poor.

The importance of Westminster is that it sets the agenda in the Scots-English branch of the Reformed tradition for the understanding and practice of the sacraments for the next three centuries. In the United States, the acceptance of Westminster was initially in terms of subscription, namely the requirement to accept it as the defining theological statement for the English-speaking Reformed church. Over time, allowance was made for clergy to articulate exceptions to particular claims in Westminster. Here, the primary point for us to note is that Westminster maintained its role as the primary explication of Reformed theology, particularly in the ways in which it articulated an understanding of the role of Scripture and the sacraments.

SCHLEIERMACHER AS A THEOLOGICAL EXCURSUS

While Westminster provided the dominant theological basis for framing Reformed theology, an alternative interpretation developed through the work of Friedrich Schleiermacher that offered significant implications for the sacraments. Schleiermacher's reinterpretation of the language of atonement is placed in the context of his attempt to reappropriate theological categories that were central to Calvin in the development of Reformed theology. In a recent article, Reformed theologian Joshua Ralston describes Schleiermacher's use of the three roles of Christ as prophet, priest, and king and the way in which Schleiermacher developed an understanding of atonement within Christ's priestly role that avoided "any notions of divine wrath and punishment, vicarious payment for sin, and the soteriological elevation of the cross over the ministry of Jesus."[27] On this point in particular, Schleiermacher clearly breaks with harsher versions of Calvinism in order to develop an alternative trajectory for Reformed theology. While Ralston notes that Calvin's own theology displays "some sort of contradiction"[28] between the role of God's grace and the redemptive work of Christ, we have seen that Calvin's liturgies do not show the same level of tension. It may well be that the centrality of soteriological claims in Calvin's liturgies, particularly in terms of the covenantal language, played a significant role in the harsher ways that his theological tensions were resolved by his followers.

In his classic work *Grace and Gratitude: The Eucharistic Theology of John Calvin*, Brian Gerrish draws out the ways in which Calvin's theology is erected on the scaffold of God's initiative in extending grace with the expectation of thanksgiving as the response that we offer for God's goodness. As we noticed in Calvin's liturgies, this implicit theology is often undertoned if not at times absent from the highly didactical prayers in Calvin's order of worship. The need for explanation of a distinctly Reformed approach as well as the determination to bring decency and order to the Reformed experiment in Geneva drove Calvin's effort to insist on the proper understanding of the sacrament and its role in the community of faith.

For Schleiermacher, then, what is the significance of the Lord's Supper? His reflections point to a middle way between those whom he claims approach the supper as magical and those who view it as merely a sign. Those who ascribe to the magical view hold that the elements of bread and wine are transformed into the body and blood of Christ, based on their literal reading of Scripture as well as their interpretation of Old Testament observances that are construed to be connected to Christ's institution of the meal. In contrast, a purely spiritual interpretation of the Lord's Supper runs the risk of dismissing the central way in which Christ "conjoined the eating and drinking with the observance" of the meal.[29] Between these two extremes, Schleiermacher makes a case for Calvin's understanding of the real presence of Christ by which participating in the body and blood of Christ builds up the community of the faithful. With this move Schleiermacher appropriates Calvin's emphasis on union with Christ by recognizing the role of the Lord's Supper as providing nourishment for our journey as disciples. Here participation in the Lord's Supper includes the forgiveness of sin through the "living relationship" between the presence of Christ in both the individual and community.[30] Furthermore, participation includes the "experience of an enhancement of powers given for the purpose of sanctification."[31] Namely, we receive strength to grow in the life of faith.

Schleiermacher's contribution to this discussion is through his use of the person of Christ in terms of a broader incarnational understanding of the life, ministry, death, and resurrection of Christ that provides the basis for a theology of redemption. Here, Calvin's emphasis on Christ's priestly office provides a distinctively Reformed way for Schleiermacher to present a theology of atonement "through themes of union and representation instead of sacrifice and substitution."[32] While Ralston's primary interests are to prompt a reassessment of Schleiermacher's contributions within the context of Reformed and ecumenical theology, as we will see in our exploration of the possibilities of a Reformed liturgical theology for the twenty-first century, it may also provide us with an important starting place in our examination of the need for liturgical renewal that addresses dominant theological issues of our time.

BARTH AND TWENTIETH-CENTURY THEOLOGICAL DEVELOPMENTS

In chapter 4, we observed Barth's effort to reframe Calvin's theology as an alternative to the dominant liberal theology of the nineteenth century. Barth's contribution to the rise of neo-orthodoxy provides Reformed theology with a new direction that will serve as the primary guide for theological conversations throughout much of the twentieth century. For our interests in eucharistic theology and practice, it is important for us to notice the way in which Barth frames the issue of atonement and the implications of this in terms of the celebration of the Lord's Supper. In contrast to Schleiermacher's emphasis on Christ as the representative model of union, Barth returns to earlier models of atonement theory to solve the primary theological question of the distinctive separation between (the wholly other) God and humanity. For Barth, the language of reconciliation provides the key in depicting the work and person of Christ. Barth describes this in *Church Dogmatics* by asserting that "reconciliation is the fulfillment of the covenant between God and man."[33] Here Barth builds on central aspects of the Reformed tradition's commitment to a covenant theology by refracting his theology through a christological lens. Rather than developing this theology in terms of an historical sequence, Barth insists that all theological questions must be framed in christocentric terms. For example, note this important declaration: "Jesus Christ is the atonement. But that means that He is the maintaining and accomplishing and fulfilling of the divine covenant as executed by God Himself."

Barth's approach contrasts with the Westminster Confession, which begins by articulating a theology that is developed through an historical lens in terms of sections on the role of Scripture, the doctrine of God, God's eternal decree (which provides a framework for the doctrine of election), and sections on creation, providence, and the fall of humanity. Only after establishing this timeline does Westminster turn to the language of covenant and Christ's role as mediator (in light of "the fall"). This approach provided the framework for the theological debates that would emerge during the development of historical-critical study of Scripture that increasingly raised questions about the historicity of the text. The point here is that if the biblical text is read as a historical timeline, then significant theological questions arise in terms of the implications of a doctrine of election and in particular the role of Christ. Barth creatively subverts these concerns by blowing up the time constructs and insisting that all doctrinal claims must be refracted through the centrality of Jesus Christ. To wit: "Apart from and without Jesus Christ we can say nothing at all about God and man and their relationship one with another."[34] Or to put this in terms of our interest in the language of atonement: "This means at once that as the beginning of all things the presupposition of the atonement is a single, self-sufficient, independent free work of God in itself, which is not identical with the divine work in creation or with the divine creative will realized in this work."[35] Barth recognizes the risks in any attempt to capture God's work of reconciliation in Jesus Christ: "There is no doctrine more dangerous than the Christian doctrine of the atonement."[36] By recentering the Reformed understanding of election through a christological prism, Barth depicts the work and person of Christ as the source of mediation that bridges the chasm between God and humanity. As we will see in coming chapters, this theological solution "from above" will have to wrestle with questions about its understanding of incarnation and its implicit docetic Christology. In spite of Barth's insistence that Jesus as "both God and man" is fully human, he declares that "Jesus Christ is man in a different way from what we are."[37] Without this distinction, Barth insists that the mediatorial work of atonement would not be possible.

The significance of Barth, particularly as it relates to the doctrine of atonement, is the theological framework that it provides for the liturgical developments in the celebration of the Lord's Supper for Reformed communities. As we will see in von Allmen's attempt to provide a Reformed eucharistic theology, Barth's own desire for a regular (weekly) celebration of the Lord's Supper presents a particular kerygmatic commitment to the proclamation of the crucified Christ at the center of the life of the covenant community.

DEVELOPING A REFORMED EUCHARISTIC THEOLOGY

We have previously noted Barth's influence on the work of Jean-Jacques von Allmen in his outline of a Reformed liturgical theology. Von Allmen builds his proposal on Barth's claim that the work of the church is rooted in the regular celebration of the sacraments, which, as we noted in the previous chapter, is the proclamation of God's work in salvation history. Citing Barth, von Allmen asserts that "the whole worship of the Church is thus embraced, determined and limited by the divine command concerning baptism and Eucharist."[38] It is important for us to note the way that Barth locates the rituals of the church within the confines of a theology that draws solely from divine revelation. In this way, the sacraments (rightly celebrated!) avoid a comparison with humanly devised rituals that are part of religious activity (which for Barth consists of human striving for salvation) in contrast to revelation, which for Barth remains the sole source of salvation. This argument follows the logic of Calvin's critique of the Roman Catholic sacramental system by identifying the true sacraments (and the proper way to celebrate them!) as those which were instituted by Christ. It is interesting to observe that by locating the sacraments within the divine decree, von Allmen uses his reading of Barth to avoid the historical challenges that Calvin faced in showing the relationship of the ritual actions between the two covenants: specifically, the relationship between circumcision/baptism and Passover/Lord's Supper.[39]

Von Allmen focuses his attention on the role that the Lord's Supper plays within worship as part of the proclamation of salvation history. For our interests, it is helpful to note the way that von Allmen incorporates the work of biblical theologians of his era along with insights from the liturgical renewal movement. One can see his interest in *Heilsgeschichte* not only in the broad strokes of his argument about the liturgy as a presentation of salvation history, but particularly in the ways in which he highlights the theological interpretations of the biblical narratives. While the results of the broader liturgical renewal movement may not be readily identifiable in von Allmen's attempt to present a distinctly Reformed approach, the questions that prompted the ecumenical convergence to bring about liturgical reform are visible in his approach and even acknowledged in the selected bibliography at the conclusion of the book. These diverse theological movements provide a basis for the broad ways in which he locates the celebration of the sacraments within the context of classical approaches to Reformed theology. We can see this in the careful way that von Allmen articulates the connection between the Lord's Supper and an understanding of sacrifice. "The Lord's Supper has not different modes of celebration, although we might specify in it the phases of Christ's passion."[40] Von Allmen begins this analysis similar to the ways in which we have seen Calvin and Westminster link the Lord's Supper with an interpretation of Christ's atoning death on the cross. However, he quickly recognizes the danger of focusing on the "memorial aspect" of the service since it carries the risk of reifying a "sacrificial idea of the service"[41] by [over] emphasizing the role of the priest as the one who presents a judicial case to God on behalf of the people. In contrast, von Allmen outlines the alternative risks of devaluing the Eucharist as a meal of fellowship (an approach he associates with both Zwingli and liberal Protestantism) or eliminating any eschatological aspect to the celebration.

In order to provide a fuller picture of the Reformed approach to the celebration of the Lord's Supper, von Allmen returns to the defining role of Scripture. He helpfully extends the biblical citations beyond the narrow confines of 1 Corinthians 11 by drawing on Acts 2:42 and 20:7 as indicative of the rationale for the weekly celebration of the Eucharist. While von Allmen shares this goal with the broader liturgical renewal movement, he proceeds by offering three reasons for the importance of a distinctively Reformed service of Word and sacrament: (1) The celebration of the service is a matter of obedience, particularly since "Christ instituted and commanded the Church to celebrate it."[42] Here the argument directly follows the claim that the sacraments are part of the divine decree. Hence, our regular celebration of them is a matter of faithful response to what God has ordained. (2) The link between Word and sacrament becomes an embodiment of the Gospel's link between the proclamation of the Word in the life of Christ and the Passion narrative that leads to the cross. Since the presentation of the life of Jesus inevitably leads to the cross, a service of Word and Table provides a fuller testimony to the revelation in Scripture. It is important for us to note that with this move von Allmen aligns the Communion liturgy exclusively with the passion narrative. (3) Finally, von

Allmen insists that the celebration of the Lord's Supper provides a form of discipline that marks a point of distinction between the church and the world. "Listening to the Word is for all, but Communion is for those who have not only listened to the word, but have received it and keep it."[43] Such an understanding of the exclusive nature of the eucharist provides continuity with the history of a fenced table within the Reformed tradition that is open only to those who are truly repentant and found in good standing within the covenant community. Once again, we can detect a reliance on a Pauline understanding of worthiness, which was connected by John Knox and others to the role of discipline as the third mark of the church in the Church of Scotland.

What we can take from this important work is the way in which von Allmen draws a distinction from the language of sacrifice in the Communion liturgy while still asserting the primary theological connection to atonement and the passion narrative as primary to the gathering at the Table. In summary, von Allmen offers a distinctively Reformed approach that draws on the liturgical-theological contributions of Calvin and Barth in order to develop a broader sacramental theology in response to the insights of biblical theologians and the liturgical renewal movement.

THE SHIFT IN CONFESSIONAL AND LITURGICAL LANGUAGE

We have traced significant theological options within the context of the Reformed tradition in order to note the historical distinctions in the way that the language of sacrifice and atonement have dominated the discussion of a Reformed eucharistic theology. Calvin's liturgies establish a clear basis for the major trajectory in which atonement theory provides a central lens within the Communion liturgy. While particular theological voices advocated for alternate perspectives, notably the way that Knox's Communion liturgy presents explicit claims of penal substitutionary atonement theory or Schleiermacher's effort provides an alternative understanding of atonement from within the framework of Calvin's Christology, subsequent Reformed liturgical resources have been guided by the theological language of Westminster. Barth and other neo-orthodox voices provided theological language that reasserted classic Reformed approaches focusing on the language of the Communion liturgy around the death of Christ on the cross. For example, the primary Communion liturgy in *The Book of Common Worship of the Presbyterian Church in the USA* (1946) presents a service that summarizes this dominant liturgical pattern within the Reformed tradition. The Communion liturgy begins with a biblical warrant: the recitation of 1 Corinthians 11. While the prayer that follows the words of institution has a loose Trinitarian framework, the major focus of the prayer is clearly christological, with a specific focus on sacrificial atonement. The opening reference to God as Creator quickly moves to giving thanks for the gift of Jesus Christ who took "our nature upon Him, and to suffer death upon the cross for our redemption, who made there a full, perfect, and sufficient sacrifice for the sins of the whole world."[44] The liturgy continues by asserting its role in remembering Christ's passion as "we Thy humble servants, pleading His eternal sacrifice" present the gifts of bread and wine as Christ commanded us to do.[45] A brief invocation of the Holy Spirit requests that the bread and wine may be the communion of the body and blood of Christ. The liturgy clearly traces the contours of the language of the Westminster Confession (as well as the Directory for Publick Worship) that the Lord's Supper is "a commemoration of that one offering up of himself, by himself, upon the cross, once for all, and a spiritual oblation of all possible praise unto God for the same."[46]

Before we turn to examine the development of new confessional and liturgical resources during the second half of the twentieth century, we should also note that many evangelical and nonliturgical Reformed congregations carried a similar theological emphasis in their celebrations of the Lord's Supper. Typically, the words of institution provided the biblical warrant for the celebration of the Lord's Supper. While these congregations avoided Calvin's pedagogical and explanatory prayer or the use of formal liturgical texts in favor of an extemporaneous prayer, the minister offered a prayer asserting the theological claim of substitutionary atonement in Christ's death as the primary function of what is remembered in the Lord's Supper.

Westminster continued to dictate the terms of theological debate even as questions grew about its status and relevance as a summary of Reformed faith. The decision to write a new confession to mark the union of the United Presbyterian Church of North America and the Presbyterian Church in the U.S.A. in 1958 is noteworthy for two particular reasons. First, the decision to augment Westminster by creating a book of confessions that included a new confessional statement marks a new hermeneutical approach to the role of confessional statements. The decision underscores the historical context of confessional statements by placing them into conversation with one another. On the one hand it allowed Westminster to remain a central part of the confessional canon, while at the same time providing limits to the ways in which Westminster could be used to enforce certain interpretations of Reformed orthodoxy. Equally important, though, was the effort to create a new summary of faith that spoke to the issues of the day. The Confession of 1967 (C-67) draws on the theological influences of the time. Both the structure and the vocabulary of the confession are heavily influenced by Barth's theology. Note the distinctive way in which the starting place and outline of the confession are christocentric. Similarly, the language of reconciliation is primary throughout the confession. Within this theological framework, C-67 breaks new ground. For example, the paragraph on "God's reconciling act in Jesus Christ" begins by naming the work as a mystery and noting a variety of "expressions of a truth" that are found in Scripture "which remain beyond the reach of all theory in the depths of God's love for man."[47] An array of interpretive images about Christ's death includes the language of sacrifice, payment of debt, and satisfaction of a legal payment (models of atonement theology which we have noted in our analysis of liturgical texts), each of which is rooted in a singular commitment to a theology of God's love of humanity. Gone is the attempt to identify a specific explanation for Christ's death.

Additionally, C-67 reframes the role of the sacraments by locating them in the mission of the church and identifying them as part of the "equipment" of the church. In many ways the shift is subtle, yet it carries with it significant consequences for how to present central aspects of the celebration of the sacraments in the life of the church. While the confession asserts that "Jesus Christ has given the church preaching and teaching, praise and prayer, and baptism and the Lord's Supper" as the way to live out its mission, it immediately balances this claim by stating that "the church is obliged to change the forms of its service in ways appropriate to different generations and cultures."[48] This claim opens the doors for the development of liturgical resources that provide new ways to experience the gift of the sacraments. Equally surprising is the way in which C-67 summarizes the Lord's Supper:

> The Lord's Supper is a celebration of the reconciliation of men with God and with one another, in which they joyfully eat and drink together at the table of their Savior. Jesus Christ gave his church this remembrance of his dying for sinful men so that by participation in it they have communion with him and with all who shall be gathered to him. Partaking in him as they eat the bread and drink the wine in accordance with Christ's appointment, they receive from the risen and living Lord the benefits of his death and resurrection. They rejoice in the foretaste of the kingdom which he will bring to consummation at his promised coming, and go out from the Lord's Table with courage and hope for the service to which he has called them.[49]

First, note that the description of the Lord's Supper has been framed by the language of celebration and joy. Gone is the introspective language of penitence and the obsession with worthiness that provided the dominant mood throughout the history of the Reformed tradition. Gone as well is any attempt to describe a Reformed understanding *vis a vis* Roman Catholic doctrines and practices. C-67 does preserve classic Reformed language that historically guided its interpretation: the Lord's Supper as remembrance of Christ's dying as well as the reception of the benefits of Christ's death and resurrection (even here, though, note the theologically expansive language that unites death with resurrection). Finally, C-67 reclaims eschatological language as central to the celebration of the sacrament, thus shifting the focus primarily from the past event of Christ's death to the hope of the consummation of the kingdom of God.

The impact of C-67 is immediately recognizable in the liturgical resources that are included in *The Worshipbook* (1970). The preface provides a list of primary influences and goals in the preparation of new worship materials. This includes the use of contemporary language in the liturgy and an attempt to balance distinctly Presbyterian approaches alongside the contributions of the broader ecumenical church. As we have already seen in chapter four, this includes an early version of a common lectionary as well as ecumenical versions of prayers and creeds.

In terms of the liturgy for the Lord's Supper, *The Worshipbook* embodies many of the theological claims that we outlined in our sketch of twentieth-century developments. It locates the Communion liturgy within the context of the Service for the Lord's Day as a structural way for advocating for a weekly celebration of Word and Table. Even the rubrics reinforce this understanding by noting that "when the Lord's Supper is omitted" the service moves toward its conclusion. In this way, the liturgical text presents the eucharistic celebration as normative and not as an addition to be included only on special occasions. It captures the hope of Calvin while channeling the vision through the insights of the liturgical renewal movement in its advocacy for weekly Communion.

Our analysis of the Communion liturgy in *The Worshipbook* begins by noting the way that the invitation to the table reframes the actions at the table. The invitation marks a dramatic shift in Reformed liturgical practice. In place of an extended reading from 1 Corinthians 11, the liturgy draws on a compilation of texts from Luke's Gospel to provide a biblical warrant for the celebration. Gone is the problematic use of Paul's analysis of eucharistic malpractice in Corinth with its focus on the significance of worthiness, which historically dominated the tenor of Reformed worship. In its place is an attempt to foster a sense of joy (rather than fear) by naming the actions at the table as a joyful feast before citing a curious text from Luke 13:29: "Then people will come from east and west, from north and south, and take their places at the banquet in the kingdom of God." Already we can note significant theological changes at play in the opening words of the Communion liturgy. Beyond the emotive change, the use of a verse drawn from an eschatological section of Luke's Gospel prompts a shift in the understanding of time as it relates to the focus of the liturgy. On the one hand, the opening claim that "Friends, this is the joyful feast of the people of God" directs our attention to the present moment and the communal gathering around this table. Here we already see a shift from classic Reformed Communion liturgies that purposefully focused on the past in terms of remembering the redemptive action of Christ's death on the cross as a point of contrast to the fear that the Mass was engaged in a form of re-sacrificing Christ.

The verse chosen from Luke 13, though, is taken completely out of context. What we have here, in my opinion, is a classic example of the attempt to identify a biblical warrant that suits our own purposes whether or not it does justice to the text itself. While there is language of eating (which seems to provide the primary rationale for the use of the text), the verse is drawn from a larger eschatological teaching of Jesus on his journey to Jerusalem. As an invitation to the present actions at the table, the future orientation of the text seems largely overlooked. Fortunately, the liturgical citation of Luke 24:30–31, a selection from the Emmaus road narrative, is on much stronger hermeneutical grounds. Here is a eucharistic text that was historically overlooked in contrast to the reliance on the 1 Corinthians 11 text. It is also noteworthy that it draws from the resurrection narratives and thus expands the focus beyond the cross to include the resurrection.

The liturgy then turns to the *Sursum Corda* in call and response form before offering a full prayer of thanksgiving that is structured in a distinctly Trinitarian outline. Here we can clearly see the influence of the liturgical renewal movement as well as the proposals on salvation history from biblical theologians. The Trinitarian framework for the prayer is developed in terms of an historical timeline. The opening section focuses on the first person of the Trinity and God's work in creation and in the gift of the commandments to Moses. Seasonal prefaces that are suggested as alternatives tend to move more quickly to a christological focus (given their connection to the church year with its focus on the life of Christ). Following the *sanctus*, the prayer turns to its christological section with expanded incarnational language, similar to what we saw in C-67, by mentioning the life of Jesus as teacher, healer, and friend. As in C-67, the mention of the cross is immediately linked with language of resurrection which is followed by the hope of eschatological victory in the coming of God's kingdom. This serves as a prompt for the congregational response: "Remembering the Lord Jesus, we break bread and share one cup, announcing his death for the sins of the world and telling his resurrection to all men and nations."[50] There are several important aspects of this response. First is the way that the language of remembering, as a central component of the gathering at the table, is placed in the mouth of the congregation as a way in which they participate in the prayer. Second, the prayer uses the language of breaking bread and sharing one cup even though it is unlikely that many congregations actually participated precisely in this way, given that the common mode of Communion was pre-cut bread and individual cups. Third, theologically it is the congregation's words that proclaim the effect of Christ's death "for our sins" while at the same time linking it with the promise of resurrection.

Finally, the prayer moves to a brief section on the Spirit as the one who draws us together and to Christ in the celebration of Communion. Here the influence of Calvin's theology, both in terms of the role of the Spirit and the emphasis on union with Christ, can be clearly seen. Following the recitation of the Lord's Prayer, the minister at last recites the words of institution as s/he breaks the bread and pours the wine. Note that this use of 1 Corinthians is solely limited to the institutional narrative and does not include the sections of warnings on worthiness that had become a standard part of the Reformed liturgy.

What we can detect from our analysis of C-67 and the new liturgy is a remarkable change in mood, language, and shape to the eucharistic prayer. While there is continuity with theological themes from earlier Communion liturgies, we can identify significant new directions of the way that Reformed eucharistic theology is evolving in conversation with ecumenical partners and diverse theological and cultural influences. Looking back at these landmark works, we can see the tide shifting in terms of what constitutes a Reformed eucharistic theology.

ECUMENICAL INFLUENCES ON REFORMED WORSHIP

The publication of the Presbyterian *Book of Common Worship* (BCW) in 1993 provides a clear portrait of the influence of the liturgical renewal movement alongside the contributions of biblical theology. As the last in a generation of new worship books by mainline Protestant denominations, this version of the BCW built on the liturgical insights from other Christian communities in an era in which hopes for increased ecumenical cooperation were high. The preface to the service book highlights the commitments that undergird the liturgies: (1) a Reformed emphasis on form and freedom in worship; (2) an era of ecumenical convergence that strives for unity at the font, pulpit, and table; (3) an understanding of worship as Reformed (defined primarily in terms of a biblical emphasis) and catholic (rooted in early liturgical practices from the church's history).[51]

The Communion prayers in the BCW build on insights that we highlighted in the liturgies in *The Worshipbook* and extend these developments by drawing heavily on the work of the liturgical renewal movement alongside insights from biblical theologians. A Trinitarian structure for the prayer is filled out by a recitation of salvation history (selected themes are coordinated to the days and seasons of the church year). In looking for Reformed distinctives in this liturgy we can find the following: (1) the use of the *Sursum Corda*, which is placed in call and response form at the beginning of the prayer of great thanksgiving; (2) a choice of three locations for the Words of Institution—as invitation to the table, in the middle of the prayer (which is the ecumenical placement), or at the breaking of the bread at the conclusion of the prayer; (3) an expanded christological section that emphasizes the life and ministry of Jesus alongside his death and resurrection; (4) calling on the Spirit's presence (*epiclesis*) so that the bread and wine may be the communion of the body and blood of Christ. Here, the Spirit's work is identified as the source of bringing us into union with Christ.

Equally striking is the shift away from sacrificial language in the prayer. Explicit atonement imagery is absent. The main prayer includes the following reference in the christological paragraph: "Dying on the cross, he gave himself for the life of the world."[52] These words point to the distinct Reformed emphasis on the Lord's Supper as a remembering of the one-time death of Christ. Yet, even here, we should note the dramatic move away from the atonement language which we have seen was stressed throughout much of the history of eucharistic prayer in the Reformed tradition. Reformed theologian Martha Moore-Keish notes the concerns raised by some scholars that the new liturgies are more reflective of ecumenical consensus than of distinctive Reformed insights.[53]

In summary, we will note the ways in which diverse theological movements have significantly influenced Reformed prayers and practices at the Communion table. Ecumenical and liturgical movements found the theme of salvation history as fruitful in providing direction for reform to the church's worship. The result of these joint efforts has brought dramatic changes to the worship life of the broader church and particularly to those within the Reformed tradition.

6

Baptism

Calvin's defense of infant baptism established the boundaries of the debate on the role of baptism in the Reformed tradition. As we noted in chapter 3, Calvin faced both theological and cultural pressures that supported his decision to continue the practice of infant baptism as normative in the church. On the theological front, his commitment to the sovereignty of God and an understanding of grace as God's generous act toward us provided the primary rationale. Calvin unfolded this theological commitment in the context of his ecclesiology as covenant community. Thus, the baptism of children into the church provided a structure in which we grow into our baptismal vows together. More challenging for Calvin was wrestling with the biblical texts and their silence on the topic of infant baptism.

Calvin's creative interpretation of Old Testament texts provided a broader rationale for his approach to sacraments and particularly his understanding of baptism. As we noted in chapter 3, Calvin's solution, following Zwingli, was to claim the practice of circumcision as providing precedence for infant baptism. Within the context of a covenant community, Calvin saw circumcision as analogous even though the practice was only for infant boys. In the absence of any clear biblical warrant, Calvin's baptismal liturgy cobbled together a collection of texts from diverse biblical references.

At the same time, Calvin removed any connection between baptism and salvation, which is solely determined by God and not assured by our actions. This understanding created cultural pressure in Geneva, particularly from parents who wanted assurance that their infants were not in danger of eternal condemnation. Calvin stood firm on this point and insisted that the benefit of baptism was our inclusion into a community that nurtured and encouraged us to grow into the likeness of Christ. Trust in Mother Church provided sufficient support for our shared journey.

Those who followed Calvin started from his general theological convictions. The Scots Confession runs closest to Calvin's logic when it declares that the "fathers under the Law, besides the reality of the sacrifices, had two chief sacraments, that is circumcision and the passover."[1] It is worth noting that other forms of sacrifice are portrayed as separate rituals from the Jewish practices of circumcision and Passover. The goal of both of these additional "Old Testament sacrifices" is to establish a clear identity of the Hebrew people. Baptism and the Lord's Supper, which "alone were instituted by the Lord Jesus," serve a similar purpose in terms of establishing the identity of a covenant community. In terms of baptism, the Scots Confession asserts that "we assuredly believe that by Baptism we are engrafted into Christ Jesus."[2] In terms of the right administration of the sacraments, Scots develops two criteria: (1) baptism by an ordained minister (specifically to counter the practice of baptism by midwives in the Roman Catholic Church); and (2) a simplified rite that does not taint "Christ's original act." Here the confession follows closely on Calvin's pointed rejection of the Roman Catholic baptismal practices that included exorcism, anointing, and other associated actions. One must wonder, though, how the Scottish Church defined their understanding of Christ's original act? Is this Jesus's baptism by John in the Jordan River or is this a reference to Jesus's command to baptize and create disciples in Matthew 28? In either case there are a wide range of theological issues that need to be addressed, including how the ritual of baptism for the repentance of sin came to be a primary sign of Christian communities or how the Reformed church chose infant baptism as its normative pattern.

Knox's lengthy baptismal liturgy provides his own theological slant. The liturgy assumes that the one presented for baptism will be an infant and unfolds the liturgy in terms of the language of the child's adoption by God. Knox notes that this action happens in the context of the community as a holy sign that marks the infants as separate from "Infidells and Pagans."[3] The liturgy seeks to find a balance between offering words of assurance to the parents of the one being baptized with warnings to any parents whose negligence in presenting their children for baptism may cause "injurie to your own children, hydinge from them the good will and pleasure of Almyghtie God their Father, but also heape damnation upon your selves, in suffering his children, boght with the bloode of his deare Sonne, so trayterously (for lack of knowledge) to turn backe from him."[4] As we noted in the preceding chapter, Knox's liturgies portray the struggle for salvation as a cosmic conflict between God and Satan in which Christ's death provides the satisfaction for God to receive us in spite of our unworthiness.

THE SACRAMENTS IN THE EARLY REFORMED CONFESSIONS

A tension emerges among other early Reformed confessions in terms of how closely to follow Calvin's logic of using Old Testament texts and actions as primary biblical warrants for Christian worship practices. For example, the Heidelberg Catechism follows the general trajectory we have outlined from Calvin and Knox when it notes that baptism is "the sign of the covenant" that "distinguished" the children of believers from those of unbelievers. Immediately following this statement, though, comes a clear demarcation: "This was done in the Old Testament by circumcision, which was replaced in the New Testament by baptism."[5] Here a shift from Calvin's attempt to allude to Passover and circumcision as anticipatory signs that point toward Christ changes to a more dispensational view of signs for particular eras that comes with its own version of supersessionism (that the new Christian signs are superior to the older Jewish ones).

The Second Helvetic Confession develops this perspective on the sacraments while beginning to shape a Christian understanding of the sacraments in a new direction. The confession notes the role of Ministers as "Stewards of the Mysteries of God," which it defines in terms of preaching and the sacraments. The primary biblical warrant for this definition is Ephesians 3, where the apostle Paul describes his role in receiving and sharing the good news of God's grace in Christ that now extends to the Gentiles. The confession explicitly notes that the Greek word for mystery (*mystērion*) is linked in the early Church to the Latin word sacrament (*sacramentum*). Thus, the initial description of the sacraments in the Second Helvetic is explicitly in the context of Christian sacraments of the church.

The chapter on the sacraments provides a fuller context and unfolds the presentation in a way similar to other Reformed confessions. The sacraments are instituted by God, and signs given to the church to fulfill God's promises to strengthen our faith. Participation in the sacraments "distinguishes us from all other people and religions."[6] The Confession then refers to circumcision and the paschal lamb as the Old Testament sacraments (with a note contra the claim in the Scots Confession that the Paschal lamb was part of the sacrificial system "from the beginning of the world"). Second Helvetic goes on to proclaim that the "principal thing which God promises in all sacraments and to which all the godly in all ages direct their attention . . . is Christ the

Savior—that only sacrifice and the Lamb of God slain from the foundation of the world; that rock, also, from which all our fathers drank, by whom all the elect are circumcised without hands through the Holy Spirit, and are washed from all their sins, and are nourished with the very body and blood of Christ."[7]

What we have in this description then is a claim of a latent christological aspect of the Old Testament sacraments which are depicted as connecting to an understanding of atonement theory that will be more fully developed in the two sacraments "of the new people" (baptism and the Lord's Supper) while the acts of repentance, ordination, and matrimony are classified as "profitable ordinances of God."[8] While the outward signs are different, the spiritual meaning (Christ) is the same. However, the Christian sacraments "have been fulfilled or perfected in Christ" which causes the former signs "of the old people" to be "abrogated and have ceased." They have been replaced: "Baptism in the place of circumcision, the Lord's Supper in place of the Paschal Lamb and sacrifices."[9] The Confession asserts that the sacraments of "both peoples are equal" since Christ is the "chief thing and very substance of the sacraments in both."[10]

We need to pause here and consider the enormous consequences of these claims. While one cannot expect modern historical-critical interpretations of biblical texts in the sixteenth century, nevertheless there is a troubling case of dismissing and denouncing central celebrations of our Jewish brothers and sisters. The process begins with the failure to recognize the rites in their own context and integrity before moving into more questionable theological territory by declaring their illegitimacy following the incarnation of Christ. Certainly, the medieval practice of typologically interpretating Scripture was a familiar practice that supported this hermeneutical approach. While this version of antisemitism may not be as blatant as the rhetoric that supported pogroms against Jewish people and communities as "killers of Jesus" in many places during the Middle Ages or as disturbing as Martin Luther's virulent denunciation of the Jews published late in his life, nevertheless this form of biblical eisegesis fed a toxic system of oppression and vilification that supported an ongoing persecution of Jewish communities.

The question that we must ask is, Why was this position necessary? Why was it important for early Reformed theologians and confessional statements to identify sacraments in the Old Testament only to declare them no longer valid? One of the key reasons is the challenge that Calvin and other Reformed theologians faced in terms of identifying the required biblical support to distinguish Reformed practices from Roman Catholic ones. While there are certainly Jewish practices that significantly influenced the development of early Christian sacraments, liturgical scholars are increasingly clear about the diverse forms of baptismal and eucharistic practice in the early church as they analyze ancient texts and artifacts that shed light on early Christian communal practices. Of course, Calvin and other sixteenth-century scholars did not have access to this knowledge. What the Reformed community longed for was to find biblical texts that supported their worship practices. For Calvin, it was important to identify a role for covenant between God and humanity that provided a unitive reading of Scripture. Given the way in which Calvin and other Reformed leaders viewed the Old Testament as a positive witness to our experience and understanding of God's redemptive work in the world, then perhaps these typological readings of Old Testament texts should not be so surprising. To be fair to Calvin, there was justification in the way certain New Testament texts appropriated Hebrew Scripture as well as in the writings of Augustine and the preaching and commentary of many of the early church fathers. Yet for all of the claims of returning to the practices of the early church, it remains surprising that the Reformed approach to the sacraments as outlined by Calvin and the early Reformed confessional statements shows little in common with the understanding and practices of the early church.

Other early Reformed confessions wrestle with similar questions. Second Helvetic outlines its understanding of the sacraments by describing the way that the signs of bread, wine, and water are "consecrated by the Word." These ordinary things become holy "when the Word of God is added to them, together with the invocation of the divine name, and the renewing of their first institution and sanctification, then these signs are consecrated, and shown to be sanctified by Christ."[11] Note again how this description places the emphasis on the Gospel portrait of Jesus's action as the birthplace of the sacraments even though the confession previously outlined a version of the sacraments from Old Testament rituals that pointed to Christ. This approach allows a christological warrant to provide the basis for the efficacy of the sacraments that in turn diminishes the validity of the Old Testament practices. When Second Helvetic presents a chapter on baptism, it does so as an explicitly Christian practice drawn solely from New Testament texts. The institution of baptism is depicted at Jesus's baptism by John (instead of through a reference to circumcision). Second Helvetic uses Calvin's language of "mystical union" to describe the role of sacraments as participants "spiritually and inwardly partake" in the gatherings at table and font.[12] Jesus's command to go and baptize in Matthew 28 and Peter's instructions at Pentecost in Acts 2:37–39 are added as biblical warrants that fill out the start of Christian baptismal practice. Its purpose is defined as removing the "filthiness of sins" from us since "we are all born in the pollution of sin [and] are the children of wrath."[13] In baptism, "God freely cleanses us from our sins by the blood of his Son," and adopts us as children to share in the covenant life together.[14] Once again we can see the connection between atonement theory and the sacraments as central to the early Reformed understandings of both the Lord's Supper and baptism.

Interestingly, the section on the form of baptism proclaims its fidelity to the way that Christ was baptized. The distinction made by the confession is in terms of denying the role of human additions to the rite: exorcism, candles, oil, salt, and spittle. Curiously, though, the confession overlooks the primary characteristics of Jesus's baptism as an adult who was immersed in the Jordan River. Finally, the confession denounces the Anabaptists for withholding the sign of the covenant from infants, which is summarily declared as "contrary to God's word."[15]

As we have seen, these early Reformed confessions stay mostly within the confines of Calvin's biblical and theological approach to the sacraments. They collectively emphasize the sacraments as given by God and distinct from human or religious rites. Together the confessions seek to articulate a theology and practice that contrast with the Roman Catholic Church by appealing to Scripture even when the biblical texts provide little correlation to the Reformed approach. The theology of baptism is primarily characterized in terms of its portrayal of covenant life shared by those within the community of faith.

WESTMINSTER'S APPROACH TO THE SACRAMENTS

By the time of the writing of the Westminster Standards in the seventeenth century, we can see that a Reformed understandings of the sacraments had settled into regular congregational practice. Westminster provides a brief chapter on the sacraments that offers a Reformed orientation without the polemical need to contrast the understanding from Roman Catholic or Anabaptist practices. Westminster uses the language of sacraments as "holy signs and seals of the covenant of grace, immediately instituted by God, to represent Christ."[16] The biblical support for this claim (which was added after the confession was written) cites four passages: (1) Genesis 17:9–11 with its rendering of the connection between circumcision and the Abrahamic covenant; (2) Exodus 13:9–10 with its alternate rendering of the celebration of Passover in relation to the consecration of firstborn among the Israelites who are marked by a sign, namely the words of the Shema from Deuteronomy 6:5: "You shall love the LORD your God with all your heart, and with all your soul, and with all your might"; (3) Romans 4:11 with its description of Abraham's justification by faith as a "seal of righteousness before he was circumcised;" and (4) Exodus 12:3–20 which provides the main account of the initiation of the celebration of Passover. It seems likely that the first three biblical references are intended to support the practice of infant baptism whereas the Passover meal reference is interpreted as a typological parallel to the Lord's Supper. It is important for us to note the theological claims and associations that are offered here. The initial biblical warrant claims the Abrahamic covenant, with its initiation rite of circumcision, as establishing precedence for the role of sacraments as gifts from God within a community of faith. Exodus 13 seems chosen for its language of the initiation of the first born who are marked by a sign (a particularly curious choice given its role as an alternative account of the Passover narrative to Exodus 12). The use of Romans 4 is a way of undercutting the external role of the signs in order to emphasize the role of faith as primary, which serves the purpose of affirming a positive role for the use of Old Testament text while at the same time placing the stress on faith rather than on the significance of external signs. Finally, Westminster turns to Exodus 12 as the primary Passover narrative as a way to develop an interpretive link to the celebration of the Lord's Supper. What is particularly striking in this definition of sacraments is the intentional decision to avoid Gospel texts as primary references for the origin of the sacraments which are "instituted by God to represent Christ and his benefits."[17]

More specifically, Westminster declares that baptism is a New Testament sacrament "ordained by Jesus Christ" (using Matt. 28:19 as the biblical warrant) that serves as "a sign and seal of the covenant of grace."[18] Water is named as the "outward element" of the sacrament for those who profess faith in Christ and for the infants of one or more believing parent. Following Calvin's lead, Westminster notes the significance of baptism while also distinguishing salvation from the act of baptism itself (both for those who are unbaptized who may be saved as well as for those who are baptized who are not "regenerated").

While the theological claims for baptism in the Westminster Confession are fairly restrained, the Directory for Publick Worship that was part of the Westminster Standards was much more explicit. Similar to other Reformed depictions that we have noted, baptism is portrayed as a sacrament for children that is to take place within the context of congregational worship. The Directory suggests that the minister should provide words of instruction before the baptism that clarify the proper meaning of the rite. This explanation begins by announcing that baptism was instituted by Christ (although the liturgy provides no biblical warrant to support this claim). Baptism is a seal of the covenant of grace which portrays our union with Christ. Particularly significant is the way the Directory develops this understanding in conjunction with its theory of Christ's atonement:

> That the water, in baptism, representeth and signifieth both the blood of Christ, which taketh away all guilt of sin, original and actual; and the sanctifying virtue of the Spirit of Christ against the dominion of sin, and the corruption of our sinful nature: That baptizing, or sprinkling and washing with water, signifieth the cleansing from sin by the

blood and for the merit of Christ, together with the mortification of sin, and rising from sin to newness of life, by virtue of the death and resurrection of Christ.[19]

The Directory develops this theological interpretation alongside a portrayal of covenant theology that looks to the Abrahamic covenant as a model for the role of baptism within the Christian community. Immediately following this Old Testament reference, the Directory describes the Gospel portrayal of Jesus's welcoming of the children as the basis for infant baptism (no citation, but an indirect and descriptive biblical warrant). The role of baptism as seal of the covenant relationship established in the work of Christ prepares the recipients to "fight against the devil, the world, and the flesh."[20]

The Directory explicitly develops the rite of baptism as primarily depicting a covenantal theology. The act of baptism by water is depicted as an external rite by which children are received into the visible church. This act is not salvific since the children to be baptized "are Christians, and federally holy before baptism, and therefore are they baptized."[21] In addition, the minister's prayers both before and after baptism articulate an understanding of covenantal theology that provides the theological foundation for the sacrament. Both the Larger and Shorter Catechisms that were written as part of the Westminster Standards provide biblical and theological grounds for the theological orientation and claims that we have described from our overview of the Confession and the Directory.

As we have previously noted, the significance of Westminster can be seen in the way that it held sway for three centuries. While in recent years Westminster has been characterized as more representative of summing up the theological direction of the Reformed movement during the seventeenth century than it was of laying the groundwork for a theological vision that would connect with the development of new philosophical and theological insights, nevertheless, Westminster remained an important touchstone for its commitment and defense of a particular theological interpretation of the Reformed approach to the sacraments.[22]

ALTERNATIVE INTERPRETATIONS OF BAPTISM

At the time of Westminster, significant changes were already underway that would lay the groundwork for several shifts in terms of the ways in which Reformed communities interpreted the role of baptism. We noted in our discussion of Scripture in chapter 4 the rise of biblical criticism and the significant ways in which it questioned the method of biblical interpretation, especially in the use of biblical warrants. As we will see, this became particularly significant in terms of the Reformed tradition's acceptance of infant baptism and the lack of direct New Testament evidence to support this practice.

Theological developments within the nineteenth century provided a basis for questions about the role of baptism within the Reformed tradition. As we have seen, confessional documents assume the practice of infant baptism as normative. In fact, the Church of Scotland passed a law in 1672 that required the baptism of infants within thirty days of their birth.[23] On this point, one can see ways in which the cultural significance of infant baptism continued to provide a basis from which theological arguments to support it were developed. The difficulty of identifying a direct line of critique on baptismal practice may largely be due to the lack of a robust baptismal theology among Reformed communities.[24] Nevertheless, the rise of biblical criticism and the emergence of new theological methods would slowly raise critical questions around the biblical and liturgical assumptions that were offered to support a Reformed baptismal theology.

The reliance on the historical-critical method raised additional questions about appropriate ways to read and interpret Scripture. Significant concerns emerged about the use of typological and allegorical readings of Old Testament texts as a primary basis for interpreting Christian baptism. Similarly, the historical research into the life of Jesus prompted new questions around the centrality of baptism in the ministry of Jesus. This critical work laid the foundation for significant questions about the use of Scripture to defend doctrines and practices of the church. For example, we noted previously in chapter 5 how Schleiermacher's rejection of Anselm's theory of substitutionary atonement had enormous consequences for the liturgical portrayal of the Lord's Supper. Similarly, any liturgical attempts to directly link the water of baptism with the blood of Christ became increasingly problematic. Before looking at the immediate consequences of this theological debate, we will note the way Schleiermacher carefully crafted questions about baptismal practice.

In his section on baptism in *The Christian Faith*, Schleiermacher deliberately develops an approach to baptism that outlines a theological understanding of its role. He begins by pointing to baptism as signifying the act of an individual "being taken up into Christian community."[25] Following Calvin's emphasis on pneumatology, Schleiermacher insists that the regenerative effect of baptism is the work of the Holy Spirit. The link to Christ instituting this rite is provided indirectly via the role of the Spirit in Christ's ministry rather than an attempt to provide a biblical warrant (like Matt. 28). This move also allows Schleiermacher to immediately recognize the possibility of diverse baptismal practices within the New Testament and the early church. Schleiermacher couples this insight with a critical awareness of the distinction between John's baptism of

Jesus and the development of Christian baptism. Rather than search for a biblical warrant to prove the case for a particular form or understanding of baptism, Schleiermacher proceeds to analyze the relationship between faith in Christ and baptism. Baptism provides a sign of the regenerative work of the Spirit in and through the "divine grace [that] is secured through the community."[26] This careful way of articulating a baptismal theology allows Schleiermacher to avoid what he calls the "magical effects" of baptism, where the application of water provides the effect of cleansing, as well as the "degrading" of baptism as an unnecessary external practice (that is seen as inferior to the internal spiritual baptism).[27]

Schleiermacher forcefully asserts the integral relationship between faith and baptism as central to its integrity in the life of the church. The result of this move leads to a series of questions about the assumption of infant baptism as the normative practice of the church. Schleiermacher concludes that "All things considered, at the time of the Reformation it could have been quite convenient to let go of child baptism so as to draw nearer to Christ's institution of baptism once more."[28] Schleiermacher calls on households to reach their own conclusions about when their children should be baptized—either as infants or later upon their own profession of faith. In the end, Schleiermacher's work is as significant to baptismal theology for what he leaves out as for what he endorses. Gone is the attempt to provide typological texts or biblical warrants to prove the right baptismal practice. Schleiermacher avoids the association of atonement theory with baptism by reclaiming the practice of baptism as central in terms of establishing the identity of the baptized through their union with Christ in the context of the confessing faith of the church. In this sense, covenant theology is neither dismissed nor elevated, but placed in the context of the broader life of the community. Schleiermacher picks up on Calvin's pneumatological emphasis and his teleological focus on union with Christ as central to baptismal practice and identity.

We can detect one result of Schleiermacher's theological conclusions in the debate over liturgical reform of the baptismal liturgy of the Reformed Church in Zurich. In his critical analysis of the debate, historical theologian Theodore Vial shows the influence of Schleiermacher's theology as well as the ways in which the critical study of the life of Jesus (particularly through the controversial work of David Friedrich Strauss) provided significant impetus for those arguing to change the baptismal liturgy. The inability of traditionalists and progressives to reach an agreement led to a compromise arrangement with the approval of two distinct baptismal liturgies that were approved for use in the Canton of Zurich in 1868. The traditional liturgy reaffirms that Christ "instituted baptism as a symbol of the covenant of the New Testament."[29] The claim is followed by the recitation of Matthew 28:18–20 as the biblical warrant before citing Mark 10:14–16 with Jesus's welcoming of the children as the basis for infant baptism. This liturgy stresses the importance of the Apostles' Creed as a summary of faith for those being baptized. The prayer following the creed reasserts baptism as the sign of the covenant before identifying the link to atonement theory by invoking these words: "Give it the spiritual treasures and blessings, through which the power of the blood of Jesus for the forgiveness of sins and the operation of the Holy Ghost for sanctification are marked and affixed with a seal."[30]

In contrast, the second baptismal rite begins by noting God's movement through creation to call and gather us into one flock. The rite provides a briefer version of Matthew 28 and Mark 10 as biblical warrants for baptism. Baptism is described as an act of consecration where we "bear witness" to God "who has called us to a filial relationship."[31] The baptismal rite avoids the use of the Apostles' Creed and instead stresses the importance of raising children in the community of faith. The minister's prayer invites God's blessing on the child: "Immerse it in the life-stream of your grace and sanctify it to your possession. Take it into your Kingdom. Let it be your child in imitation of Jesus and impress the image of his life and death from early on its soul, so it might not live for himself, but for him who has paid a high price for it. Fill it with your holy spirit, the spirit of truth and of love."[32]

In contrasting these divergent baptismal rites, Vial highlights three important distinctions: (1) the contested role and interpretation of the Apostles' Creed;[33] (2) whether or not the language of the rite should directly address Jesus Christ; and (3) questions around the use of language about the blood of Jesus as part of the baptismal liturgy.[34] The decision to approve dramatically different baptismal rites demonstrates the divergent theological streams that were emerging within the Reformed tradition.

DEVELOPMENTS AMONG PRESBYTERIANS IN THE UNITED STATES

We can see similar ways that the theological struggle described in the debates over liturgical reform in Zurich played out among Presbyterians in what would become the United States. We previously noted the decisive role that the Westminster Standards played in defining Reformed theology and practices within the United States. While subscription to Westminster "in all essential and necessary articles" was required of Presbyterian ministers by the Adopting Act of 1729, the influence of continental theology was also increasingly felt in the United States. One can see the shift away from a strict acceptance of Westminster in a series of theological skirmishes: (1) the debate over higher criticism and biblical inerrancy headlined by Charles Briggs at Union Theological Seminary in the 1890s; (2) the decision by both the Northern and Southern Presbyterian church to approve revisions to Westminster (in 1903 the Northern church added two sections in an attempt to balance the emphasis on election, which were later approved in 1942 by the Southern church); also in 1903 the Southern church added a statement to clarify "certain inferences drawn from statements" in the Westminster Confession; and (3) the Old School–New School debates that led J. Gresham Machen (and others) to split from Princeton Seminary in 1929 over the role of Westminster.[35]

The effect of these ongoing debates can be seen in the different ways in which the southern and northern church shaped their baptismal liturgies. In the South, the baptismal liturgy in the *Book of Church Order* included three questions to ask the parent(s) of the child presented for baptism:

1. Do you acknowledge your child's need of the cleansing blood of Jesus Christ and the renewing grace of the Holy Spirit?
2. Do you claim God's covenant promises on (his) behalf, and do you look in faith to the Lord Jesus Christ for (his) salvation, as you do for your own?
3. Do you now unreservedly dedicate your child to God, and promise, in humble reliance upon divine grace, that you will endeavor to set before (him) a Godly example, that you will pray with and for (him), that you will teach (him) the doctrines of our holy religion, and that you will strive, by all the means of God's appointment, to bring (him) up in the nurture and admonition of the Lord?[36]

These three questions remained constant in the baptismal rite up until the time of reunification with the northern church in 1983. The questions show a continuity with the theology of Westminster with its emphasis on linking baptism and atonement theory, a stress on baptism as initiation into God's promises of covenant, and an acknowledgment of the significance of teaching doctrine as central to formation in Christian faith.

In contrast, the *Book of Order* for the northern church simply outlines a basic understanding of the sacraments as instituted by Christ where Christ is present with those who are gathered. As an essential part of public ministry, the church commemorates the redemptive acts by which we are united to Jesus Christ and made one in him.[37] Within this context, baptism provides a sign of God's power and mercy to cleanse people of their sins.[38]

It is interesting to note how these two descriptions of baptism roughly align with the theologies of the baptismal rites adopted in Zurich. The southern church shows its adherence to a traditional understanding of Westminster whereas the northern church increasingly reflects the theological influence of Schleiermacher and nineteenth-century liberal Protestantism.[39]

DEBATING THE ROLE OF BAPTISM IN THE REFORMED TRADITION

While much of the discussion centered on theological claims and liturgical language for a Reformed approach to baptism, Karl Barth led a spirited attack on the understanding of baptism and the acceptance of infant baptism. His 1943 lecture lays out the case for a reevaluation of baptismal theology and practice. Central to Barth's argument is a reliance on Romans 6, particularly verse 4: "Therefore we were buried with him by baptism into death, so that, just as Christ was raised from the dead by the glory of the Father, so we also might walk in newness of life." In this text, Barth recognizes that baptism claims to be a sign of regeneration that portrays a passage from death to life through a participation in the death and resurrection of Jesus Christ. For Barth, this primary understanding of baptism provides the basis for his interrogation of the baptismal rite, mode, and practice of infant baptism. While Barth's inquiry dramatically diverges from Calvin and the trajectory of Reformed theology, he curiously begins his study by noting the correlation between baptism and circumcision: "Primitive baptism carried out in this manner as its mode [submersion in water] had in its mode, exactly like the circumcision of the Old Testament, the character of a direct threat to life, succeeded immediately by the corresponding deliverance and preservation, the raising from baptism."[40]

For Barth, the primary goal of baptism is the proclamation and participation in the saving death of Jesus Christ. Barth connects this witness with his commitment to salvation history: "One does no honour to baptism by interpreting it as if it were in essence more than the representation of the sacred history (*Heilsgeschichte*) which comes to pass between God and man in Jesus Christ."[41] This basis for baptism allows Barth to focus on a Christocentric approach while at the same time affirming a central role of covenant that prophetically links together Old Testament texts with their fulfillment in Jesus Christ.

Barth's concern centers on the way that a basic understanding of baptism has been compromised by "the innocuous form of present-day baptism" which has obscured the dramatic power of baptism to witness to Jesus Christ.[42] Barth develops a Reformed understanding of baptism that rejects a Roman Catholic reliance on the rite itself as well as avoiding what he identifies as a Zwinglian tendency to emphasize the faith of the baptized as the grounds for baptism. In place of these approaches, Barth asserts the central role of God's covenant as the sole source of grace (here Barth studiously avoids what we do and what we believe as the basis for a Reformed baptismal practice). Barth concludes that the meaning of baptism is "the glorifying of God in the building up of the Church of Jesus Christ, through the pledge given to a man, with divine certainty, of grace directed towards him. . . ."[43] Since this work is solely God's action, Barth connects it to the redemptive work of God in Jesus Christ in which the "blood of Jesus Christ and the Holy Ghost cleanses us from all sin."[44]

The regenerative work of baptism occurs within the context of a community of believers where the one baptized professes their faith in the redemptive work of Jesus Christ. For Barth, the work of baptism is God's declaration of deliverance in the life of the baptismal candidate so that through the work of Jesus Christ they are freed from the bondage of sin. As a free and responsible decision to rely on God's redemptive work in Jesus Christ, believers are received by baptism into the covenant community. On this basis, Barth rejects the practice of infant baptism as "a wound in the body of the Church," since infants do not come as willing and obedient participants.[45]

Barth buttresses his critique by noting the lack of biblical evidence for infant baptism and pointing out inconsistencies in Calvin's teachings on baptism in the Institutes.[46] Barth concludes that: "From the standpoint of a doctrine of baptism, infant-baptism can hardly be preserved without exegetical and practical artifices and sophisms."[47] It is the power and allure of Constantinian Christianity and the *Volkskirche* (national church) that has corrupted baptismal practice by obscuring the meaning of baptism.

Barth's rejection of infant baptism was picked up by the German Reformed theologian Jürgen Moltmann, who offers a contrasting vision for the role of baptism as a sign of eschatological promise. Moltmann understands that this represents a shift from a traditional way of approaching baptism via soteriology, where the primary questions revolve around either the salvific effect of baptism itself or are closely aligned with christological claims. Moltmann observes that within this schema, "Baptism is justified through a founder christology and legitimated by the fact that it was instituted by Christ himself."[48] As we have seen, this understanding of baptism in the Reformed tradition is usually linked with a theology of covenant so that baptism as initiation for infants or adults provides an initiation into the community of faith, the church. In agreement with Barth, Moltmann notes that there remains uncertainty about the relationship between faith and baptism. In infant baptism it seems that baptism precedes faith, whereas adult baptism follows upon the testimony of faith.[49] This inconsistency prompts Moltmann to question the legitimacy of infant baptism particularly in light of the way that the practice has aligned with an understanding of "Christian society," which was often portrayed as analogous to the role of circumcision among the people of Israel in the Old Testament. On these grounds, Moltmann calls for a reform of baptismal theology and practice in order that baptism might clearly point to the prophetic witness of the church.[50]

Moltmann's reading of the New Testament clearly identifies the primary impetus for the development of Christian baptism as grounded in the "resistance movement" of John the Baptist as he issues a call for repentance in hope of experiencing the coming of the kingdom of God. On this point, Moltmann clearly distinguishes this basis for baptism from circumcision or other purification practices by Jews or members of ancient mystery religions. By contrast, Jesus's baptism by John is immersion into an expanding vision of the coming of God's kingdom in terms of judgment, forgiveness, and the hope of new life. Moltmann concludes that "Christian baptism is eschatology put into practice. It manifests the advent of the coming God through Christ in human life and is the sign of life's conversion to the life of Easter."[51] Seen from this perspective, baptism depicts the life of Christ by the work of the Spirit. How baptism pictures our participation in the life of Christ is expressed with different emphases within the New Testament. These varied portraits prompt Moltmann to insist on the importance of identifying baptism within the broader contours of an incarnational theology rather than locating it at a particular moment in the life of Christ. Moltmann proposes reclaiming the central component of baptism as a calling upon the life of individuals who through baptism receive a Christian identity within a community that works for liberation within the world.[52]

In spite of the efforts of Barth and Moltmann to question the practice of infant baptism, Reformed congregations have shown limited interest in addressing their concerns.[53] While the theological influence of Barth has been decisive in terms of establishing neo-orthodoxy and reaffirming key insights from Calvin and the early Reformed confessions, his influence on a Reformed understanding of baptism is part of a complicated legacy. While there is renewed interest in terms of baptismal rites for adults (particularly given the demise of Christendom), Reformed congregations continue the practice of infant baptism primarily through its commitment to the "teaching of the free antecedent grace of God." Here again, though, Barth notes that this theological justification is not one that was offered by the reformers themselves.[54] The question that has been prompted by Moltmann is how baptism can portray God's initiative in ways that provide Christian communities with a clear witness to the role of Christian faith.

LITURGICAL AND THEOLOGICAL CHANGE TO BAPTISMAL PRACTICE

The Confession of 1967 (C-67) points in the direction that baptismal theology and practice is moving for Presbyterians in the United States. The brief paragraph on baptism highlights Jesus's baptism by John as central to Christ's work of reconciliation. Barth's influence is seen in terms of both the language of reconciliation as well as a new focus on baptism as the mark of Christ's dying and rising (an indirect reference to Romans 6). In baptism, the church celebrates God's covenant and assumes the responsibility of nurturing individuals in Christian discipleship.[55] C-67 affirms the practice of infant baptism but notes the responsibility of parents and the congregation for raising children in the life of faith.

These themes from C-67 are further developed in the baptismal rite in *The Worshipbook*. The rubrics which precede the service note that the rite is designed for either the baptism of "mature believers" or for infants. The liturgy opens with Matthew 28:19–20 as the biblical warrant for the service. It portrays baptism as the sign by which God's promises in Jesus Christ are known to us through the forgiveness of sin, by inclusion into the family of faith, deliverance from darkness, and participation in the dying and rising with Christ. The rite includes questions for the baptismal candidate or for the parent(s) of the infant receiving baptism, but notes that "other questions may be required in the Cumberland Presbyterian Church and in the Presbyterian Church in the United States:"[56]

1. Who is your Lord and Savior?
2. Do you trust in him?
3. Do you intend (your child) to be his disciple, to obey his word and show his love? And if the baptism is for an adult it includes the question: Will you be a faithful member of this congregation, giving of yourself in every way, and will you seek the fellowship of the church wherever you may be?[57]

The prayer before baptism offers thanks to God for the gift of baptism and for the hope we have in Jesus Christ while also invoking the Spirit's presence to make us one with Christ. Following baptism using the Trinitarian formula, the prayer references Acts 2 with the language of adding to the number of those who are called into the body of Christ.

There are several important developments in this liturgy. Note that the word covenant is not explicitly used nor is there any reference to Old Testament passages with descriptive renderings of baptism as part of salvation history. Gone as well is any use of the Gospel account of Jesus's welcoming of children as justification for infant baptism. In place of these themes, the language of the reconciling work of Christ gets prominent attention, along with particular attention to the Romans 6 image of baptism as dying and rising with Christ.

In 1983, the reunion of the northern and southern Presbyterian churches brought significant change to the description of baptism through the language adopted in the Directory for Worship. The definition of the sacraments from the United Presbyterian Church provides a basic orientation to the sacraments. In place of the questions used by the southern church, the new directory provides two questions for those presenting infants for baptism: (1) Do you reaffirm your own faith in Jesus Christ as Savior and Lord? (2) Do you claim God's covenant promises on your child's behalf? The Trinitarian baptismal formula does include the language of "child of the covenant," which was historically used in the southern church. In addition, the new *Book of Order* includes a section on the baptism of believers (adults) that includes instructions on the meaning of the sacrament: "The minister shall affirm that the water of the sacrament symbolizes that in Christ God washes away the sin which is inseparable from the human condition."[58] In addition, the language of C-67 is invoked by the declaration that baptism enables them to share in the reconciling work of Christ.

Given the concerns about the theology and practice of baptism that we have seen in the writings of Schleiermacher, Barth, and Moltmann, it seems appropriate to wonder how the Reformed tradition maintained its traditional approach to baptismal theology and practice and what signs we can detect that point to a renewed consideration of the role of baptism in the liturgical life of our congregations. We begin by noting again that for the most part questions of baptismal theology have been largely absent from the discussion of congregational renewal. To cite one striking example that lies at the center of our broader investigation, Jean-Jacques von Allmen's seminal work on worship in 1968 largely excludes an examination of baptism since it is not part of the regular Sunday worship of the congregation. While von Allmen builds on the insights of Barth in terms of the primary role of covenant and salvation history, he remains mostly silent on the place of baptism in this vision of community life.[59] The occasional asides in von Allmen's work primarily reflect the priorities we have seen in our survey of Reformed confessions. For example, von Allmen echoes the interpretation of circumcision as a Jewish practice that has been superseded by Christian baptism, which serves as "the mark of initiation into the people of the promise."[60] One can surmise from this observation that von Allmen understands baptism to serve as a clearer sign of the covenant life that reaches fulfillment in the life and death of Jesus Christ. Since von Allmen's primary commitment is to a vision of salvation history that is proclaimed, reflected, and enacted in the life of the community, it seems striking that the role of baptism remains undeveloped. Here, von Allmen simply cites Barth's declaration that baptism establishes the place where "the Church comes [in]to being."[61] Furthermore, von Allmen develops this insight in terms of the place of the baptized as participants in worship ("the cult") and thereby to rehearse the story of God's redemptive work in the world. Here, the priority of the baptized to participate in the witness of the community takes precedence over Barth's questions about responsibility and obedience. Von Allmen describes this in terms of the catholic church's commitment to baptism as a "sign of prevenient grace" rather than as a "demonstration of grace."[62] In the end, von Allmen leaves us with an effort to restore a sacramental theology of the Reformed tradition that follows the theological trajectories of Barth and biblical theologians but that provides limited insights on ways that a Reformed baptismal theology can contribute to congregation renewal.

LITURGICAL RENEWAL THROUGH REVISIONS TO BAPTISMAL RITES

Where von Allmen remained largely silent, the liturgical renewal movement (particularly following the period of success following Vatican II) provided significant impetus in terms of pressing for revised baptismal rites that articulate their own theological priorities. This dramatic shift is evident in the new baptismal rite provided by the *Book of Common Worship* (1993) that strives to hold together historic affirmations alongside new theological emphases in the liturgy. The service begins with the traditional use of Matthew 28 as a biblical warrant (but offers a series of other optional New Testament texts for inclusion in the service). The minister offers a brief description of baptism where God claims us, seals us, and frees us from sin and death. The liturgy is marked by the inclusion of a series of questions for baptismal candidates, their parents or sponsors, and the congregation. The baptismal questions begin by asking the candidate (or the parent(s) of the candidate) if they want to be baptized. The desire for baptism is balanced by asking the congregation if they will nurture the baptismal candidates in their faith.

The liturgy shifts to the profession of faith, which uses the language of covenant four times in rapid succession to assert a central theological claim. In this context, the liturgy invokes the questions of renunciation adopted from the liturgical renewal movement, which has influenced this baptismal rite so that it is more reflective of the baptismal rites in the worship books of other denominations. Following the renunciations is the recitation of the Apostles' Creed. For those who are professing their faith, two questions are included: (1) "Will you be a faithful member of this congregation, share in its worship and ministry through your prayers and gifts, your study and service, and so fulfill your calling to be a disciple of Jesus Christ?" (2) "Will you devote yourself to the church's teaching and fellowship, in the breaking of bread and prayers?"[63] A prayer of thanksgiving over the water follows these questions. The prayer recalls the role of water in salvation history from creation through Jesus's baptism and links baptism with Christ's death and resurrection. The prayer also calls on (*epiclesis*) the Spirit's presence in the baptismal water in order that the Spirit's presence may bring redemption and new birth. Following baptism with the Trinitarian formula is the laying on of hands, which includes an invocation of the Spirit as well as an optional anointing with oil.

The new baptismal liturgy represents a significant change in baptismal theology for Reformed congregations. Specific biblical references are drawn from the New Testament (while Mark 10 is carefully avoided as a reference for infant baptism). The liturgy reasserts the language of covenant and also connects it with a theme of salvation history while avoiding language associated with atonement theory. The influence of baptismal rites from ecumenical sources can be seen throughout the service, but particularly in the use of the renunciations and in the prayer of thanksgiving over the water. There is heightened attention to the role of the Spirit in baptism that recaptures a major theme in Calvin's theology. We will look more closely at these developments and what they may suggest when we turn our focus to contemporary expressions of a Reformed baptismal theology in part 3.

PART III

The Future of Reformed Worship

7

Scripture

The reading of Scripture was central to the theological and liturgical reform that led to the Protestant Reformation. For Calvin and others in the early Reformed movement, Scripture provided a weapon to combat what they identified as abuses and malpractices of the church. Scripture was wielded as a two-edged sword: the reading of Scripture opened their eyes to the possibilities of different understandings of Christian faith while also serving as the basis for their attacks on Roman Catholic doctrine.

Let's begin by reviewing key insights from the Reformed tradition that can continue to guide us as we examine options for the future role of Scripture in worship. In our overview of Calvin, we noted the influence of humanism on his theological approach. His reading of Scripture was influenced by the commitment to study texts in their original language. A distinguishing feature of his approach to the riches of Scripture was the belief in the integrity of the Old Testament as a witness to God. This aspect of Calvin's reading of the Bible is evident in the regular singing of the Psalms as well as the decision to read and preach regularly through books of the Old Testament. Calvin's use of the *lectio continua* method served as a distinguishing mark of the Reformed approach to Scripture. The goal of promoting biblical literacy in order to prompt growth in Christian piety is founded on the practice of hearing Scripture read and proclaimed regularly. For Calvin, this included not only a Sunday service but also regular weekday services. Similarly, Scripture's role in the formation of new liturgies provided the framework for the significant shifts that Calvin made to the interpretation and celebration of the sacraments. All of these practices were fundamentally based on Calvin's theological conviction that the Holy Spirit is the One who brings life and understanding to our words and actions as we gather in hope and thanksgiving to acknowledge our dependence on God's grace.

When we look at Reformed worship today, we can see how these distinguishing theological marks continue to influence our liturgies. However, we have also noted ways that theological change and the rise of the historical-critical method of studying Scripture challenged many of the dogmatic assumptions that supported traditional liturgical texts and practices. While the new critical methods for reading Scripture were based on many of the humanistic assumptions that initially distinguished Reformation approaches from Roman Catholic doctrine, they were also influenced by significant philosophical shifts (particularly beginning with the work of René Descartes and its appeal to the primacy of reason) that led to new theological approaches. For example, we noted the significance of personal experience in the work of Friedrich Schleiermacher. The primary point to note here is how theological shifts led to changes in the liturgy over time.

As we begin to ponder what changes are necessary for Reformed worship, we should be aware of philosophical and theological shifts that are prompting us to see ourselves and the world around us from different perspectives. The first major shift is the awareness that the age of Christendom is over. We live in a multifaith world where the assumptions of Christian identity and a privileged place for Christian faith are no longer viable. While the process of the demise of Christendom has been going on for decades, the nostalgia for the way things used to be continues to hold sway in many congregations. Often the way in which we read and interpret Scripture remains culturally captive to the language and mythology of the American dream. A latent Christian triumphalism permeates our prayers and hymnody. The painful process of acknowledging our place as one faith among many options (increasingly including no faith) prompts a need for a careful examination of our assumptions and language. The dominance of secular neocapitalism has provided its own agenda with particular values (e.g., accumulating wealth as a sign of success) and joined with other forces on insisting that religious faith is solely a private matter. In contrast, Calvin's attempt to establish a form of theocracy in Geneva where the church and state promoted (and at times enforced) a shared moral vision of life together continues to haunt our imaginations. Since our history in the United States is closely intertwined with political power and money, it is difficult for congregations to accept a countercultural place outside the halls of power and the allure of wealth. Particularly at this juncture, a careful rereading of Scripture can help us identify with the witness of those on the margins.[1]

A second major philosophical shift that carries significant consequences is the rise of postmodernity. I am using the term postmodernity here as a way to note significant shifts from the central tenets of modernity. For our interests, we will pay attention to certain key characteristics of this movement in response to the primary commitments that defined modernism. We have already noted the questioning of human progress that rose up as a response to the horrors of WWI. Accompanying this shift is a growing suspicion of the role of reason and certainty in determining objectivity and the ability to make universal claims. Postmodern approaches reject the dualisms inherent in modernity (e.g., subjective/objective, mind/body).[2] In place of these approaches, a variety of postmodern approaches emphasize the role of difference in the midst of the diverse nature of interpretation that is integrally connected to one's cultural and personal experience. This sense of skepticism is also focused on metanarratives that propose to offer grand overarching models that seek to guide/determine interpretive options. Theologian Stanley Grenz characterizes the different approaches in these words: "The modern understanding linked truth with rationality and made reason and logic arbiters of right belief. Post-moderns question the concept of universal truth discovered and proved through rational endeavors."[3]

In place of the search for rational certainty and the desire to show progress, postmodern approaches emphasize relativity and interplay as open-ended ways in which we construct meaning in our lives and world.[4]

APPROACHES TO READING SCRIPTURE

The question for Reformed communities is not *if* we will read Scripture, but *how* we will read it. Liturgical theologian Graham Hughes notes the challenges that face the church in terms of the ability of Christianity "to portray itself as a viable source of meaning" given the rise of secularism and what he terms (via Max Weber and Charles Taylor) as the "disenchantment of the world."[5] Once again, we come face to face with Karl Barth's description of the strange, new world of the Bible. While Barth's renewed emphasis on Scripture as God's revelation harkens back to Calvin, his understanding of the Word of God as event shows a more nuanced approach to the way Scripture speaks to us. Barth recognized the danger of the attempts to control the reading and interpretation of the Bible. He went so far as to name these risks as the search for history, morality, and religion in Scripture.[6] Instead, Barth's emphasis on the Bible as a place to encounter the Word of God places the reading of Scripture beyond our control. In the early years of the development of what became known as dialectical theology, Rudolf Bultmann's approach to the reading of Scripture as a moment of existential decision shared a similar emphasis. While Bultmann's use of demythologization of what he identified as the three-story universe of the ancient world (heaven, earth, and hell) provided a way for modern readers to hear and respond to the existential message in Scripture was a major cause for the division between Barth and Bultmann, it is helpful to note the similar concern that motivated their study of Scripture.

We should acknowledge the challenges of reading Scripture in worship. While Barth may relish the strangeness/otherness of the biblical texts, Hughes (and others) worries that the distance and foreignness of Scripture may make the text unfathomable both to those who still come to worship (bringing with them their modernist assumptions) and those who have distanced themselves from any form of Christianity. In light of these challenges, we will begin by noting several significant features of Scripture that can guide our deliberations about the choices we make in terms of the public reading and interpretation of biblical texts.

First is an obvious concern around the cultural bound elements in all texts. The historical-critical method provided a major effort by acknowledging the *Sitz im Leben* behind the world of the text. The growth of information about archeological and other ancient texts has brought new light to the cultural practices and norms of the ancient world. Yet even as these new resources provide a wider perspective on practices and customs, they also expose the different assumptions of ancient people from those of us who live in a highly technological and increasingly diverse world. To cite but one obvious example of the disparity in cultural norms: issues in gender identity and roles are vastly different. No amount of Bultmann's demythologizing a three-story universe (heaven-earth-hell) is going to make a difference in terms of addressing the vast differences between the ancient world and contemporary expectations and assumptions. In fact, I would argue that problems have been exacerbated by the lack of acknowledgment of the differences between the ancient world and our own. Conservatives have selected certain preferred cultural norms from the vast biblical world and tried to enforce them as requirements (no to polygamy but yes to submissive women). Liberals have tried to either sweep aside cultural differences by extolling deeper spiritual meanings of the text or picked and chosen texts that are interpreted to support their own cultural perspectives (Galatians 3:28 as a liberative text over and against other Pauline texts). My point here is to simply acknowledge that not all Scripture is edifying or appropriate for reading in public worship.

If we are going to continue the historic commitment to the centrality of Scripture, it is critical for us to consider our cultural contexts in order to determine what choices we will make. In *Reformed Sacramentality*, liturgical theologian Graham Hughes reflects on Calvin's preference for the auditory sense amidst his fear that reliance on other senses runs the risk of idolatry. Hence, there is a propensity in Calvin's liturgies for an overabundance of words (a condition that continues to preoccupy Reformed liturgies). Hughes concludes, "The dominance of language over every other human communicative or sentient faculty is thus prominent in Calvin's sacramental theology."[7] This conviction prompted Calvin to prioritize doctrine, preaching, and Scripture. As we saw in our analysis of Calvin's liturgies, the result was a highly didactic approach to worship that appealed primarily to reason by providing an explanation of the liturgical practices. One only needs to look at the highly structured, overly wordy church bulletins in many congregations today to see the way that this legacy has continued. Even among Reformed congregations that have opted for versions of contemporary worship, the preference for the auditory persists (often seen in the lengthy sermons that offer bullet point outlines for the listeners to follow). In a broader cultural context that is increasingly visual, the nearly exclusive reliance on the auditory sense raises critical questions about our practices. While some congregations are exploring ways for art to illustrate the meaning(s) of a text, the primary focus remains textual. Even Hughes notes that "in recent years many people have discovered it *is* enough, in reading Scripture for example, to listen to *the texts in themselves* and *for their own sake* to find the stories' meanings not in truths external to them but rather within their own narrative configurations of reality."[8] How can we affirm the significance of biblical texts while recognizing the need to engage our senses more holistically?

In reflecting on how we read Scripture in worship, there are three important questions for us to explore: (1) Given the open concerns about an overreliance on the auditory senses, how much Scripture will we read each week? (2) What choices will we make in terms of the texts that we read? and (3) What hermeneutical presuppositions guide the choice of texts and the connection between texts?

First, in terms of the amount of Scripture to read regularly in worship there are critical questions about the use of the Revised Common Lectionary that must be raised. Is it reasonable or appropriate to read an Old Testament, Epistle, and Gospel lesson each week (in addition to reading or singing a psalm)? One concern here is about the length of readings and the ability for listeners to absorb difficult and diverse texts. We should also note the impossibility for sermons to deal with the nuances and differences between these texts. Thus, it seems wise to limit the number of readings in order that we may focus on the richness of a particular text.

As we saw in chapter 4, the Revised Common Lectionary attempted to deal with issues of textual difference by imposing a thematic link between the texts. Old Testament and Epistle readings were selected to complement the Gospel reading (except in the semi-continuous option during ordinary time). Thus, our hearing and interpreting of biblical texts is based on a preferential or coerced hermeneutic that both guides and restricts our understanding of the rich diversity within the Bible.

Liturgical renewal and biblical theology brought their own set of theological presuppositions that has reshaped the role of Scripture and changed the liturgical scripts for the celebration of the sacraments. Together they provided support for the development of a common lectionary that was widely used among Roman Catholic, Anglican, and mainline Protestant congregations. This lectionary addressed the pressing need for biblical literacy by organizing readings around themes within the church year. Critics of the lectionary noted the absence of significant portions of the Bible as well as the hermeneutical lens used to coordinate readings. While some of these concerns were addressed in the revisions to the common lectionary, particularly the inclusion of additional readings that featured stories of biblical women (Revised Common Lectionary in 1994), concerns continue to grow.

However, we have also named another aspect that was central to the development and use of the (Revised) Common Lectionary. The lectionary is firmly committed to supporting a metanarrative rooted in a particular interpretation of salvation history. We noted the congruency in the twentieth century between those advocating for liturgical renewal and a movement among biblical theologians who saw *Heilsgeschichte* as a way to create a unitive theological framework from the diverse witnesses within the biblical canon. To be fair, the biblical texts provide models for this approach. For example, note the recitation of the works of God in the psalms. The point to be made here is that there is a myriad of patterns within the biblical text rather than one particular overarching theological framework that is imposed on the text. The distinction between encouraging thanksgiving for God's faithfulness as an on-going pattern of life versus a theological/liturgical list is important. By superimposing the church year as a thematic device, the lectionary addresses the concern for biblical literacy by directing the readers/listeners to follow *the story* of God's saving history that is narrated in the biblical canon. While this effort provided a source of significant cooperation among ecumenical partners, it came with the cost of accepting tenets of modernity that insisted on searching for a unitive meaning.

Within the framework of Christendom and the assumptions of modernity, there was a coherence to the liturgical renewal agenda that provided biblical, liturgical, and theological foundations. As a pastor, I wholeheartedly accepted and supported this approach to congregational renewal (that was not without some success). The shifting landscape of the twenty-first century prompts me to question whether this approach continues to be viable for many congregations. Given the rapid rise of the nones (religiously unaffiliated individuals) and the secular insistence on faith as a private matter, congregations will need to wrestle with how to maintain a sense of historical and theological identity in a way that allows visitors access to the strangeness of the world of Scripture as well as the congregational customs and liturgical habits that we so often take for granted.

ADDITIONAL OPTIONS FOR SELECTING SCRIPTURE

Given growing questions about the Revised Common Lectionary (RCL), several alternative lectionaries have recently appeared that attempt to address particular concerns. This includes approaches that augment or serve as alternatives to the RCL. Year D offers an additional year to add to the RCL as a way to expand the common lectionary (with a particular focus on the Gospel of John and the Epistle to the Hebrews).[9] The narrative lectionary provides a list of texts for the Sundays from September through May that "follow the sweep of the biblical story, from Creation through the early Christian church."[10] The Season of Creation recommends selected readings for Sundays and holy days between September 1 and October 4 (feast day of St. Francis of Assisi) that focus on our relationship with the Creator and all of creation.[11]

Biblical scholar Wil Gafney created *A Women's Lectionary* to focus on readings of Scripture that highlight the role of women in Scripture. This important resource offers a corrective vision for reading patriarchal texts by focusing on the stories of women in the margins of the stories.[12] The lectionary is available both in a three-year version (as an alternative to the RCL) or as a one-year addition (that augments the RCL). As congregations awaken to the ways in which our reading of Scripture perpetuates racism and patriarchal perspectives, Gafney's work provides a critically needed resource that provides a more expansive and inclusive vision of Scripture.

In addition, there are thematic lectionaries that are developed to address particular issues or serve the needs of specific congregations: for example, the African American lectionary offers a six year cycle of readings that focuses on the traditions of the African American church and connects to the "joy, freedom, and the challenges of being both African American and Christian."[13] I will add one additional popular method of selecting readings for worship—the minister's choice of creating thematic series in which texts are chosen by the pastor as the basis for a sermon series on a particular topic.

Each of these methods has its own advantages. For our purposes, we are reflecting on the role of Scripture in light of contemporary and cultural issues. Our primary question is this: To what extent do we come to the text with an implicit or explicit expectation for the text(s) to support a theological perspective or to address a particular topic? Here, the role of a metanarrative or thematic units provides a broad framework into which particular theological interpretations are developed. We should be aware of the tendency to impose themes on the text(s) as a way for us to control the multiplicity of interpretations that are inherent in any given text.

Is there an alternative way to come to Scripture that lessens the risk of imposing meaning on the text(s)? It is worth noting that Calvin's preference for the *lectio continua* method may still provide a helpful pattern. Clearly, Calvin and other reformers brought their own theological agenda to the texts that were read and proclaimed. Yet if a primary goal of reading Scripture in worship is to build biblical literacy, then focusing on one particular book of the Bible may be critical in helping members of the congregation cultivate piety and grow in the life of faith. A primary criticism of *lectio continua* is the challenge of getting mired in long and difficult books of the Bible that may not correlate with contemporary issues. It seems to me, though, that Calvin's optimism about the Spirit's presence and direction in understanding the rich and complex witness of Scripture provides an important antidote that should not be quickly dismissed.[14]

How one interprets Scripture, particularly in light of the theological priorities that one brings to the text, shifts over time. I believe there are important lessons for us about ways that we select and read texts in this era of post-Christendom and postmodernity. In the end, I am not proposing we should be required to use any particular way of choosing texts, but I am suggesting that we examine our priorities and assumptions to the patterns we have inherited and adopted. As we will see in the various proposals offered in this section of the book, individual congregations will need to discern what is appropriate for their particular contexts. The return to the diversity of worship practices of the early church can serve as a helpful pattern for us to follow.

BIBLICAL HERMENEUTIC 1: SCRIPTURE AND CREATION

We have noted in our survey of Reformed practices ways in which theological beliefs and assumptions have dictated the direction of Reformed worship throughout its history. Thus, there is a basic question to ask in terms of the Scripture that we hear read and proclaimed each week: What theological priorities are directing our hermeneutical and liturgical choices? Our goal is to discover how central theological claims within the world of the biblical text address significant sociocultural issues that we are collectively facing today. We will explore two key issues that are grounded in Scripture and respond to the needs of our time: (1) the centrality of the earth in the witness of Scripture; and (2) Scripture's commitment to the preferential option for the poor.

While Calvin might not immediately identify these as the theological priorities that he brought to his reading of Scripture, I will argue that both play central roles in Calvin's theology. First, given the current ecological crisis that threatens the future of planet earth and all of its inhabitants, we must ask ourselves what resources the Reformed tradition can draw on that can help us navigate these perilous times. The witness of Scripture and the writings of Calvin offer us guidance to help us reclaim our relationship with the earth. In the preface to the French translation of the Bible, Calvin observes: "It is evident that all creatures, from those in the heavens to those under the earth, are able to act as witnesses and messengers of God's glory. . . . For the little birds that sing, sing of God; the beasts clamor for God; the elements dread God; the mountains echo God, and fountains and flowing waters wink at God. . . ."[15]

This sentiment is not unusual for Calvin, who is consistently prolific in his praise of creation as the theater of God's glory. Calvin's concern is not that there is a danger in extolling the goodness of creation, but that humans, who are blinded by sin, are unable to recognize the presence of the divine in the world around us. Given Calvin's fear of the human propensity toward idolatry, he is concerned about the temptation to substitute the image of the divine found in nature for God the Creator. Remember for Calvin, it is the witness of Scripture (special revelation) that allows us to see ourselves rightly and recognize our dependence on God for all of life. There are important threads in Calvin that connect to the urgent need for the church to recognize our responsibility to serve as stewards of creation.

As we have seen in the twentieth century, though, Barth's complete dismissal of natural revelation (contra Brunner) prompted a deepening suspicion in Reformed circles of positive portrayals of creation. The result further isolated Reformed liturgies from references to nature. One can see the effects of this theological shift in the diminished use of the Psalter in worship, which until the early twentieth century served as the primary source of hymnody in many Reformed congregations. The Psalter's eco-centric vocabulary and earth imagery gradually receded from congregational memory.

Thus, we return to our primary questions about the role of Scripture in the regular worship life of Reformed congregations. How can a biblical hermeneutic that focuses on the central role of the earth draw on the richness and diverse witness of Scripture while also addressing a major issue that the planet (including us) must face? In particular, how can a recognition of the agrarian culture of the ancient biblical world address urban, technological people?

Two recent works have offered alternative perspectives on the relationship between nature and Scripture in the broader Reformed tradition. We will look briefly and critically at these two approaches before proposing an alternative way of reclaiming the central role of the earth in the witness of Scripture.

First, in *When God Was a Bird*, Reformed theologian Mark Wallace makes the case for Christian animism as a forgotten voice within the witness of Scripture. According to Wallace, the biblical witness to the divine presence in all of creation has been overshadowed and submerged by a theological tradition that posited an otherworldly God and saw creation as fallen and evil. A rereading of Scripture with attention to the revelatory encounters within nature provides the grounding for a Christian re-enchantment of nature as the place of the divine. "The natural world, and its many divine, human, and animal denizens, is the primary locale of the biblical God's revelation of peace and fecundity. *Above all else, nature is God's preferred habitat in the Bible.*"[16] Thus, sustained attention to the role of the earth in Scripture serves as an antidote to the implicit Gnosticism that shapes much of American Christianity.[17] The tendency to spiritualize nature is readily identified by the ways in which our reading and preaching of Scripture uses images of the earth as metaphors for deeper spiritual truths: for example, the significance of the Jordan River as a place and ecosystem is dismissed in preference of the spiritual lesson that can be gleaned from our reading of Scripture. In this way, our method of reading Scripture reflects the spiritualization of the sacraments that we identified in Calvin's and the Reformed tradition's fear of the materiality of baptism and Communion. We will explore in the coming chapters the need to reclaim the prominent place of the earth in Scripture as a locus for encountering the divine presence that is central to reclaiming the sacraments as a celebration in which we acknowledge Christ's presence in, with, and through these gifts of the good earth.

Wallace's attempts to highlight the richness of biblical images that are integrally linked to nature is accompanied by a challenging attempt to sympathetically re-narrate the theological tradition in order to advocate for an historical commitment to the central role of the earth in Christianity. For me, his creative reinterpretations of the theological tradition stretch credulity in his desire to name a cloud of witnesses who support his commitment to Christian animism: for example, claiming Augustine as a natalist theologian ignores the vast writings of Augustine on the fallenness of creation. Wallace's roll call of saints includes mystics like Hildegard of Bingen and John Muir. This collective of testimonies leads Wallace to conclude that "God is not, in the biblical neo-animist worldview, a bodiless heavenly being divorced from the material world but is manifested instead as the winged Spirit who protectively alights on Jesus at the time of his baptism and thereby infused the world with sustaining love."[18] For Wallace, reclaiming this part of the Christian tradition provides a symbiotic way of aligning biblical texts with our encounter with the divine in creation. Whether or not one completely agrees with Wallace in his broader proposal to reclaim what he identifies as the animistic roots of

Christianity, his work points to the possibilities and importance of rereading Scripture from different perspectives.[19]

A second recent approach to the relationship of Scripture and nature comes from the Reformed liturgical scholar Cláudio Carvalhaes, who recognizes an inherent tension between nature and Scripture. For Carvalhaes, the anthropocentric assumptions in Scripture are compounded by the ways in which the Christian tradition used the Bible to justify a theology of dominion that provided the logical grounds for the subjugation of nature, the conquest and consumption of the earth, and the process of colonization. Given this history, Carvalhaes believes that any attempt to reclaim Scripture's primary witness to the earth is likely to come up short in light of the dominant cultural influences of neocapitalism. Once again, we note the distance between the influences, customs, and cultural habits that shape our daily lives and the attempt to reclaim a counter narrative from Scripture that could compete for our attention. In light of these vast differences, Carvalhaes's solution is to default to the book of nature as providing an essential correction to our corrupt reading of Scripture. The book of nature provides an essential alternative to the way in which we have read Scripture to support cultural and economic practices that threaten the earth's future.

If our goal is "for the Christian religion to reconnect us to God we need to *religare* (bind together) with the earth," Carvalhaes says.[20] It is important to note here the way in which Carvalhaes posits the disconnect between Christianity and God. This fundamental separation is the result of our estrangement from the law of nature (*lex naturae*). For Carvalhaes, our reading and interpretation of Scripture as well as our liturgical practices have separated us from the essential ingredient, which is our relationship to the earth. The loss of this grounding has accelerated the diminishment of materiality while shifting the focus to an amorphous spirituality that is detached from the earth. On this point, Carvalhaes echoes the insights of Wallace, who traced the shift from the divine presence in nature to the distant sky god who is distinct and remote from the earth. Thus, recovering the primary role of the law of nature is the starting place for promoting the well-being of the earth and ourselves. "We are at a point where no book of common worship or new liturgical practices can be created without the guidance and needs of the earth."[21] Where Wallace recognized a minority voice that had been submerged over the course of historical and theological development, Carvalhaes insists on an *a priori* focus on the law of nature to provide the urgent correction to our present disastrous course. Here, Carvalhaes shows an acute awareness of the environmental crisis that we presently face as well as a keen sensitivity to the issues of postmodernity with its critique of the role of reason and human progress that we have highlighted. For the church to reclaim a voice and witness that responds to the needs of the earth and the questions of those outside the church, then surely dramatic change is needed. Carvalhaes charts the course of this change by highlighting a series of ways in which attending to the primacy of *lex naturae* challenges the assumptions and malpractices that are ingrained in our current practices. Rather than operating within a relational perspective, humans have objectified nature as that which is different and distinct from us. Akin to this insight is the acceptance of a strict hierarchical order, with humans at the top of the pyramid and creation as a resource to tame or support human life. The benefit of a shift toward *lex naturae* is to recognize and attend to that which is suffering and whose life is threatened.[22]

Perhaps the key point for our purposes is to note that for Carvalhaes "*Lex naturae* then challenges the sole use of the Bible in our communities...."[23] Thus, what we see here is a call for more than to turn our attention to alternate renderings. Instead, the earth takes precedence and instructs/challenges our reading of Scripture, our theological claims, our liturgies, our creedal statements, our approach to the sacraments, and our entire way of constructing our ecclesiological practices. Carvalhaes concludes that "new theological frameworks must be proposed and complicated, beyond the duality of God's immanence/transcendence, Jesus' humanity and divine nature, and the eschatological discourse of time as separate from space."[24] Christians will need to reject their reliance on rationality and adopt insights from traditions that have prioritized a sacred relationship to creation.

Our exploration of the role of biblical hermeneutics revolves around our diagnosis of the relationship between our reading of Scripture and our relationship to the earth. For Wallace, the reclamation project involves a rescripting of the tradition that salvages/appropriates the ancient way of encountering the divine in nature. In contrast, for Carvalhaes our reading of Scripture has become so corrupted by our captivity to the values of the empire that led to colonialism, consumerism, and neocapitalism that it is only through a radical reorientation to nature that will help us create new rituals that provide a basis on which we may be able to reengage with Scripture.[25]

Our exploration of this first priority of biblical hermeneutics will close by proposing an alternative option to the need to develop the relationship between Scripture and creation. Our interest here is in terms of exploring ways to read Scripture in light of the demise of Christendom and the rise of postmodernity. It is imperative for us to find ways that connect our experiences of nature with our reading and interpretation of Scripture.[26] On this point, it will be crucial for Reformed theology to clarify that any form of special revelation occurs in the context of general revelation (which in light of our survey of Wallace is understood in terms of the divine presence in creation). While Calvin's discussion of the relationship between general and special revelation can be read in terms of a dialectical relationship between these forms of revelation, more often than not the Reformed tradition has interpreted Calvin in a dualistic way that preferences special revelation at the expense of general revelation. Hence any attempt to find a middle way between the proposals of Wallace's submerged symbiotic reading of Scripture and creation or Carvalhaes's radical reorientation to the priority of *lex naturae* must begin with an insistence on a unitive approach to revelation that avoids the destructive dualisms that have contributed to the spiritualized readings and interpretations of Scripture from inside our church buildings and exacerbated the ways in which Christian faith is understood as removed from the world and inattentive to the needs of the earth.

To be fair, this hermeneutical project of reclaiming the relationship between Scripture and creation may require all the tools that we have identified; at times drawing on Wallace's appropriation of alternative theological positions while at other times insisting with Carvalhaes on tearing down structures that prohibit our relational realignment with God, neighbor, and the earth. Yet I believe that there are ways to maintain the centrality of Scripture with an openness to receiving a new word that disrupts and connects with our daily lives and our experiences of the divine.

Over the last decade, I have engaged in a series of conversations with congregations about their experience of God in creation and the relationship of these experiences to their participation in worship and the ongoing life of the church. Consistently, individuals clearly articulate places where they have experienced God in nature. However, when asked how these experiences correlate to their reading of Scripture, participation in congregational life, or their understanding of Christian faith, they generally have a very limited theological vocabulary on which to draw.[27] Their participation in worship through the regular reading and proclamation of Scripture and the celebration of the sacraments has not provided them with the language or skills to connect their experiences in the world with their life inside the church.

What is needed, in my estimation, is a reclaiming of the complementary ways that Scripture gives witness to God's presence in creation. For Reformed congregations, the starting point for this journey is a return to the regular singing/reading of the Psalms, particularly with an emphasis on the psalms that underscore the role of nature as a prominent voice of praise to the Creator (book 5 or Pss. 107–150).[28] Two caveats should be noted: (1) as we reclaim Scripture's emphasis on creation we must be careful not to romanticize nature (one can see this tendency particularly in nineteenth-century hymnody), but to point equally to the joy and suffering in nature and its dependence on the Creator as the source of all life. In this way, the earth provides a model of witnessing that we have often overlooked, which is a point made by Jesus in the Sermon on the Mount as he speaks of the birds of the air and the lilies of the field (see Matt. 6:25–30); (2) As we hear and recognize the witness of creation to the Creator, then we must respond by making space for our testimonies of experiencing the presence of the divine in nature. As an initial step, preachers can provide models of this witness in sermons that include experiences of encountering God outside the confines of the walls of the church. Much more is needed, though, in terms of opening up and listening to the stories of others and encouraging one another to develop the biblical and theological vocabulary that helps us speak of our experiences in ways that are connected to the church's proclamation and practices. In the coming chapters, we will explore ways the sacraments (particularly by highlighting the elements of the earth in grain, grape, and water) can support us on this journey.

The potential for this change requires us to open up space in our worship services where we regularly acknowledge our dependence on God. It will require us to take risks by breaking the routine ways that we have maintained decency and order. We will need to gather for worship outside the walls of the church more often and discover how the earth can disrupt our patterns and habits as well as support our experiences.[29] We will need to find ways for elements of the earth to more regularly be a part of our worship services as we gather inside the church (currently cutting flowers and watching them die seems to be at the top of the list of ways that the earth is included in worship!). And we will need our understanding of discipleship and mission to radically expand so that we engage in responding to the earth's wounds, which we have created.

On this journey, we are guided by Calvin's conviction that it is the Spirit who brings us life and is the source for our understanding of this strange, new world of the Bible. By reclaiming the first hermeneutical principle of the centrality of the earth in the witness of Scripture, we are drawing on key commitments from the Reformed tradition in a way that responds to the urgent need of our time. Careful attention to the text of Scripture will serve as a guide for us in our present contexts.

BIBLICAL HERMENEUTIC 2: PREFERENTIAL OPTION FOR THE POOR

There is a second hermeneutical emphasis that is drawn from Scripture that is imperative for our renewal. When we reflect on God's preferential option for the poor, our first thought is of the way that this phrase serves as the defining point of liberation theology. While this may at first seem incongruous to Calvin's theological emphases, it is worth noting that Calvin's continued emphasis in the practice of almsgiving and caring for the poor were central in both his liturgy and his commitment to the church's witness in Geneva. We noted previously that Calvin's eucharistic liturgy concluded with a word of admonition: "You are commended to have love among yourselves, and especially towards the poor."[30] In certain ways, we can recognize these as historical links to a reemergence of this hermeneutic in contemporary Latin America. The historic meeting of the Latin American Episcopal Conference (CELAM) in Medellin in 1968 declared this statement as central to the church's mission and identity. Similarly, the classic work of Gustavo Gutiérrez, *A Theology of Liberation*, provided a clear articulation of the importance of this principle for theology. It would be easy for us to conclude that this theological theme, with its sociological and economic emphases, is being used as a theological filter to control the text and its interpretation. Indeed, critics of liberation theology consistently point to the significance of Marxist theory in guiding the critique of liberation theologians. It is essential, though, to not move too quickly to criticize liberation theology before weighing how it developed the primary theological claim of God's preferential option for the poor. Obviously, there is not space in this work to present a history of liberation theology. Instead, what we will explore is the relationship of Scripture to this hermeneutical/theological claim as a way to assess its significance in shaping the future of Reformed worship.

The identification of the tragic conditions of poverty throughout Latin America was paramount to developing the question: "how to say to the poor, the least of society, that God loves them?"[31] Clearly this sociological observation and its accompanying political and economic analysis were foundational in terms of asking the question of how the Gospel addresses the needs of those on the underside and at the margins of our contemporary neocapitalist system. Here, though, liberation theologians offered two important insights that have often been overlooked or casually dismissed. First, all theology grows out of specific contexts and is derived from one's experiences. As James Cone, the father of black liberation theology, wrote: "Theology is always done for particular times and places and addressed to a specific audience. This is true whether theologians acknowledge it or not. Although God is the intended subject of theology, God does not do theology. *Human beings do theology*."[32]
On this point, different expressions of liberation theology (Latin American, black, feminist, womanist, etc.) came together to reject the possibility of universal theological claims that are detached from our lives and experiences. This subjective turn of theology drew on the great insights of the theological tradition (note the parallels to Augustine's *Confessions* and the works of Kierkegaard) while pointing out the ways that modern western theology was held captive by its over-reliance on the rationality of man. In its place, liberation theologians insisted on naming one's identity and social location as integrally connected to one's perspective and experience of the divine.

Second, liberation theology discovered its guiding tenet of God's preferential option for the poor through its careful rereading of Scripture. Mexican theologian Elsa Támez observes "that if all the texts in the Bible that speak of the poor were cut out, very few pages would be left."[33] She goes further in noting that the attempts to isolate that which is "purely spiritual and theological" in Scripture runs the risk of producing a "limited and insipid text, inapplicable to the real struggles of human life."[34] Instead, by reading Scripture through the lens of the poor, we discover God's preferential option for them: "the option for the poor is not one of a multitude of virtues, in case it could be optional, but a biblical principle."[35]

Similarly, Jon Sobrino argues that the option for the poor is first and foremost based on a faithful response to the Gospel. This claim grows out of the depiction of Jesus as one of the poor and the call to follow Jesus as requiring us to attend to those who are in need. For Sobrino, "An affinity between Jesus and poverty is abundantly evident throughout the Christian scriptures. In fact, that Jesus himself is the historical sacrament of God's option for the poor, and that he himself implements that option in his concrete life, appear altogether clearly."[36] We should note two important aspects of this claim of the preferential option for the poor as they relate to the role of Scripture. First, Sobrino centers it directly on his christological reading of Scripture. Sobrino develops his case out of a close and careful examination of the Gospel texts.[37] Secondly, Sobrino articulates this insight in terms of the theological significance of the sacramental presence of the divine that is denoted by Jesus's incarnation as one of the poor. Jesus's poverty is neither accidental nor metaphorical but is fundamental to the biblical witness of God's presence in and with the poor. As Sobrino concludes, "From a historical viewpoint, there can be no doubt that Jesus' life, mission, fate, and even resurrection would lack its internal logic without an essential relationship between Jesus and the poor of the world, or without his option for them."[38] Similarly, Gustavo Gutiérrez describes the significant ways in which the Gospels are addressed to the poor as providing the hermeneutical basis for the church to discover its mission with the poor.[39]

Other liberation theologians have broadened the reading of Scripture beyond the Gospels to show ways in which God's preferential option for the poor is central throughout Scripture. James Cone's emphasis on the liberation of the Hebrews from slavery in Egypt provides a key biblical witness that guides his portrait of black theology.[40] The Brazilian Dominican theologian Gilberto da Silva Gorgulho provides an extended explication of Scripture in his important essay on the role of biblical hermeneutics in liberation theology. Gorgulho identifies two central components in the way that liberation theology approaches the Bible. First is the commitment to a popular reading of the Bible that is grounded in the correlation between the experience depicted in the text and our own experiences. It is precisely at this point that he notices the centrality of suffering and the plight of the poor as endemic to Scripture. Second, the reading of Scripture provides the basis of identifying the Spirit's word to our own settings.[41] Gorgulho develops these insights by elucidating their significance in his reading of both Old and New Testament texts.

For liberation theology in general, the depiction of God's commitment to and presence with the poor is grounded in the experience of poverty found in the world of the biblical text as well as in our present-day communities. Here is not an abstract idea of poverty but the painful reality of those who are crushed by systems of oppression and whose only source of hope is God. This correspondence between the biblical text and our contexts resides at the methodological center of liberation theology's commitment to reading Scripture with and for those who are marginalized and led to the ways in which base communities read Scripture in order to discover ways their lives were portrayed in Scripture.

While the historical attachment to power and money certainly provides enormous obstacles for many Presbyterians in recognizing the contributions of liberation theology, the theological disclaimer most often provided is in terms of the need to maintain a Reformed commitment to the sovereignty of God. Liberation theology's emphasis on our participation in building the kingdom of God on earth has been seen as conflicting with Calvin's emphasis on God's providence and initiative. As we consider this theological tension, we should recall again Calvin's commitment to the central practice of almsgiving and the importance of providing for those in need. Similarly, Martha Moore-Keish notes the historic importance of the connection between holiness and ethics in Reformed theology when she describes the attention to worthy participation in the Lord's Supper in terms of connecting the "holiness of the table with the holiness of all of life."[42]

Reclaiming these ethical practices is an important step in the direction of showing how faithful discipleship draws on the witness of Scripture to address the needs of our world. The gift of our relationships with one another and with the earth provides the basis for a liturgical solidarity in which we discover ways to read Scripture, pray together, and work with and for one another. This vision of shared life challenges the carefully constructed and guarded power of the *ordo* by requiring us to open up space in our worship in order that the Spirit may bring us new life.

Far too often a Reformed stress on the spirituality of Word and sacrament has pointed worshippers away from the suffering of our neighbors and of the plight of the earth. Even when significant Reformed voices (like Katie Geneva Cannon and Alan Boesak) have articulated liberation perspectives and challenged the ways in which we have interpreted biblical texts, the use of Scripture in Reformed worship remains largely confined to the historical practice of biblical warrants and to the attempt to portray universal elements of worship as grounded in and dictated by Scripture has gained momentum.[43]

In this chapter, we have been exploring ways that Reformed congregations can read Scripture in light of our post-Christian, postmodern era. In keeping with our historical and theological identity, we have insisted on the importance of highlighting and wrestling with the biblical witness in order to discover ways that the Spirit is prompting us to experience and respond to God's presence in our lives and in the world. Central to this task, we have identified two key biblical hermeneutical claims that must guide us: an attention to the role of the earth and a recognition of God's preferential option for the poor. Before concluding this chapter, we will examine the role of Scripture in terms of how we will construct new liturgies in light of the commitments that we have identified.

THE PATH TO LITURGICAL REFORM FOR REFORMED CONGREGATIONS

There is a broader issue for Reformed worship in terms of the use of Scripture that supports our worship services. We have seen the problems that the Reformed reliance on biblical warrants has created in terms of the way that the interpretation of these texts seems to contradict both the plain sense of the text as well as the critical standards of biblical interpretation. From the defense of infant baptism to the narrow reliance on interpretations of 1 Corinthians 11 to justify Reformed eucharistic liturgy and practice, serious questions have emerged through the process of liturgical change. As we have noted throughout the course of this book, the primary method for liturgical development employed within the Reformed church has been to start from theological concepts that provide the direction and the claims of the liturgy. This was certainly the case in terms of Calvin's liturgies, which took the form of expanded tutorials on the proper theological understandings of the sacraments. Likewise, we noted ways that the implementation of the liturgical renewal movement within the Reformed context was driven primarily by theological understandings gleaned from a consensus of the ecumenical movement as well as from commitments to biblical theology.

Along the way, though, there have been significant theological voices within the Reformed tradition that have pointed out alternative directions. One can point to the works of Schleiermacher, Brunner, and Moltmann to name a few. Our interest here is in terms of exploring the way theology can be used not to simply overlay and control a predetermined, proper understanding of a particular liturgical form but in terms of opening up new space in order to encounter the Word through the reading of Scripture and the celebration of the sacraments. In this regard, there is another important lesson for us to learn from the work of Friedrich Schleiermacher. In a recent essay, historical theologian Theodore Vial describes Schleiermacher's role in advocating for liturgical renewal in the nineteenth-century Prussian Church. In his effort to bring together the Reformed and Lutheran Church, King Fredrich Wilhelm III advocated for the development of a new liturgy that would unite Protestants. On Reformation Sunday in 1817 Schleiermacher co-presided with Lutheran theologian Philipp Marheineke at the Nicolai Church in Berlin. It provided the king (who was Reformed) with an opportunity to receive Communion with his Lutheran wife (Queen Louise).[44] Schleiermacher shared the king's interest in uniting the two traditions, particularly since he was convinced that any creedal distinctions were no longer of primary significance. King Wilhelm established a commission to revise the liturgy in the hopes of creating a unified Protestant church in Prussia. The king's attempts to enlist Schleiermacher in this effort were rejected. Schleiermacher insisted that liturgical renewal should not be imposed from the top down but must come from the "bottom up."[45] According to Schleiermacher a liturgy "is an expression, a representation, of communal piety. As such it must be produced by the community and not commanded from the top."[46] For Schleiermacher, the liturgy provided an opportunity for "shared piety in a particular community."[47]

Schleiermacher points us in a surprising new direction that has been often overlooked within the Reformed church. What does liturgical renewal from below look like? What resources can congregations draw on to support the work of developing worship materials that grow out of our experiences of God and point to connections between worship and daily life? Here again, the Reformed tradition has historically turned to Scripture as its primary resource. Calvin described the Psalms as a mirror for the emotions of the soul, and his regular use of the Psalter in worship provided an important bridge for the development of household piety that was central to his understanding of growth in the life of Christian faith. Perhaps Schleiermacher's own commitment to the centrality of the experience of the divine as primary in cultivating the feeling of our dependence upon God may serve as an important basis that will resonate with our reading of Scripture. We noted earlier in this chapter the importance of encouraging those in our congregations to name their experience of the divine in creation. What I am suggesting is that the liturgy grows out of a dialectical movement between our reading of Scripture and our experience of the divine. In a similar way that follows our discussion of biblical hermeneutics, how does our engagement with the poor teach us about God's presence with those who live on the margins? In his recent collection of liturgical texts, *Liturgies from Below*, Cláudio Carvalhaes highlights the practice of teaching "your church to pray with the poor" as a central way to develop relationships in which we become aware of the suffering of those around us.[48]

With our senses open to the beauty and suffering of the earth and our hearts and hands open to the poor, we come together around the reading of Scripture in hope that the Spirit will make sense of the strange worlds in which we live (and according to Barth the strange new world of the Bible). Corporate worship provides a model for this pattern of spirituality to take shape in our daily lives. The role of the liturgy is to open up space in our lives by naming these moments and feelings of God's presence and absence. The task of the preacher is to show ways that the biblical text(s) provides us with patterns for living in which we acknowledge our dependence on God as the source of life, our relationship to one another, and our interdependence with all of creation. In this context, hearing biblical texts of the recitation of God's mighty acts in history is a way of prompting ourselves to ask the question: Where is God in the midst of the joy and pain of our lives?

This approach to Reformed worship grows out of the historic commitment to form and freedom with its recognition of the value of particular forms of worship alongside its reluctance to accept required liturgical texts. As we saw in our exploration of the Prayer for Illumination, Calvin's preference was for an extemporaneous prayer to call on the Spirit to bring us an understanding of the Scripture. This approach to worship, with its emphasis on free expression, requires the worship leaders to have a deep familiarity with liturgical forms of prayer while inviting worship leaders to infuse them with their own idioms. Ironically, this practice encourages us to leave behind our attachment to decency and order and to trust liturgical leaders to guide us on a hopeful journey of encountering God's word to us in this time and place. With no divine liturgy from above to draw on, this risky approach inevitably means that sometimes our worship will fall short, lapse into heresy, and border on incoherence. Here again the culturally bound elements of Scripture (with its grand poetry and powerful testimonies as well as its incoherent passages and internal inconsistencies) provide the template for Reformed worship. We gather to encourage and support one another as we dare to imagine ways of life that liberate us from the tyranny and idolatry of our temptation to accept the myths of individualism, self-reliance, and success (always at the cost of our neighbor, the earth, and ourselves). The subversive witness of biblical texts paints a portrait of a communal way of life in which we acknowledge our dependence on God and our kinship with all of creation. With Scripture as our guide, we long for a liberative word that shows us ways to live in right relationship with God, one another, and the earth.

8

The Lord's Supper

In the opening chapter on the Lord's Supper, we noted the development of Calvin's approach to the sacrament in contrast to the Roman Catholic Mass. Calvin's theological commitment to the regular celebration of the sacrament provided a visible word that complemented the reading and proclamation of Scripture (together these served as the marks of the true church) as a witness to the saving death of Jesus Christ. In contrast to the Latin Mass, Calvin's liturgy used Scripture (primarily 1 Corinthians 11) to provide a rational explanation of the significance of remembering the passion of Christ. In terms of ritual action, there remains much to admire about the dramatic transformation in the Communion liturgy and practice spearheaded by Calvin and the early Reformers. The use of the vernacular language in the liturgy, the shift from the altar to the table, partaking of both bread and wine in Communion, and the dramatic increase in regular participation by the congregation are all hallmarks of a new Reformed approach to the sacrament. Yet in terms of liturgical text, early Reformed Communion liturgies come across as theological diatribes. Even more troubling is the way in which Calvin's theology became codified as a new form of Reformed neo-scholasticism took hold. Reformed liturgies after Calvin followed this trajectory, venturing even further into theological explanations that supported an interpretation of Christ's work on the cross through the lens of substitutionary atonement. Knox's liturgy in particular draws on images of the work of Christ as a contest between God and Satan where Jesus's death is necessary to appease God's wrath. Even when Reformed liturgies moved away from the harsher language of these interpretive explanations, the tone of the liturgy remained primarily penitential.

While the language of thanksgiving was central, the purpose was to recall the reason for gratitude as dependent on the atoning work of Christ. Calvin's eucharistic liturgies linked this with the need for careful introspection in order to avoid the danger of unworthy participation. Thus, good standing in the community became a hallmark of the Reformed tradition and in some places led to the practice of fencing the table from those who were deemed unworthy.

We also noted a number of diverse influences in the nineteenth and twentieth centuries that eventually led to significant changes in Reformed Communion liturgies. Primary factors include the influence of Schleiermacher's theology (particularly his critique of the prominent role of substitutionary atonement); the rise of biblical criticism, with its rejection of the use of biblical warrants and its suspicion about a reliance on typological interpretations of Scripture; and the contributions of the liturgical renewal movement, particularly through the study of descriptions of eucharistic practice in the early church. While Vatican II led to a massive transformation in the celebration of the Mass, it also contributed to liturgical renewal among Protestants, who began the process of writing new liturgical texts in light of the growing awareness of the diversity of liturgical practices in the early church. The study of documents of the early descriptions and patterns of early Christian worship led to the recognition that an emphasis on sacrificial language was a later addition to the eucharistic prayer.[1]

In addition, we noted the significance of theological movements in providing language and themes that provided direction for the development of new liturgies. For example, the focus on reconciliation in Barth's theology became a prominent theme in a new confessional statement (C-67) as well as in new Communion liturgies. Similarly, the emphasis on salvation history provided a theological template for the eucharistic prayers in the 1993 Book of Common Worship.

We previously noted that the changes in the Communion liturgy and practice since C-67 and *The Worshipbook* are in many ways shockingly dramatic. This includes tone (from penitential to celebratory), frequency (with a shift from quarterly to the description of weekly celebration as normative) language (from didactic to poetic metaphors that also provide an increased number of congregational responses), theological focus (particularly with the significant shift away from sacrificial language), a new emphasis on embodied gesture (in the rubrics), and the importance of the material elements of bread and wine. This amount of change should not be diminished or quickly dismissed. In many ways, it represents the culmination of the influences of the ecumenical, liturgical renewal movement, which continues to push for reform, mutual recognition, and co-operation between historic divisions of the church. It is still important to note the significance of the World Council of Church's publication of *Baptism, Eucharist, and Ministry* (Lima document) in 1982 as a template for the ecumenical movement. We are all beneficiaries of the ongoing, tireless effort to foster reconciliation in the celebration of the sacraments between the divided body of Christ.

RECENT SHIFTS IN EUCHARISTIC LITURGIES

In the preceding chapter on the role of Scripture, we observed the importance of reflecting on the future of Reformed worship in light of the challenges and opportunities presented by post-Christendom and postmodernity. Our consideration of the future of eucharistic prayer and practice will correspond to insights that were raised in light of the emergence of new cultural contexts and philosophical movements. To begin with, we should note that recent revisions to the 2018 Presbyterian Church (U.S.A.) *Book of Common Worship* (BCW) provide insight into the challenges that the church is facing. The primary set of eucharistic prayers in the 1993 BCW closely follows the form of a strict outline that makes the theological case for eucharistic prayer as a presentation of salvation history. Seasonal foci provide particular points of emphasis, but otherwise the tone and form of the prayers remain consistent. The 2018 BCW begins with an abbreviated eucharistic prayer as part of the service for the Lord's Day. While it follows the general pattern of eucharistic prayers in the 1993 edition, its emphasis on brevity limits the theological portrayal of salvation history that was prominent in the previous prayers (and was a shared focus of eucharistic prayers in other denominational worship books). While I believe that the shift away from a fuller description of salvation history was not theologically intentional, it does suggest the diminished influence of this form of biblical theology with its stress on a meta-narrative that closely followed the logic of modernity.

Similarly, the set of sixteen additional eucharistic prayers in the 2018 BCW provides a new emphasis on diverse language and images. While the prayers generally follow a shared Trinitarian framework with distinct paragraphs for each member of the trinity, the language of the different prayers offers distinct theological values.[2] Here again we can see the subtle influence of postmodernity with its emphasis on subjectivity and diversity. The gradual shift away from one specific form of praying opens up space for exploring new language with a particular focus on addressing issues of gender and diversity. We should also note the significant transition from a reliance on didactic and explanatory language in the early reformed liturgies of the sixteenth century to the use of more poetic language with an abundance of metaphorical images.

A second important aspect that deserves our attention is to observe the way in which these eucharistic prayers further erase an emphasis on sacrifice and atonement as central to the celebration of the Lord's Supper. The brief, primary eucharistic prayer in the service for the Lord's Day collapses the distinctive focus on Christ's death with the following words in the christological paragraph: "He shared our pain and died our death, then rose to new life that we might live, and all creation be restored."[3] With these words, the historic Reformed stress on atonement as central to the celebration of Communion and presentation of Christ's death as the one-time event that allowed for the satisfaction of God's wrath is eliminated. In its place is thoroughly incarnational language of solidarity between Jesus and humanity. This striking theological shift echoes again in the *epiclesis* where the Spirit is called upon so that the bread and wine "may be for us the body and blood of Christ and that we may be his body for the world."[4] With these words, the transformation of the elements provides a christological model for the lives of the participants. As the bread is broken and wine is poured, so too our lives become a source of renewal for the world. Here, the ghost of Schleiermacher peers through the liturgical text with its stress on "themes of union and representation instead of sacrifice and substitution."[5]

Similarly, other eucharistic prayers in the BCW offer a muted interpretation of Christ's death, particularly in contrast to Calvin and early Reformed liturgies. For example, while Prayer 3 includes the christological language "Dying on the cross, he gave himself for the life of the world,"[6] it avoids providing any further theological interpretation. The text of Prayer 5 asserts, "Obeying you, he took up his cross and died that we might live"[7] but offers no further description. In fact, language of sacrifice is primarily absent in most of the prayers. The exceptions are the prayer attributed to Hippolytus of Rome (third century CE) and the eucharistic prayer drafted by the ecumenical group the International Commission on English in the Liturgy (ICEL). Additionally, some new prayers virtually erase any connections to the passion narrative. The text of Prayer 8 frames the life of Christ in this way: "Remembering his love for us on the way, at the table, and to the end, we proclaim the mystery of faith."[8] It leads me to wonder if Calvin would even recognize these texts as eucharistic prayers!

The question for us, though, is whether or not even this amount of change is significant enough to address the broader theological, cultural, and philosophical issues facing the church. In many ways, these efforts at sacramental renewal remain based on the claims and assumptions of Christendom and modernity. The desire to create a unified liturgy with universal claims that would be shared and understood rationally by all participants and provide a persuasive form of evangelization to those outside of the church is suggestive of the hopes and underpinnings of these efforts. We can now see that these forms of change do not address the deeper structural reform that is imperative for the church to acknowledge if we are committed to congregational renewal in ways that acknowledge the needs and demands of our times. In an age of religious pluralism and secularity that rejects the philosophical foundations of modernity, new directions for liturgical renewal are required.

DECONSTRUCTING COMMUNION

Calvin began writing a new liturgy for the Lord's Supper by blowing up the Mass. He could find little resemblance between his reading of New Testament texts and medieval Communion practices. Unlike Luther's German Mass, where revisions were minor by comparison, Calvin decided that nearly everything in the Mass other than the Words of Institution should be eliminated. Ironically, Calvin kept the words attributed to Jesus since they provided the basis for a dominical command. "This is my body" (*hoc est corpus meum* in Latin) served as the high point of the Mass when the bell was rung to draw attention to the miracle on the altar when the bread and wine became the body and blood of Christ. These magic words (the expression "hocus-pocus" may be related to the Latin words) were indispensable even in Calvin's radical reorientation of the actions and liturgy of the Lord's Supper. As we saw in chapter 2, Calvin's inspiration for his Communion liturgy came almost entirely from 1 Corinthians 11, which portrays the Apostle Paul's attempt to correct Communion malpractices in the church in Corinth. Reformed liturgies grew out of descriptive texts about eucharistic malformation. There's an important lesson for us in this history. I believe that the well-intended efforts to transform eucharistic practice and liturgies that emerged in the 1960s and continue to this day have failed to learn this lesson from the past. While there is much to admire in Calvin's liturgical experiments as well as from the efforts of the liturgical renewal movement to reorient sacramental practices in ways that more closely connect the sacraments to daily life, they were based on biblical and theological assumptions that are increasingly questionable. In making this claim, I am not denying the value and significance of these worship services. I, myself, as a disciple of the liturgical renewal movement, grew through my participation in these experiences. What I am disputing is that these efforts at congregational renewal and growth can actually lead to the change that is needed in the church and the world. While we continue to produce new and improved liturgical texts, it has, to date, not stemmed the rapid decline in the PC(USA) or produced widespread congregational renewal. We will not attain new eucharistic practices by placing them on the faulty foundations of the past. To cite but one example, we have observed that the attempt to substitute biblical warrants as a way to shift and reshape the emotive experience of Communion is insufficient.

Declaring that the gathering is a "joyous feast" does not make it one.[9] Similarly, while I believe that deleting the didactical explanations of atonement theory is a step in the right direction, it has left us with significant questions about the ethical claims on our lives as we participate in the liturgy and particularly about how we will speak about sacrifice in a society that is obsessed with success and instant gratification.

THE CASE FOR A REFORMED SACRAMENTALITY

In his important book *Reformed Sacramentality*, Graham Hughes wrestles with the question of how Reformed communities can develop a robust understanding and practice of the sacraments in what he describes as a time of late modernity. Hughes begins his assessment by noting that Reformed sacramentality takes a "disseminated" form by rejecting notions that particular moments/occasions present a heightened or "condensed" presence of God. We have seen this in the debates about Christ's presence in the bread and wine at Communion. Calvin's concern about the temptation of idolatry led him to reject any form of locating the presence of the divine in the Communion elements. While this theological move avoided the concerns about idolatry (one can note the continued debate among Roman Catholics about the adoration of the reserve sacrament as a lingering problem), it came at the high price of skepticism of the value of any form of materiality (including our own bodies!) as a place to encounter the divine. The problem for Hughes is that the Reformed commitment to a dispensed sacramentality left it without any center or basis for identifying the presence of the divine. Instead, locating the presence of God in one's own experience served as a kind of mirror in which one reified/deified one's self (and thus succumbed to an original form of idolatry!). Hughes draws on the work of Charles Taylor, who proclaims that Calvin's commitments to humanism led to the "disenchantment of the world." Taylor claims, "We can see the immense energy behind the denial of the sacred if we look to Calvin."[10] This analysis persuades Hughes to conclude:

> My contention is that Reformed Christianity's predilection for the diffused sacramental type leaves it dangerously exposed to a "cultural colonization" by modernity (or, in fact, by postmodernity; ...) Otherwise expressed, this is suggesting that Reformed Christianity, and most especially its present day contemporary-worship mutation, is now insufficiently in touch with its tradition to be able to summon the necessary critical acumen in face of the modernist threat.[11]

For Hughes, the Reformed tradition must reclaim forms of condensed sacramentality in order to provide a healthy correction. Otherwise, Reformed Christians lack the sacramental substance that allows us to locate and experience the divine in ways that actually confront and challenge the presuppositions and beliefs that dictate our increasingly self-determined identities.[12]

For Hughes, the condensed approach underscores the role of the church's sacraments as the means of grace for Roman Catholics. In contrast, Hughes describes the Reformed movement as "a style of Christian awareness that locates God, or the sacred in everyday experience."[13] As a Reformed theologian, Hughes is quick to ground a disseminated sacramental approach in his reading of the Gospels: "What we have in Jesus' proclamation is pretty much the paradigm of 'disseminated sacramentality,'"[14] which could connect with his analysis of contemporary culture and its desire for immediacy and emphasis on individuality. At the same time, Hughes underscores the major challenge of a distributed approach to sacramentality: namely, the lack of a controlling center that is guided by a commitment to tradition and becomes captive to "an *ideology* of novelty."[15] Hence Hughes's work represents his attempt to find mooring for a Reformed commitment to dispersed sacramentality.

Hughes confirms our concern about the dangers of linking Reformed sacramentality to theological insights grounded in modernity. He clearly recognizes the need to reorient sacramentality from what was at times a circuitous reading of Scripture to provide adequate biblical support for a sacramental act (as we have seen, what does infant baptism really have to do with Jesus's welcoming of the children in Mark 10:13–15?). Equally important, Hughes is keenly aware of theological and philosophical shifts that make the reliance on a constructed narrative like *Heilsgeschichte* highly problematic. However, Hughes also remains anxious about allowing a dispersed notion of sacramentality to roam free. Thus, the turn to Catholic authority represents the compromise that he is willing to make to preserve the integrity of the sacraments while maintaining space for a more qualified understanding of dispersed sacramentality.

In order to traverse this vast landscape and find a way to connect these different approaches to sacramentality, Hughes weaves together a selection of liturgical definitions of sacramentality ("the fusion of spirit and physical form"[16]) representative of a Catholic approach with the classic Reformed suspicion of the dangers of idolatry. In some ways, it is a clever dialogue guided by a particular anthropological approach that begins by naming sacramentality as that which responds to the universal needs of the human condition, but one that is guarded by a Reformed commitment to Jesus as the primordial sacrament (via Barth). For Hughes, "images *occupy an intermediate point* between the spirit realm and the physical world."[17] Here the image of Jesus becomes the controlling factor in mediating the experience of sacramentality by the participants and offers a distinct advantage of recognizing the material forms of sacraments apart from conceptual understandings of the sacraments as key to their meaning.[18] The question remains, though, how do these material elements of bread and wine point us toward Jesus Christ?

For Hughes, the solution to challenges facing the Reformed emphasis on a dispersed sacramentality is to call for a recognition of "particular bearers of holiness"[19] that provide hermeneutical lenses through which one interprets and discerns a broader diversity of religious and spiritual experiences. These challenges are heightened in these postmodern, individualistic times by the weakened form of ecclesial guidance that connects the experience of sacramentality with communal Christian discipleship. Hughes holds on to the dispersed sacramental emphasis while also designating three significant criteria: (1) the "physicality *must be able to bear* the significance we want to attribute" to the sacramental event; (2) a particular meaning is "invested" in these events; and (3) the events are designated through an "order of canonicity" with a received *Christian* view of God.[20]

Hughes's strongest contribution is his insistence on balancing the historical emphasis on spirituality with a strong commitment to the materiality of the sacraments. It is here that Hughes insists that physicality should not be confused with idolatry. The Reformed tradition's insistence on the Word and its accompanying stress on language comes with its own commitment to the possibility of transformative encounter in the events of worship. The experience of encounter provides Hughes an important bridge to reclaiming an active place for sacraments and sacramentality within the Reformed tradition. However, in opening this door to materiality, Hughes wants to guard against what he perceives as the dangers of our postmodern times. Ultimately, the presiding minister provides the "pivotal role" in mediating the encounter of the transcendent God with the community gathered for worship through the material gifts of the sacraments.

While I am convinced that Hughes is asking many of the important questions in terms of what Reformed liturgical praxis has to offer in light of its approach to the sacraments, I am not willing to endorse an arrangement that elevates the role of the minister as the guarantor and protector of the sacraments. Nor is this a deal that I believe is representative of the normative strains within the Reformed tradition. To locate the significance of the sacraments in the "order of canonicity," that is, to cede their proper location to the ecclesial locations and the primary actors (in this case the minister as presider) is, in my estimation, to give away the distinctive Reformed practice and understanding of the sacraments and to allow the dictates of an anglo-catholic, ecumenical liturgical renewal movement to take precedence. With this move the Protestant commitment to the priesthood of all believers is sacrificed on the altar to which only the clergy have access.

Here, again, we must face a primary liturgical conundrum of the Reformed tradition. Is it actually possible to correct our malpractice by reinserting what we have previously rejected? Can a reliance on insights from the ecumenical, liturgical renewal movement provide the corrective that is needed without diminishing the distinctive and generative Reformed insights that have been central to our tradition? Can Calvin's liturgical practices be salvaged with a better (more catholic) liturgy? While Calvin and the early reformers advocated for the unity and wholeness of the church by a reliance on the guidance of Scripture (and in this sense provided a positive model of catholicity), they rejected hierarchical models that located the authority of the church's teachings in those who held pastoral offices.[21] How will a reliance on past ecumenical liturgies help us address the cultural and theological questions that the church is facing? Or to ask these questions in the language of Paul Tillich's theology: Can the Catholic substance and the Protestant principle actually coexist within a liturgical community without becoming mutually destructive? Hughes's work pushes us to look for alternative answers to these queries by proposing that the two models of sacramentality belong together and mutually enrich one another. How can condensed sacramentality that draws on the rich encounter with the divine in worship be held in dialectical tension with a disseminated sacramentality that seeks the divine in the world in ways that allow the community to experience and absorb the sacramental moments that prompt them to connect to other experiences of the divine in their lives?

There's another way that we could pose the question in response to Hughes's proposal for clerical oversight of worship: Do the sacraments actually need us to protect them? Is there an inherent sacramentality that Reformed Christians can identify and reclaim from our theological history that might serve us well in the twenty-first century? I believe that Calvin's theological and liturgical commitment to a prominent place for pneumatology provides an important clue: Can we trust the Spirit's presence in the actions of the assembly's gathering around Word, water, bread, and wine to bring definition to our experience of the sacraments and sacramentality? I offer this insight not as a naive riposte to Hughes's assessment but as a broader question of our assemblies. In my estimation, to champion such an approach requires a form of fierce bravery that we let go of our carefully constructed texts and our rigidly prescribed routines in order that the Spirit might actually bring *new* life to us. I fully acknowledge such a move is one that will lead to mistakes, failed experimentation, cultural misappropriation, and at times theological heresy. Thus, the question for a contemporary Reformed approach to sacramentality is whether to put the emphasis on the role of presiders in mediating proper and primary experiences of grace at the table and font or whether to trust the primacy of the Spirit as that which brings new life in a surprising abundance of ways and forms.

Calvin clearly articulated that our experience of grace in the sacraments was solely a result of the Spirit's presence as we gather around these ordinary gifts of creation that point us to Christ. To be fair, Calvin's own willingness to accept certain aspects of a hierarchical understanding of ministry within the church when it comes to Word and sacraments provides a basis for Hughes and others to explore. A traditional Reformed approach to sacramentality is filled with risks and missteps. The central commitment to balancing form and freedom has followed conflicting paths from those who gleaned important insight from the liturgical renewal movement and who insist on a fixed textual approach to preserve the meaning of the sacrament to those whose dalliance with extemporaneous utterances may cause one to wonder what theological messages are heard and interpreted by the participants. Somewhere, though in the midst of these divergent options, I believe that a recovery of the sacraments, sacramentality, and a sacramental life can take root in our liturgical communities in ways that are distinctly Reformed and increasingly local. The historical evidence of the sacramental practices during the early centuries of the church shows a highly diverse and adaptive approach to theological understandings of both the acts of washing (baptism) and shared meals (Lord's Supper). Equally important is the growing recognition of a much broader range of biblical texts from which to draw in terms of our liturgical actions. For example, we will turn next to the wide range of New Testament texts that shows the influence of Greco-Roman meals as a template for the Christian assembly and provide for both cultural continuity and Christian particularity in its celebrations of meals that brought together the early followers of Jesus. Here the antecedents of a Reformed liturgical commitment to form and freedom can be clearly found. Yes, there are immense dangers to this approach to the sacraments. The question that we must ask is this: Are these risks that are worth taking? Or, given the increased theological, political, and cultural tensions of our time, is this simply too great of a risk for liturgical leaders and communities of faith?

RECLAIMING MATERIALITY FOR REFORMED CHRISTIANS: THANKSGIVING AS SHARING WITH THE POOR

Hughes's work underscores the critical importance of reclaiming materiality in our worship services. As we saw, Calvin's insistence on a liturgy that contrasted with the Mass and his fear of idolatry reinforced the Reformed predilection to define the sacraments primarily in terms of spirituality. The result was to present the experiences in terms of inner meanings (often cognitively defined). Calvin and the early Reformers turned to the New Testament as the basis to develop the stark contrast to the celebration of the Mass. Two aspects of this approach are especially significant for our study. First, while the early Reformed liturgies and confessions were quick to claim links to the Jewish celebration of Passover, Reformed liturgies developed in ways that were distinct from these Jewish rituals. The Reformers noticed that the early Christian meal gatherings portrayed in the New Testament did not rely on the traditional food of the Passover meal and that early Christians gathered regularly (weekly or at times daily) rather than annually. Thus, while pointing in the direction of Jewish Passover rituals for typological and theological references, the Reformers developed practices that were entirely different.[22] A second curiosity about the development of Reformed Communion practices is that while there was an expressed interest in biblical texts to support the sacramental practices (including a deep commitment to the language of the Table as opposed to the altar), there was no interest in developing a liturgical practice of an actual meal in spite of the fact that the primary biblical text of 1 Corinthians 11 that provided the biblical warrant for Reformed practice clearly depicts the congregation in Corinth as sharing a full meal (in this case resembling our potluck supper).[23] As we will see, a vast number of meal texts in the New Testament were simply ignored as the Reformed liturgy concentrated on a particular theological explanation for the celebration of the Lord's Supper.

In contrast to this approach, a Reformed emphasis on the materiality of the Lord's Supper begins with the elements of bread and wine. With no doctrine of transubstantiation, Reformed practice gathers around the table to break bread and eat it and to share the cup of wine in memory and thanksgiving for the life of Jesus Christ. In doing so, we reclaim the etymological origin of the Latin word *sacramentum* with its link to taking an oath to follow a leader as well as the connection to the Greek word *mystērion (*mystery). This shift in the focus of eucharistic practice allows us to build on the biblical hermeneutics of caring for the poor and the earth.

Recent research into the practices of early Christians provides us with new portraits of the origins of the sacrament. We will explore three areas of study that provide important insights for eucharistic renewal for Reformed congregations: the significance of food, the role of Greco-Roman meals, and the focus on thanksgiving as Christians gather around the table. While these recent areas of research on early eucharistic practice generally align with the Reformed commitment for worship practices to be based on Scripture, the findings have produced relatively little change to Reformed Communion practice (either at the theoretical, theological, or practical level).

In his analysis of the economic uncertainty of life for poor people in an ancient Mediterranean world, liturgical scholar Andrew McGowan draws attention to the importance of gaining access to bread as the staple food in the diet of both the rich and the poor. McGowan notes "that the eucharistic practice of the first two or three centuries would have been understood in relation to other processes by which people gained access to food and in particular access to bread, in circumstances where hunger was an ever-present threat."[24] Thus in order to understand the origins of eucharistic meals, we need to begin by recognizing the pervasive presence of poverty in the ancient world where the typical meal for poor people consisted of bread, wine, and greens. Access to daily bread was often dependent on the distribution of it by local politicians and benefactors. In Rome, eligibility for free bread was linked to citizenship, thus increasing the fragility of those who lived on the margins and underside of society. To understand the role of Christian eucharists, then, we must recognize the pervasive role of food insecurity in the daily lives of the poor. "Christian distributions of bread, at and outside meals, will inevitably have been perceived in some relation to these practices and certainly as having some economic and dietary appeal as well as wider symbolic significance."[25] All of this points to the fundamental significance of bread as food where the broken bread in the Eucharist provided the meal portion for participants. McGowan links this distribution of daily bread to the descriptions of early Christian gatherings in Acts 2: both in the breaking of the bread (verse 42) and sharing of food (verse 47). Similarly the daily distribution of food in Acts 6:1 underscores its role in the emerging Jewish-Christian identity.[26]

McGowan concludes his essay by noting the practical implication of these insights for reading other New Testament texts. In light of his analysis, he recognizes the petition for daily bread in the Lord's Prayer links with the anxiety of food insecurity that hovers over daily life. "Bread does not stand for anything else here."[27] Instead, our focus turns to God as the patron and provider whom we trust to provide for the daily, material needs of our lives. Similarly, McGowan describes how the mention of "barley loaves" in the feeding of the five thousand in John 6 relates to the agrarian economy where barley bread is the staple food of the poor (as opposed to the urban production of wheat bread). Once again, the broken bread (*klasmata*) signifies meal portions that are gathered. For McGowan, the theological significance of this text is to underscore that the ministry of Jesus includes providing for the daily needs of poor people while insisting that "this is not just a feeding program."[28] McGowan concludes, "To make bread the central substance in the characteristic ritual meal of the community was not to invoke a mere sign that pointed outside of itself; rather the bread of the Eucharist was itself an array . . . and part of that wider reality of creation and community."[29]

What insights can Reformed congregations draw from reclaiming a focus on the materiality of bread in our Communion celebration? On the one hand, we should note that a primary contribution of the liturgical renewal movement has focused on recovering the centrality of the elements of real bread and wine/juice in our Communion practices. The revised Directory for Worship emphasizes this point in describing the sacraments: "They employ ordinary things—the basic elements of water, bread, and wine—in proclaiming the extraordinary love of God."[30] Similarly, the description in the 2018 *Book of Common Worship* states that the bread "should be common to the culture of the congregation" while the service rubrics underscore the visibility of breaking the bread and pouring the cup so that the congregation can see the elements.[31] While these point to a growing interest in the materiality of the bread and wine at Communion, there is no mention of connecting this practice with the needs of hungry people in our congregations and broader communities.[32]

It is precisely at this juncture that we turn to one of the insights of the biblical, hermeneutical commitments that we outlined in the preceding chapter: the preferential option for the poor. In a world of food insecurity where increasing numbers of households lack resources and access to healthy food, we must connect the ways in which we gather around the Communion table with the need for all people to have enough to eat and drink.

St. Gregory of Nyssa Episcopal Church in San Francisco serves as an inspirational model of showing ways to make this connection. In her wonderful memoir, *Take This Bread*, Sara Miles narrates the story of her own conversion to Christian faith through her involvement in a food pantry at the church.[33] What began with participation in the congregation's outreach ministry by responding to the needs of those in the community who lacked access to food led to her service as Director of Ministry in the congregation and evangelist through her writing and preaching. It is particularly interesting to note that worship at St. Gregory's follows a set eucharistic text from the *Book of Common Prayer* for its form of prayer, but embodies it in ways that allow participants to make connections and experience Communion in new ways. Surrounded by an eclectic array of icons of dancing saints and participating in a fully embodied liturgy that appeals to the senses of the worshipers, the weekly eucharistic service weaves together the breaking of the bread and sharing of the cup with the congregation's commitment to feeding its neighbors and its own sense of hospitality to members and guests (coffee hour occurs around the Communion altar after the service).

Reclaiming the central role of bread and wine is a significant starting place for a Reformed commitment to materiality. A second and related area for us to consider involves the growing body of scholarly work about the diversity in eucharistic practice in the early church that underscores the central role of Greco-Roman meal customs that shaped early Christian gatherings. This research came from the work of New Testament scholars who noticed similarities between meal texts in the Gospels and the early descriptions of Communion practice in Christian communities and compared them with the gathering practices of ancient associations, clubs, and religious communities in the Greco-Roman world. New Testament scholars Dennis Smith and Hal Taussig authored important works to show how widely accepted meal customs of their day were adapted by early Christian gatherings.[34] The banquet tradition, shared by both religious and civic organizations, offered a familiar pattern for gathering around a shared meal. The meals were provided by a sponsor and held in homes or public spaces. They offered a time for conversation and at times even debate around stories and presentations (for Christians, around the shared memories and teachings of Jesus). These gatherings were also important ways to promote core values shared by the community—including hospitality and koinonia.

As we have already noted, Andrew McGowan's research demonstrates that most Christians were among the working poor in the first couple of centuries following Jesus's death, and that the daily meal usually consisted of bread, wine, and water. Thus, what we have come to consider as the basic eucharistic elements were the staples of daily existence. Sponsors for the Eucharist banquets/gatherings might provide other food for participants. For example, Paul describes the eucharistic meal of the church in Corinth and notes the different amounts of food and wine that are consumed by the rich and poor (which provides the grounds for his ethical indictment that unequal sharing is unworthy of the name of the Lord's Supper). Different Christian gatherings included a wide variety of foods beyond the basics of bread, water, and wine: oil, vegetables, salt, milk, honey, and olives, just to name a few. The variety of food included in the meal was largely dependent on the sponsor and affluence of the community. The diversity of these practices was widely accepted until the Synod of Hippo in 393 C.E. restricted Communion to bread, wine, and water.[35]

Sharing food and providing for the needy are common ingredients in this history of eucharistic development. While scholars continue to debate theological interpretations and sociocultural influences, there is a growing consensus that the basis of early eucharistic practice consists of gathering for a meal and serving the poor, either by inclusion in the meal itself or by collecting food and funds to take food to those who were hungry.[36]

One congregation whose worship reflects learnings from this research is St. Lydia's in Brooklyn, where the emphasis on supper church emerged as an attempt to fully reclaim shared food as central to Christian worship and as open for all who came. The importance of the full meal as an integral component of Christian gathering and a basis for communal identity were highlighted. In their own words:

> We place practice before belief, trusting that eating, praying and singing together moves us deeper into faith. Instead of trying to figure out what we believe, we're trying to live what we practice. St. Lydia's is a church that gathers to share a sacred meal, as the first followers of Jesus did. Simple unaccompanied music is sung, scripture explored, and prayers offered, all in the context of a home-cooked meal.[37]

Other congregations adapted a simpler version of this approach known as "brunch church" as a way to keep food at the center of the eucharistic liturgy but ran the risk of highlighting a liturgical trend to serve the appetite of those who already had ample access to food. The question remains whether a return to materiality through a renewed emphasis on bread and wine or a full meal will be integrally connected to the needs of the poor and hungry in our communities.

CULTIVATING THANKSGIVING

In his brilliant book *The Eucharist*, Roman Catholic scholar Thomas O'Loughlin extends these insights by linking them with the ways food is central to rituals and the creation and sustenance of relationships within communities. O'Loughlin points to the ways in which these practices provide a roadmap for the emerging practices of discipleship within the early Christian communities by weaving together the human desire for meal sharing and the meal practices of Jesus (and its emphasis on inclusion and hospitality) with an active way of remembering the story of Jesus and exploring its significance for the life of the community.[38] This act of remembering as a blessing around the table took the pattern offered by the historical Jesus in giving thanks and expressing our dependence on God the Father/Creator as the source of life and as the one who provides us with our daily bread. These meal practices sustained the life of the community and its radical hospitality and commitment to providing for the poor and served as a major source of growth during the first couple of centuries. As Christian communities grew in size, it became increasingly difficult to preserve the centrality of the meal with its emphasis on food. O'Loughlin concludes, "Because the meal, given its place in practice and memory, could not be abandoned altogether, so it was curtailed until it reached a minimal point and which was then re-validated by a theological narrative."[39] In place of the shared eating and drinking connected to the practice of giving thanks to God, "the Eucharist became one more memory-producing ritual that could prompt minds to think of the truths of revelation where the encounter with the divine had only a mnemonic origin in something actually done by Christians."[40] Or to put it another way, the question of who gets to eat was largely left behind—both for those who participated in these gatherings and especially for those who depended on the sharing of the food that was a central part of Christian evangelism. The symbolic tokenism of food was used as a link to reinforce a prescribed theological message that took shape around an imaginative historical version of Jesus's Last Supper. Increasingly, eating and drinking were primarily seen as practices offered for and by the clergy who served as guardians of the sacred memory that became reenacted at the altar.

A new Reformed vision of eucharistic prayer and practice connects the opportunity to eat and drink together in community with thanksgiving for God's presence in the life, death, and resurrection of Jesus Christ. A renewed focus on following the pattern of Jesus's spirituality by offering thanksgiving to God (the Creator) pairs nicely with Calvin's stress on the significance of worship as a way to cultivate piety and on Schleiermacher's notion of the role of worship in prompting us to experience the feeling of absolute dependence. This shift reclaims a historical emphasis for Christian discipleship in following the patterns of Jesus's faithfulness while it avoids the dangers of creating an image of Jesus who does not relate to our lives.

A NEW EUCHARISTIC PRAYER

For those who are looking for a liturgical text that builds on the insights of O'Loughlin's research, I offer the following eucharistic prayer:

> *Blessed are you, God of creation, whose Spirit breathes life into all creation.*
> We give thanks for the beauty of this earth: for sun and moon, rivers and oceans, plants and trees, amoeba and animals. You create us to care for one another and to live in harmony with all of creation. When we wander away, in your mercy, you continue to call us to follow your path of love and justice. And so with glad and generous hearts we join our voices in songs of praise with all creation:
> **Holy, holy, holy Lord, God of power and might. Heaven and earth are full of your glory. Hosanna in the highest. Blessed is the one who comes in the name of the Lord.**
> **Hosanna in the highest.**
> Blessed are you, God of creation, in Jesus Christ we see your presence and hear your word.
> We give thanks for your Spirit's presence in Christ's ministry of teaching, healing, feeding, dying, and rising again.

Great is the mystery of faith: **Christ has died, Christ is risen, Christ will come again.**

Blessed are you, God of creation, for giving us grain and grape from which we make this bread and wine to celebrate your presence in our lives. Pour out your Spirit on us and these gifts of food and drink so that we will see the ways that your grace sustains our lives each day.

We give you thanks for this bread and this cup that we share. May your Spirit move among us and lead us to share our food with all who are hungry. Strengthen us to work together for a world of justice, peace, and hope until the day of your reign fully comes.

And now let us pray as Christ taught us . . . **Our Father . . .**

The text of this prayer includes the biblical hermeneutics of earth care and sharing with the poor that we have identified as central to renewal in congregations. By cultivating the practice of thanksgiving, the prayer guides us in ways to embody this practice in our lives by sharing what we have with those who are in need and by paying attention to our relationship with creation.

THANKSGIVING AS CARING FOR THE EARTH

This central commitment to thanksgiving also extends to the second of our biblical, hermeneutical priorities, linking Christian faith with caring for the earth. To give thanks is to recognize our dependence on Mother Earth and for the ways in which she sustains our lives. This begins at the Communion table around the bread made from the grain that grows up from the earth and the grapes that provide us with wine that gladdens our hearts. While our diets may be more complex than those of first-century Mediterranean peasants, nevertheless we remain equally dependent on the health of the soil, sufficient water, the goodness of the sun, and the presence of clean air. We will examine this more closely in the chapter on baptism with a focus on Christian discipleship and caring for the earth. Here we will simply note that the sacraments are dependent upon the earth for providing us with bread, wine, and water. Thus, what we celebrate with is not composed of otherworldly, ethereal, or spiritual elements. It comes from the earth, which desperately needs our care. To proclaim that "these are the gifts of God for the people of God" is to confess God's incarnational presence that is woven into the fabric of creation.

If we are not relating to the earth and to the poor, then our worship will continue to wither and become increasingly parochial and irrelevant. What we say and do in our sanctuaries is often incoherent or hypocritical in a rapidly increasing post-Christian world. This is not a call to jettison all forms of tradition or to use relevance as a litmus test for our liturgies. It is, however, an ethical plea for us to clearly articulate and show links between worship and daily life. This was part of the rapid growth in the early church where collecting food for widows, prisoners, and the poor was a normative part of weekly Communion.[41] Similarly, we noticed the importance of this question for the early Reformers: How does worship provide a basis for cultivating piety? Calvin recognized the central role that Word and sacrament provide in shaping and nurturing Christians. As we saw, he expected household piety to grow out of the rich experiences shared in worship. The *table, bread, and wine* at the Lord's Supper were named as both ordinary and extraordinary. They provided linguistic and embodied links that subtly connected worship with the daily household meals. Families gathered to give thanks for their daily bread, to sing psalms at home together, and to read Scripture. These practices provided ethical expectations for ways to live as followers of Jesus Christ. Furthermore, the consistory in Geneva backed up these expectations by disciplining individuals whose behavior was deemed as egregious. While I am not calling for a twenty-first-century consistory, I am insisting that sacramental practice must be clearly linked to daily life.[42]

THE FUTURE OF COMMUNION

In the previous chapter I described the importance of reclaiming Schleiermacher's vision of liturgical reform from below. What will the Lord's Supper look like when change comes on a local, congregational level? Let me sketch out a few examples that point in the direction that I believe is necessary. In many congregations, change in worship comes at an incremental pace. In these settings, new eucharistic prayers led by the minister will provide the initial impetus for change. As we have seen, the new eucharistic prayers in the 2018 *Book of Common Worship* already provide models of texts that demonstrate the importance of diverse voices, images, and language.

For better and for worse, there is a long history in the Reformed tradition of extemporaneous Communion prayers connected to the commitment between form and freedom in the liturgy. There is significant potential in smaller, informal gatherings to explore the possibilities of new ways of praying and celebrating around the table. For over twenty years, I have led groups by using forms of bidding prayers as the basis for extemporaneous prayers that follow the traditional form of eucharistic prayers in the 1993 BCW (Prayer J provides rubrics so that the presider can offer the prayer in their own words). In services that I led, I invited worshipers: (1) to name experiences or places in creation where they witnessed God's presence; (2) to share stories from the life of Jesus that were meaningful to them; and (3) to name people and places where we ask for the Spirit's healing presence. This approach to eucharistic prayer usually requires preparing participants ahead of time so that they come ready to include their voices in the prayer around the table.

The rapid spread of COVID-19 in 2020 caused a dramatic shift in Communion practices. While some congregations were already experimenting with virtual Communion, the pandemic accelerated the trend that quickly became widely accepted in Protestant communities. When the COVID pandemic began to spread rapidly, virtual Communion moved from the margins to the center of most congregations. Whatever questions some may have about it, it is not going away.[43] My point is not to question the practice of virtual Communion but to raise the question about the role of food in its current iterations.

Two central concerns emerge from my analysis of wide-spread virtual Communion practices. First is the tendency to try and recreate the congregation's previous Communion practices. For example, one congregation provided directions that included buying grape juice, pouring it into small cups, and cutting up small cubes of bread in preparation for the virtual Communion. Minimalized elements were used to provide a continuity between in-person and virtual Communion. A second strategy is to encourage congregation members to simply choose what they want to eat and drink and to have it ready alongside their computers. While this method expands the options, it runs the risk of commodifying Communion according to our individual tastes.

Ironically, both of these approaches to virtual Communion are dependent on the clergy for saying the "proper words" that allow the gathering to be recognized and experienced as an authorized (by the session) version of the Lord's Supper. Protestants who have long criticized the hierarchical dominance by clergy have adopted a practice that reifies the pastor's words as that which provides the link for the virtual service to be recognized as Communion.

Alongside the concern of clergy dominance lies our question of who gets to eat? The current forms of virtual Communion reinforce the predominant practice of eucharist as serving our own appetites. In minimalized versions of distance Communion, token amounts of food and drink deprive everyone of material sustenance and underscore a gnostic spirituality that denies the needs of our own bodies while also failing to acknowledge the rising food insecurity that plagues our communities. In alternative versions, we satisfy our hunger by simply sating our own appetites while giving little thought to the growing lines at food banks in our neighborhoods. Surely the proponents of virtual Communion need to take a closer look at current practices and make adjustments that connect our Table fellowship to the hunger of the world.

Another important question that Reformed Christians should be asking is: Who gets to preside at Communion (and what does it mean to preside)?

Ironically, most Reformed churches have readily recognized the gift for preaching and provided ways that acknowledged those in their community who had skills. A local session can approve a guest preacher. This practice regularly includes adults and youth from the congregation. I am puzzled about why our polity does not allow us to recognize the skills that are central to presiding at the table. Why is it that members from our congregations who have gifts for public prayer and hospitality are not allowed to use their gifts, especially in a time where small congregations lack ordained ministers? Clearly, training would be required to support this change (we are already moving in this direction in terms of approving commissioned pastors).

REGARDING ATONEMENT AND SACRIFICE

Finally, we must address the issue of the Reformed tradition's approach to atonement and the use of sacrificial language in the eucharistic liturgy. Given the long-term effect of Schleiermacher's theology as well as growing critiques of the implications of substitutionary atonement, particularly by feminist scholars, Reformed liturgies finally began to explore new options for the way they spoke of Christ's work on the cross. Beginning with the eucharistic prayers in *The Worshipbook*, Communion liturgies in the PC(USA) moved away from explicit language and images that emphasized substitutionary atonement. Instead, eucharistic prayers began to draw on language that relates to alternative biblical and theological understandings of atonement. In the twelfth century, Peter Abelard described the significance of Christ's death in terms of the way in which it shows God's love to us. Similarly, Schleiermacher developed this approach in terms of portraying the life and death of Jesus as a moral example of dependence on God. More recently, the work of feminist and womanist theologians has been particularly significant in drawing attention to the theological consequences of substitutionary atonement theory in terms of its implications on the doctrine of God. For many, the work of feminist scholars burst into the broader consciousness of the ecumenical church at the first Re-imagining Conference in Minneapolis in 1993. The session on re-imagining Jesus included presentations by Delores Williams, Kwok Pui-lan, and Barbara Lundblad, each of whom raised critical issues about the need to address ways that patriarchy and violence are deeply imbued into our theological doctrines.

Liberation theologian Jon Sobrino notes the importance of avoiding conservative interpretations that portray Jesus as a scapegoat far removed from our own contexts and cultures. The danger of theological voyeurism and valorizing the suffering of Jesus are evident in popular forms of Christianity. One need only consider Mel Gibson's film *The Passion of the Christ* as a primary portrayal that relishes in the violent death of Jesus with little concern for the violence and death that dominate our culture.

At the same time, we must also be wary of the temptation to sanitize the witness of the Gospel by making its story conform to our desire for comfortable forms of Christianity that do not require us to change our lives. For Sobrino, the significance of the death of Jesus as an historical event is in terms of God's involvement with the suffering and identification with all those who suffer. Jesus's life and his death provide an example and service for others—a showing of dependence on God. Jesus got in the way because he stood up for the kingdom of God (over and against the anti-kingdom). "To be faithful to the end is what it means to be human."[44] Once again, the Gospels show us a countercultural witness to the claims of empire. For white Christians who must acknowledge and confess the ways that we have co-opted Scripture to support white supremacy, racism, and patriarchy and have perpetuated violence against women and people of color, reclaiming the language of suffering includes recognizing and repenting from our role as oppressors. The eucharistic prayer serves as a witness and a call to solidarity with all, especially the poor and the earth. In the midst of our prayers around the table, the Spirit "intercedes with groanings too deep for words" (Rom. 8:26) that cry out for the healing of all creation.

In his essay on the sacraments, liberation theologian Victor Codina emphasizes the need of linking the sacraments to the proclamation of the kingdom of God. This shift in emphasis unlocks the possibilities of the sacraments to move beyond the protected confines of the walls of the church and reclaims their prophetic role in announcing the liberative work of God in our lives. Codina describes this as "a return to the biblical and earliest historical origins of the mystery-sacrament."[45] With this move, once again the sacraments fulfill their role in serving as signs of the Gospel by (1) proclaiming the good news of Jesus Christ, (2) denouncing the sins of the world by showing us an alternative way of sharing life together (in this instance sharing our food with those who are hungry), and (3) demanding us to change our lives in order that we may work for the transformation of society that reflects the values of the kingdom of God.[46] Once again, the presence of the poor in our communities provides us with the opportunity to experience the (sacramental) presence of Christ in their midst and to participate in God's ongoing work of liberation.[47]

The renewal of Reformed eucharistic practice must include both a faithful witness in terms of remembering the life, death, and resurrection of Jesus Christ as well as a commitment to welcoming and including all in our communities who are suffering. By focusing on the materiality of the sacraments, we are reclaiming the incarnational message of the gospel. Our bodies gathered around tables filled with bread and wine provide us with a chance to embody our oath (*sacramentum*) and express our desire and commitment to follow Jesus Christ. The Spirit's presence in, with, and around us prompts us to respond to God's grace in order that we may experience and participate in the healing of ourselves and the world.

9

Baptism

The process of building a robust Reformed theology of baptism has been a long, arduous journey. Calvin provided essential pieces with dramatic changes to baptismal practice in the church in Geneva. We noted in chapter 3 the shifts in practice that included baptism as part of a regular worship service to show the integral role of the congregation in fulfilling the baptismal promises as part of the covenant community. With infant baptism as the norm, the participation by the parents in the context of the community provided a model of Christian life shared together. Calvin insisted that the primary emphasis was on the baptism by water rather than on ancillary rites that lacked biblical warrants and had been added later. Calvin's baptismal liturgies consisted mostly of lengthy theological explanations that sought to differentiate a Reformed understanding of baptism from Roman Catholic practices. He relied primarily on Old Testament texts in order to develop an analogy between the Jewish practice of circumcision and Christian baptism. This parallel provided Calvin with an emphasis on the centrality of covenant. Given the lack of a clear biblical warrant for infant baptism, the reliance on circumcision as a sign of the covenant served as the main basis for defending the practice.

While infant baptism remained normative in Reformed congregations, critiques of the practice by Schleiermacher, Barth, and Moltmann have continued to raise critical questions about the theological understanding of baptism in terms of its reliance on Scripture as well as its cultural connection to Christendom. This chapter will explore recent developments in Reformed liturgical practice amid efforts to deepen a Reformed baptismal theology that provides an alternative portrait of Christian discipleship in a world that is increasingly religiously and culturally diverse.

BROADENING BAPTISMAL CLAIMS

In chapter 6, we previously traced the shift in baptismal theology and practice to the new language about baptism that emerged in C-67. With a new focus around the Barthian emphasis on reconciliation, the confession reasserts the emphasis on baptism in terms of dying and rising with Christ as well as stresses the significance of growth in Christian discipleship as grounded in the waters of baptism. The baptismal liturgy in *The Worshipbook* builds on this foundation by moving away from the previous focus on Old Testament texts as biblical warrants and instead relying on the baptismal language in Matthew 28:19–20 as the basis for the liturgical practice. Additionally, the liturgy provides a pattern for both infant and adult baptism.

This shift in liturgical emphasis came to full fruition in the 1993 BCW, which provided a distinctly new theological grounding for the baptismal rite that drew heavily from the ecumenical liturgical renewal movement as well as from the focus on salvation history that characterized the biblical theology movement of the mid-twentieth century. The new focus for the baptismal rite included renewed attention to the Reformed stress on the theological significance of covenant language as well as to Calvin's emphasis on the role of the Spirit.

The new attention on developing a more robust baptismal theology is evident in the efforts to provide congregational resources that draw attention to baptismal practice and life on a regular basis. In 2006, the Sacrament Study Task Force published a report titled *Invitation to Christ* which included a call for reclaiming baptismal language and imagery as a vital part of focusing on life-long Christian growth and discipleship.[1] The report urged congregations to gather regularly around the waters of baptism, particularly by leading appropriate portions of the regular liturgy from the baptismal font. Pouring water each week into the font as a visible and audible reminder of our shared baptismal vows; confessing our sin and receiving the words of assurance of God's forgiveness from the font; and celebrating ordination and installation of ministers, elders, and deacons while gathered around the font were all seen as occasions for how our lives are connected by the waters of baptism. These practices pushed against the prevailing tendencies to see baptism as a one-time, contained rite usually reserved for infants. Baptism as a lifelong journey became a way to reclaim Calvin's emphasis on sanctification and the importance of cultivating Christian piety.

Accompanying this movement was a fledgling interest in a Reformed approach to the catechumenate. Once again, the work of Vatican II provided resources that prompted Christians in other churches to consider ways to incorporate and adapt key findings from these documents. In this instance, the Rites of Christian Initiation for Adults (RCIA) offered Roman Catholics a way to reclaim aspects of the process of Christian formation that were central in communities before the rise of Christendom in the fourth century. While the RCIA structured the formation process around lay-led study and mentorship that connected with specific liturgical rites, other denominations adapted the patterns in ways that addressed their own historical identities and theological understandings. While an official version of the catechumenate process has yet to take shape among Reformed bodies, the informal movement did provide another way to draw attention to the significance of baptismal preparation for adults (as well as for the parents of infants as part of the baptismal process). In an address to the North American Association for the Catechumenate (now known as the Journey for Baptismal Living), I outlined three ways in which a Reformed approach could draw on Calvin's theology in order to offer a distinct vision of Christian life as a baptismal journey: (1) connect baptismal preparation with a vision of baptismal life/discipleship—baptism is recognized as a source rather than a goal of Christian life; (2) reinforce Calvin's emphasis on the third use of the law as a guide for communal Christian living as a way of guarding against the dangers of individualistic interpretations of baptismal formation;[2] and (3) highlight the Reformed stress on the priority of God's grace as the sole source of Christian calling and life by underscoring the biblical witness: "We belong to God. We are not our own."[3]

More significantly, we can highlight the expansive use of baptismal language and imagery in the 2018 BCW. One can quickly see ways that a new emphasis on baptism has influenced the liturgies. The rubrics for the service for the Lord's Day provide suggestions for leading portions of the service from the baptismal font by including a thanksgiving for baptism as part of the gathering rite. Similarly, the rubrics following the confession of sin and before the assurance of pardon note that "the presider may lift water from the font, declaring the good news of God's grace."[4] The alternative liturgies spell out the connection between baptism and confession and the declaration of forgiveness by noting that these actions are grounded in the "baptismal call to new life in Christ." Three out of seven of the suggested texts explicitly use baptismal language and include scriptural references that buttress this connection (Col. 2:12; Rom. 5:5; and John 3:5 / 2 Cor. 5:17).[5] The rubrics for the Sunday service also note that pastoral rites (e.g., welcoming new members or ordination/installation) are associated with baptism and may be led from the baptismal font.

The section of baptismal rites includes a commentary on the theology of baptism. The description of baptism shows the shift in the interpretation of baptism that we have charted in earlier chapters. The commentary begins by clearly connecting baptism with the work of Christ. While it claims the Reformed tradition's emphasis on covenant as central to the understanding of baptism, it carefully notes that in this way baptism "like circumcision, a sign of God's gracious covenant with Israel . . . is a sign of God's gracious covenant with the Church."[6] The description of baptism notes that both children and believers are included in the baptismal rites while describing the significance of baptism as part of the worship life of the covenant community.

The primary baptismal liturgy begins with the great commission (Matt. 28:18–20) as its biblical warrant. The rite closely follows the contours of the 1993 BCW. The prayer of Thanksgiving over the Water follows a Trinitarian outline and fills out the text with a brief recitation of salvation history. The 2018 BCW includes five alternative prayers of Thanksgiving over the Water for use in the baptismal rite. Four of these prayers generally follow similar contours of the primary prayer but offer alternative images and language to describe the claims of baptism.[7] We will examine the other alternative prayer (Prayer 5) and its use of ecological language in the upcoming section on how our emphasis on biblical hermeneutics can shape our celebration of the sacraments.

The most striking development in terms of inserting expanded baptismal language is in the section on Daily Prayer. The description of these liturgies includes the following claim: "The services of daily prayer reflect the baptismal rhythm of Christian life—that of dying and rising with Christ."[8] The texts themselves make this pattern clear. The Saturday evening service for the Vigil of the Resurrection includes a prayer of thanksgiving for baptism (the text of the prayer is parallel to the prayer in the primary baptismal liturgy). Similarly, each morning prayer begins with a brief thanksgiving for baptism as a way to frame the day around our baptismal claims. Similarly, the night prayers include a time for confession of sin as part of the baptismal pattern of Christian life.[9]

Taken together, these changes to the baptismal language highlight a deliberate attempt to change the understanding of baptism so that it links more coherently with the life of Christian discipleship. Furthermore, by placing these prayers within the context of common worship, they show the integral connection to a portrait of life shared in community that is grounded in and sustained by the waters of baptism.

We must ask ourselves, though, to what extent this portrayal of baptism reflects the commitments to the priorities of biblical hermeneutics that we outlined in the preceding chapters: care for the earth and the preferential option for the poor. As we previously noted, the significance of these hermeneutical principles is that they are imbedded in the biblical witness as well as corresponding to the urgent needs of our time. How can a renewed Reformed baptismal theology provide us guidance in professing and living our Christian commitments in our contemporary world?

BAPTISM AND EARTH CARE

Just as the Reformed tradition needs to expand its understanding of baptism from a moment in time to a lifetime of discipleship, so too we need to move beyond a narrow use of baptismal water to recognize the sacred nature of all water. Water has a story to tell us if we can learn to listen to it. We can start by paying closer attention to the appearance of water in the biblical narratives themselves. Remembering the role that water plays in Scripture is a first step to finding our identity and our connection to the earth.

In fact, the sacrament of baptism is actually dependent upon the earth for its valence as a sign of God's grace. Since water serves as the primary element of the ritual, the availability of clean water is crucial in order for the act of baptism to take place. Ethicist John Hart describes the critical importance of access to clean water. Polluted and privatized water diminishes the power of baptism to embody God's generosity and graciousness. The image of living water, clean and available to all, conveys God's goodness and provision in creating a world that sustains life. Hart concludes that "Throughout the world today . . . environmental degradation and water privatization have caused water to lose its nature and role as *living water*, as a bountiful source of benefits for the common good. Water is losing also its ability to be a *sacramental* symbol, a sign in nature of God the Creator."[10] Hence, caring for the earth is also a way to preserve the integrity of the sacramental signs that point to the presence of Christ among us when we gather for worship. This understanding of baptism embraces the physicality of water as a sign of God's presence in creation. Recent emphases in the rubrics for the baptismal liturgy stress that water should be poured in the font visibly and audibly. This language takes a step in the right direction by affirming the ways in which we experience God in the material elements of creation.

In spite of this, I have noticed the tendency of preachers and interpreters of texts to quickly spiritualize references to water or the earth in order that they point to some sort of deeper, spiritual truth.[11] From this perspective, the mention of a river in Scripture is there to prompt us to higher associations of new birth or life. Consider, for example, the ways in which the text itself uses the language of living water in John 4. Even the text seems to indicate that the living water of which Jesus speaks to the Samaritan woman is superior to the regular water from the well. The living water quenches thirst whereas other water provides only temporary relief. Biblical commentaries have built further on this insight and heightened the divide. Some scholars have seized on this as a spiritual teaching of Jesus that supports the teachings of new birth in John 3. Spiritual life as a permanent condition of new birth takes precedence over the temporal needs of our physical conditions (in this case, thirst). Other scholars like Raymond Brown have argued that John is explicitly using this metaphor to point to the role of baptism in the formation of the Johannine community. In this case, the sacramental imagery of baptism takes precedence over the material elements of water.

While not denying the tension and preference for living water that exists in the text itself, I wonder if contemporary readers of this text are missing out on a key insight from the ancient world—namely, the need and preference for living water as basic to daily existence. Living water was the fresh, flowing water from a river or spring on which healthy life depended. Water that was stagnant or collected ran the risk of contamination. Thus, on one level, the emphasis in John 4 on living water as the source of life is one that would resonate easily with the hearers who themselves knew the importance of fresh water sources. In this sense, living water points to an ongoing stream/supply that continues to provide a basic necessity for life.

It is also helpful to note the way in which the early Christian practice of baptism showed its own preference for living water. The *Didache* records the following instructions about baptism:

1. Concerning baptism, baptize thus: Having first rehearsed all these things, "baptize, in the Name of the Father and of the Son and of the Holy Ghost," in running water;
2. But if thou hast no running water, baptize in other water, and if thou canst not in cold, then in warm.
3. But if thou hast neither, pour water three times on the head "in the Name of the Father, Son and Holy Ghost."[12]

These ancient baptismal instructions suggest a couple of key insights: (1) the preference for running or living water as correlative to the baptismal event, which is still officially required in Roman Catholic practice (note how even the pouring of water as a last resort seems to mimic the movement of water in nature itself); and (2) the insistence on water as a physical element that is central to the act of baptism; here any spiritual or higher understanding of baptism cannot be decoupled from the presence of living water itself. Living water was recognized as the source of all life; here physical and spiritual are held closely together.

In *From the Beginning to Baptism,* Linda Gibler makes this point clearly. In the earliest Christian liturgies, water was already recognized as life-giving. Gibler notes, "For at least the first two hundred years of Christian tradition water was not blessed for baptism. Clean, living water did not need to be blessed."[13] Early Christians understood their dependence on water. It is only over time that the presence of water is minimalized and that water is increasingly treated as a spiritual metaphor, a kind of religious-liturgical prop that will lead us to a deeper truth. This shift toward a spiritualization of water is in stark contrast to those who asserted the significance of water. The early church father Melito of Sardis interpreted Jesus's baptism as a universal baptismal liturgy for the renewal of all creation. "For Melito baptism in water is an ongoing process in which all of creation naturally participates . . . Jesus was baptized in water because everything is baptized in water."[14]

As we have turned away from the resources in Scripture and early Christian practice that point to the central and basic role of water to support life and to enrich our communal and sacramental life, we seem to have lost our basic insight into the ways in which we depend on water for life each and every day, including in our Sunday services. Thus, Christians, especially affluent, Western ones, need to recover/discover ways that honoring, preserving, and protecting water is both an environmental necessity and a basic part of Christian faith.

A renewed focus on relational and eco-centric language in our baptismal liturgies provides a guide for ways to recognize and claim our identity as part of God's good creation. Ethicist Larry Rasmussen describes this in terms of developing a clear sense of eco-spirituality that revolves around a sacramental center. "The basic ethical reorientation commended here belongs to an eco-spirituality that includes a profoundly sacramental sense. Water is the object of awe and not only the object of engineering; it is a medium of the mystical and not only a resource for a world of our own making; water is a 'thou' and not only an 'it.'"[15]

Similarly, Gibler's wonderful description of both the scientific and sacramental understandings of water provides a unified vision of a way to hold together the wisdom of ancient and modern portrayals of water. By integrating scientific and sacred stories of water, she creates what she calls a cosmocentric sacramentality. The story of water, whether told through scientific analysis or through biblical narrative and liturgical poetry, points to the deep mystery of water's role in bringing forth and sustaining life. Gibler concludes, "Integrating these two sets of stories has the potential to reawaken baptismal participants to the magnificence of God reflected in water."[16]

There is much to learn from the wisdom that recognizes the inextricable link between spirituality and materiality that is woven through creation. We noted the importance of this theme in chapter 7 by looking at Mark Wallace's call for Christianity to recover the biblical and historical witness to the divine presence in all of creation. For Wallace, only then will we be able to see that "everything is alive with personhood and relationality, even sentience, according to its own capacities for being in relationship with each other."[17]

The Reformed tradition must firmly reject any form of dualism between spirit and matter. While Calvin's fear of idolatry may be understandable in the face of sixteenth-century malpractices in the church of his time, it cannot continue to provide a rationale for denying the significance of the material world in which we live. Ultimately, this is an issue of affirming the goodness of creation and the truth of an incarnational faith. In and through the waters of baptism, God claims us as beloved sons and daughters. The dangers of spiritualizing the sacraments are (1) to diminish the goodness of the gift of water that sustains our lives and (2) to deny the gift of our own bodies that are created in the image of God. Baptismal liturgies must begin by clearly giving thanks for the goodness of water that is the source of life. Similarly, we must acknowledge and honor the role of women in giving birth to those who are presented for baptism. Feminist critiques of baptismal liturgies and practice have rightly named the sin of patriarchy that usurped the place and role of women by privileging spiritual birth (that required a male priest) over physical birth.[18]

We need new baptismal liturgies that clearly articulate our dependence on the earth and its resources and our acknowledgment of the role of women in giving birth. A small step in this direction can be found in the prayer of Thanksgiving over the Water (Prayer 5) that I wrote for the 2018 BCW.

Prayer of Thanksgiving over the Water

In the beginning,
when your Spirit moved over the face of the waters,
light and life emerged from the dark and formless void.
At your calling,
all creation came forth and you declared that it was good.
Under the presence of the same Spirit of light and life,
we give thanks for the gift of water that sustains life:
For the earth and the air
for plants and trees,
for birds and fish,
for animals and humans.

In the gift of your covenant, you led your people
through the Red Sea and out of slavery to freedom.
By the rivers of Babylon,
you offered consolation to your people in captivity.

When Jesus was baptized in the Jordan River,
all creation was blessed by you.
Through his death on the cross, Jesus' baptism became complete
and in his resurrection the gift of eternal life is available to all.

We gather around this water to give thanks for the gift of birth
and for the experience of new birth.
We take this water from the earth that you created,
[from the local rivers of ____]
to pour over our bodies, to mark us as followers of Jesus Christ,
and to celebrate our calling as beloved children of God.

We give thanks for N. [and N.],
whose call to discipleship we celebrate
in the Sacrament of Baptism.
By your Spirit, breathe new life upon those
who pass through this water.
Bind her/him/them *to your unending love*
and to the community of faith
that she/he/they *may share with joy*
this life of discipleship and mission, serving all in need.
Give her/him/them *strength to follow faithfully in the way of Christ*
that she/he/they *may serve as a sign of your redemptive love*
by caring for others and for the world that you created.

We praise you and thank you for your goodness that creates us,
calls us, and claims us as your own beloved children.
To you, Holy One, Holy Three,
be all glory and honor, now and forever. **Amen.**[19]

Two important aspects of this prayer should be noted. First, the language in the prayer highlights the central role of water in sustaining life from the witness of Scripture and connects the baptismal water with a local body of water. It is helpful to remember that this approach is consistent with the Reformed understanding outlined in the Directory for Worship that the sacraments "employ ordinary things—the basic elements of water, bread, and wine—in proclaiming the extraordinary love of God."[20] Similarly, the Directory for Worship notes that "the water used for baptism should be from a local source."[21]

Second, the prayer recognizes the importance of naming the gift of physical birth and points toward the primary role of the mother in giving birth to the infant that the parents are presenting for baptism. Much more is needed on this point, though, in order for us to root out the patriarchal biases that continue to exist in our liturgical texts and practices. We can start by developing a deeper sense of gratitude for the gift of life by recognizing our relationship and interdependence on all forms of life.

We need to move further, though, to make clear the connection between Christian faith and caring for creation. One example of this development can be seen in the baptismal liturgy of the Anglican Church of Canada, which adds an optional question on care for creation to the baptismal rite. "Will you strive to safeguard the integrity of God's creation, and respect, sustain and renew the life of the Earth?"[22] By including this question, the community underscores a commitment to earth care as a central part of Christian life and discipleship. Similarly, I have proposed liturgies for the commissioning of earth stewards as a way to link the vocational calling and gifts of particular congregational leaders with our identity as followers of Jesus Christ.[23] In this time of environmental disaster, where the health and future of the earth is threatened by climate change, Christians must find our voices and demonstrate our commitment to protecting the earth's resources. A renewed theology of baptism that values and protects the gift of water is an essential component in the church's witness in the twenty-first century.

BAPTISM AND CARING FOR THE POOR

A Reformed baptismal theology must also align itself with the biblical-hermeneutical priority of God's preferential option for the poor. The historical use of covenant language in Reformed baptismal rites underscores the vital role of community in the formation of Christian life. The promises to care for others and to encourage one another to grow in faith are central components of Reformed baptismal rites and help distinguish the understanding of Christian faith from the dangers of individualism. Baptism as a response to God's initiative in Jesus Christ provides a sign that Christian faith is not a matter of personal choice or accomplishment but is ultimately grounded in God's unconditional love of creation.

Calvin's theology developed this understanding further through his insistence that baptism was not necessary for salvation. Ultimately, salvation lies solely in the hands of God. Barth would later articulate this belief in terms of affirming God's yes in Jesus Christ as overcoming any no. While Barth rejected the label of universalism, the theological implications of his position remain clear. The sovereignty of God to act freely to redeem creation can never provide us with a reason to exclude others. This theological declaration affirms the recognition of our neighbors as beloved children of God. It is here that the Reformed preference for the language of covenant should pause and consider the way we have misappropriated this term. Covenant language sought to emphasize God's initiative and our relationship to one another. However, often we have used it to demarcate ourselves from those outside the walls of our congregations. It became a way to mark insiders as special, elect, or chosen rather than a sign of all creation's dependence on God's grace for the gift of life.

Reformed Christians can draw on insights from liberation theology to make an important correction to the temptation toward a sectarian portrayal of baptismal theology that overemphasizes the theme of the election of only some individuals. In his description of the theological significance of baptism, Victor Cordina notes the change in baptismal understanding that grew out of Vatican II. While affirming the central role of incorporation into the church (and as we will see, the importance of a renewed catechumenate in presenting a portrait of baptism as a process of Christian discipleship) Cordina declares that, "The theology of liberation considers baptism not only an incorporation into the church, but as eschatological orientation and initiation into the Kingdom of God."[24] For Cordina, the significance of this emphasis is in reclaiming the biblical link between baptism and the prophetic work of liberation that lies at the heart of the gospel. This is a call for "radical conversion" in which we orient our lives "to the values of the Kingdom as they were incarnated in Jesus."[25] Here the work of the church is guided by the prophetic ministry of Jesus in his witness "to announce the Good News to the poor and the liberation of captives" and to confront the structures of sin and proclaim the struggle for justice (especially for the poor) as God's liberative work in the world.[26]

Within the context of Latin American liberation theology, Christian formation took place within base communities where people gathered to explore the intersection between Scripture and their lives. From the connections they discovered between communal and personal practices, participants identified authentic ways to align the community with the struggle for justice against the powers of oppression. From this perspective, baptismal life becomes an immersion into and participation in God's ongoing work of liberation in the world.

Our previous summary of the Reformed interest in the catechumenate pointed to the possibility of reclaiming a vision of baptismal life that extends throughout our lives as a way of emphasizing Calvin's teaching on sanctification and growth in Christian piety. A quick look at the history of the catechumenate in the early church underscores the potential for connecting this emphasis with the care for the poor. Cordina notes that early baptismal practice that included the role of a catechumenate emphasized the significance of aligning the actions of those who were preparing for baptism in order that their values more closely reflected the witness of Jesus in responding to those on the margins of society. Cordina concludes, "The catechumenate, with its requirement not only of biblical formation but of conversion, expressed that baptism requires a clear orientation to the Kingdom."[27]

In his book *The Change of Conversion and the Origin of Christendom*, Mennonite theologian Alan Kreider describes the three essential ingredients in the process of conversion in the early church in terms of behaving, believing, and belonging. While the diversity of baptismal theology and practice in the early centuries of the church defies any attempt to present a singular, universal process, Kreider sheds light on an essential requirement within Christian communities where changing one's behavior served as a sign of growth in preparation for baptism. The goal was to assist those who were drawn to the Christian movement to identify with core values by participating in the church's witness and service to those who were poor and marginalized. Often this took the form of taking meals to widows, prisoners, and the sick. The early church understood these actions as grounded in the teachings and practice of Jesus. Hence, those who desired to join the church were required to participate in this process of formation so that their lives would more closely reflect these values. Kreider contrasts a Christian commitment to providing for the poor with the temptations of money, sex, and power that served as the dominant values of the Roman Empire.[28]

It is precisely at this point that a Reformed approach to the catechumenate has much to learn from this pattern of the early church. The roles of formation, mentorship, and communal identity can serve as keys for those preparing for baptism as well as guiding those within the congregation as they seek to follow in the path of Jesus. By recognizing solidarity with the poor as central to Christian growth and discipleship, congregations understand and claim a countercultural identity to the primary values of our current neocapitalist and consumer culture. This vision of Christian life follows the pattern of a cruciform dimension as we move from the old life into a new one. Here, baptismal identity draws deeply from the language of the apostle Paul in Romans 6:4: "Therefore we were buried with him by baptism into death, so that, just as Christ was raised from the dead by the glory of the Father, so we also might walk in newness of life."

Let me be clear about what I am suggesting in terms of a new emphasis for baptismal theology. This is not a call for a mission component that augments our current practices. Instead, this is a plea for ecclesial and personal conversion that will take place only by aligning ourselves with those who are vulnerable, poor, neglected, and at the margins of society. As I have noted in chapter 7, this vision of discipleship draws from the teachings of the prophets and the ministry and witness of Jesus, who persistently calls on us to welcome the stranger, to care for our neighbors, and to love our enemies. We commit to these activities not primarily because we have something to offer others, but in order to live into the baptismal call to follow in the path of Jesus. This reading of Matthew 25 finds its inspiration in the promise of encountering Christ in the lives of those who are sick, hungry, naked, and imprisoned (rather than in a sense of obligation to provide for those who are deemed as less fortunate). These relational practices take inspiration from the words of Gustavo Gutiérrez: "If there is not daily friendship with the poor and an appreciation of their desires and needs as human beings, we can transform the search for justice into a pretext."[29]

Liberation theology develops a deeper baptismal vision by not only clarifying connections between the church and the celebration of the sacraments, but by further asserting the sacramental identity of the poor. Here, the church's role in celebrating the sacraments includes a dimension of sacramentality as it conforms to the image of Christ. Ignacio Ellacuría, the Jesuit theologian and priest who was martyred in El Salvador, asserts this claim by contrasting the images of self-centered and self-giving churches. Self-centered congregations focus their energy and resources on their own needs and desire for survival and growth. Ellacuría concludes that,

> If the church does not incarnate its central concern for the Risen Jesus in the fulfillment of the Kingdom of God in history, it loses its touchstone and, thereby, its assurance that it is effectively serving the Lord and not itself. Only by emptying itself, in self-giving to the neediest people, unto death and death on the cross, can the church claim to be an historical sacrament of the salvation of Christ.[30]

By connecting ecclesiology and sacramental theology with the church's faithfulness in participating in God's liberative work in the world, liberation theology has identified a way to avoid the risks of separating the church from the world or of creating divisions between insiders and outsiders. Whether or not Reformed communities are willing to give up our desire for success and our attachment to power and privilege remains an open question. However, the potential for experiencing renewal through the gift of new life is consistent with Calvin's commitment to the centrality of Scripture and the sacraments that provides for a definition of the true church and the way that these priorities have been traditionally developed in christological terms.

MOLTMANN AND THE MOVEMENT TOWARD AN EXPANDED BAPTISMAL THEOLOGY

There is an important historical connection between the development of liberation theology in Latin American and the work of the German Reformed theologian Jürgen Moltmann. Moltmann's writings on what he described as a theology of hope were influential among liberation theologians. A bloody copy of Moltmann's Christology, *The Crucified God*, was among the works found in the aftermath of the slaughter of six Jesuit priests along with their housekeeper and her daughter at the University of Central America (UCA) on November 16, 1989, in El Salvador. Similarly, Moltmann's influence is readily detected in the writings of other liberation theologians, especially in the work of Jon Sobrino. We can see here ways in which liberation theology is not in opposition to Reformed theology but shares similar concerns and outlooks.

For Reformed theology, these connections between ecclesiology, Christology, and sacraments are not new. What is new, though, is a focus on reanimating baptismal practice by showing the importance of its pneumatological and eschatological connections. In his classic work *The Church in the Power of the Holy Spirit*, Moltmann reclaims these essential ingredients as central to reforming the baptismal theology and practice of the Reformed church. Moltmann begins by noting the work of the Spirit as that which births the church into existence and guides it on a journey of faithfully witnessing to the life, death, and resurrection of Jesus Christ. It is the Spirit that brings new life and is not a result of our effort or belief. Moltmann declares, "It is not faith that makes Jesus the Christ. It is Jesus as the Christ who creates faith. It is not hope that makes the future into God's future; it is this future that wakens hope. Faith in Christ and hope for the kingdom are due to the presence of God in the Spirit."[31] The presence of the Spirit provides the source for the church's identity and mission. On this point, Moltmann's theology is strongly reminiscent of Calvin's own emphasis on the Holy Spirit in both his theology and liturgies.

Moltmann's analysis of the role of the sacraments within the Reformed tradition shows a keen sense of awareness of the contested history that we have traced in terms of its theological development. While recognizing that Barth's insistence on the christological center of the sacraments provides a theological basis for their development, Moltmann stresses the need for the sacraments to point us clearly toward the future. "The use of the word 'mystery' therefore spreads beyond Christology and flows into pneumatology, ecclesiology, and the eschatology of world history."[32] For Moltmann, a renewed sacramental theology provides the church with the gifts and direction to engage in the hopeful participation of God's redemptive work in the world. In a brief section titled "suggestions for a new baptismal practice," Moltmann outlines the way in which baptism is lodged in the church's call "to the service of reconciliation and liberation."[33] Baptism as call is linked with the lifelong journey of discipleship in which we come to understand our lives in relationship to God's reconciling work in the world.

Baptismal theology presents both the beginning and the *telos* (goal) of Christian life. By extending the connections in baptism so that they include the work of the Spirit to live into the call and hope of participating in God's future, Moltmann points us beyond the narrow ways that we have constructed our baptismal theology that have primarily focused on activities inside of our church buildings.

THE FUTURE OF BAPTISM AND THE FUTURE OF THE CHURCH

Each of the Gospels presents the narrative of Jesus's public ministry as rooted in his baptism by John the Baptist. For John, the call to repent and prepare for the coming of God's reign was linked with a ritual cleansing in the water of the Jordan River, a place that had previously served as a source for a new identity for the Hebrew people as they crossed into the promised land. One can read John's call as a return to the wilderness in order that the Spirit will come again and bring new life to all who pass through the water of the river. From the beginning, this Jewish ritual of renewal is a wake-up call that affirms the identity of participants as beloved children of God while at the same time challenging the status quo of the liturgical claims and practices of its day. As a faithful Jew, Jesus's continued participation at the synagogue and temple provides a continuity to the prophetic witness with its emphasis on justice, particularly to those on the margins. Unsurprisingly, Jesus's initial hometown homily in Nazareth (coming on the heels of his baptism) stresses this vision in his reading from the prophet Isaiah: "The Spirit of the Lord is upon me, because he has anointed me to bring good news to the poor" (Luke 4:18). In this text, the proclamation of the good news is directly connected to the plight of those who are marginalized.

A renewed theology of baptism needs to reflect carefully on the integral connection between ritual participation and social justice for the earth and for the poor. As we have seen in previous chapters, though, the history of baptismal practice has struggled to maintain a focus on these essential ingredients. Given what was perceived as the problematic nature of Jesus's participation in a Jewish renewal ritual (the biblical narratives themselves show the tension around the question of why Jesus needed to get baptized as well as whether Jesus or his disciples baptized followers), the early church developed other reasons for the significance of Christian baptism. While in some places the catechumenate provided an emphasis on the importance of connecting conversion with service to the poor, the rise of Christendom and a new stress on original sin shifted the primary baptismal metaphor to the need for cleansing from sin in order to gain salvation (understood primarily in spiritual terms). As infant baptism became the normative practice, this connection took precedence. While we have discussed the ways that Calvin disconnected baptismal practice from an assurance of salvation, he continued to insist on its place as a sign of participation in a covenant community. As we have seen, there remained risks to a baptismal theology in which communal identity was indistinguishable from cultural norms. Calvin and his followers experimented with forms of discipline to address moral lapses but lacked a clearer way to address the significance of marks that distinguished the ecclesial community from its broader sociocultural surroundings. This is a major reason that critiques of infant baptism have persisted within the Reformed tradition in the writings of Schleiermacher, Barth, and Moltmann. An inability to differentiate between Christian communal values and societal norms continues to lead to confusion as to what makes Christianity distinct from other perspectives. In our global, multifaith context, it is important for us to learn ways to articulate the virtues of Christian faith without prejudice or judgment to our neighbors of different faiths or those without faith commitments.

It is in this context that a renewed baptismal theology needs to draw on a wide range of theological themes that intersect around a shared vision of Christian life and discipleship. Here again, our commitment to a biblical hermeneutic of caring for the earth and the poor provides an important distinguishing mark of Christian identity, particularly in contrast to a secular culture that is oriented to success, accumulation of wealth, and consumption. For Christians, baptism, as an initiation rite, displays our dependence on God for the gift of life, our relationship with creation, and our interdependence with one another. In baptism, we acknowledge that there is no form of self-improvement that will repair our brokenness from God, from one another, and from creation. It is only through an immersion into God's grace where we acknowledge our dependence on the divine and experience our connection with all forms of life that we gain a glimpse of ways of sharing life together; a vision that we refer to as the reign of God. In this vision that is deeply rooted in Scripture, peace and justice serve as primary guides on our journey through life.

Clearly, caring for the earth and for the poor are not virtues and responsibilities that belong solely to Christian communities. As followers of Jesus, we welcome the opportunity to work side by side with people of other faiths and those of no faith. Together, we can create a society that more closely corresponds to the vision of God's reign that moves us to work for justice for all people and all of creation. For Christians, these actions and this way of living is deeply embedded in our theological commitments and liturgical/ritual acts.

Many congregations have sought renewal by focusing on increasing the frequency of the celebration of the Lord's Supper. Statistics across Protestant denominations show a dramatic trend over the past decades as congregations have moved from quarterly to monthly and in some cases weekly celebration.

For Reformed communities, this trend moves toward the realization of Calvin's understanding of the ways in which Word and sacrament are deeply interconnected. As important as this aspect of liturgical progress might be, unless our practices are rooted in a theology of baptism that will sustain it, then communal flourishing is not sustainable. This is the challenge that our shrinking congregations must face. We want new life, but we do not want to let go of the old habits that constrain us. We long to experience healing and growth, and yet we stubbornly cling to the ways that we have always done things even when they fail to bring us life. We want to welcome strangers and the gifts that they will bring, but we are unwilling to let go of the decent and orderly way that we do things. Baptismal life is messy. It is inescapably linked with the sign of death of the old in order to make room for the new life that comes as a gift of the Spirit. This dramatic act of immersion into the waters of creation affirms our identity as beloved children of God and prefigures our lifelong conversion into the image of Christ, the one whose life showed us how to live.

Here again, the Gospel depictions of Jesus's baptism provide key clues for our theological understanding of baptismal life. First, baptism is immersion into the world through the waters of creation. As we have seen, the role of water is not superficial. The materiality of creation claims us as partners. The water that runs off of our foreheads provides an essential, physical connection to the goodness of creation that sustains our bodies. Second, baptism provides an incarnational sign that affirms our identity that we are created in the image of God. The Gospels present this in the vision of a divine declaration of Jesus as the beloved son whose action corresponds with the divine longing for the redemption of the world. The baby born in the manger whose birth is celebrated as the hope of the world is now identified as the source of God's approval. Third, baptism issues a call to a life of discipleship. Jesus's baptism marks the beginning of his public ministry. The presence of the Spirit provides the link between baptism and vocation—the call for us to orient our lives and use our gifts in ways that embody the healing and hope that God brings to our broken world.

There is a liturgical clue that sums up this vision of baptismal life. The prayer of thanksgiving in the service for a funeral. Witness to the Resurrection includes the following words: "Especially we thank you for your servant N., whose baptism is now complete in death."[34] With these words, baptism is summed up as a journey that begins with thanksgiving to God as water is poured over us and ends with thanksgiving for the gift of life amid the trust that God will continue to bring forth new life in the face of death.

This renewal of baptismal theology and practice corresponds with the vision of eucharistic renewal that we noted in the previous chapter. The church's faithful witness in remembering the life, death, and resurrection of Jesus Christ provides the pattern that marks our own baptismal lives and serves as a guide in orienting us to a life of discipleship where we join in the work for the healing of this world that God loves so dearly. Here, baptism as a celebration of the gift of life as well as the call to discipleship come together in a community that professes a shared faith in God as the source of life and hope for the future. As Moltmann proclaims: "A church of liberation lives from baptism as liberating event."[35]

Given the history of the Reformed tradition that we have traced, any critique of baptismal practice need not revolve around the deficiencies of infant baptism. Instead, we need a baptismal theology that affirms God's initiative in naming us as beloved children *and* in summoning us to participate in God's redemptive work in the world. It is precisely on this point that we can identify a convergence between Scripture as that which informs and guides us in the life of faith, eucharist as place of thanksgiving and source of sustenance, and baptism as ongoing participation in the life of Christ.

Conclusion

Liturgical scholars often relish citing the adage *lex orandi, lex credendi* as a way to affirm the integral relationship between prayer and belief. The statement, generally credited to Prosper of Aquitane in the fifth century CE, has gained traction for asserting the centrality of liturgy in terms of its influence on theological formulation. In some instances, it is understood to signify a corresponding relationship between prayer and belief, while in other cases it provides an *a priori* claim for the role of the liturgy in providing direction for theological reflection.

As we have seen, though, for Calvin and the Reformed tradition in general, this adage rarely holds true. Theological beliefs and doctrines drove the early formation of liturgical language and rites. Early Protestant reformers relied heavily on their interpretations of Scripture and their theological commitments as the basis for developing liturgies that provided a stark contrast with the liturgies of the Roman Catholic Church. In order to show this distinction, the services were heavily didactic as they sought to persuade and educate congregations in this understanding of Christian faith and life. The use of biblical warrants provided the primary rationale for the choices that were made and the articulation of the meaning of the sacraments was heavily guided by theological doctrines that placed significant emphasis on atonement language and images.

Similarly, the historical survey of Reformed liturgies and confessions has shown that liturgical change has primarily been the result of shifts in hermeneutical and theological positions. The rise of the historical-critical method brought new methods of reading Scripture that raised significant doubts about the use of typological approaches, particularly in terms of the citation of Old

Testament texts to support theological claims. The emergence of modernism, with its distinctive focus on reason, challenged the dogmatic claims of the church and prompted theologians to explore ways to speak of God that were more closely aligned with the development of new methodologies. Whether we look at Schleiermacher's emphasis on religious experience or Barth's insistence on divine revelation, the consequences of theological positions impacted the development and use of liturgies. We chronicled these connections and showed their theological implications that are clearly visible in the nineteenth-century liturgical debates in Zurich and in the changes to confessional and liturgical language among Presbyterians in the United States during the 1960s.

Given the historical role that theological doctrine has played in the development of Reformed liturgy, I am arguing for the importance of making conscious theological choices for the language and images that we use in worship. Reformed communities will need to determine the extent to which we want to express theological diversity. We will have to come to terms with prominent issues that face us in the twenty-first century including issues of social justice around climate change, racism, white supremacy, colonialism, gender, sexuality, and our continued attachment to economic injustice fostered by neocapitalist market systems. While the use and repetition of language in the liturgy in the context of communal rituals provides a vocabulary and direction for ethical and theological decisions, the creation of liturgical and ritual patterns of gathering continues to be shaped and directed to support particular theological claims.

This is why it is critical for us to pay close attention to how and when liturgical changes happen. The most conservative Reformed congregations, even those insisting on strict adherence to the Westminster Standards, are not using the historic liturgies from Calvin, Knox, or Westminster in their worship services. Instead, the language of worship is driven by a commitment to particular theological doctrines and the importance of teaching participants to understand and articulate (usually in cognitive terms) the essential elements of Christian doctrine. Similarly, the liturgies of progressive congregations reflect their own theological and cultural commitments in ways that seek to convey a summary of Christian faith.

A primary task for liturgical theologians, then, is to come to terms with the primacy of theology in order to assist congregations in developing rituals that authentically speak of God in the midst of our culturally diverse and increasingly secular time. By speaking of God, I am referring to the way in which worship offers embodied rituals that gesture toward our hope for God's presence in our lives and world. This is precisely why I believe it is critical to develop hermeneutics that can guide our language and action. The biblical hermeneutics outlined in chapter 7—care for the earth and God's preferential option for the poor—provide theological commitments that are grounded in

Scripture and that correspond to the urgent needs of our time. The task of Christian worship is to explore ways that these commitments take shape in our lives as we seek to faithfully follow Jesus Christ.

Calvin's determination to chart a new theological path guided the liturgical direction in which he travelled. His heirs were bound and determined to adopt a rigid course and so the Reformed exploration became confined to certain territories. Course correction came with the decision to chart a new theological direction and subsequently the liturgy once again followed in its path. Whether it was the theological agenda of the liturgical renewal movement or that of biblical theologians who hoped that an emphasis on salvation history would allow them to navigate the rough waters of changing times, liturgies adapted to reflect these changing theological commitments. As new theological maps were charted by Schleiermacher, Barth, or Moltmann and new confessional statements were written, liturgical language shifted to include these theological emphases.

Yet in the midst of all this significant change and in spite of shifts in the prevailing winds, word and sacrament remain as the stars that guide us on our journey. The role of Scripture in worship is central even when we wrestle with how to read and interpret the witness that it provides. The sacraments of baptism and Communion provide occasions for us to express our longing and gratitude for the grace that sustained us. And so we continue to gather to

> Give thanks for the witness in Scripture of those who have experienced God's grace;
> Give thanks for the water that cleanses us as it runs over our bodies to celebrate our acceptance as beloved children of God;
> Give thanks for the meals that sustain us on this journey;
> And to commit ourselves to embody this grace as we work for change in the world around us.

While this is not a prescribed program that will produce rapid growth in our congregations, maintaining a central focus on word and sacrament and exploring new ways to embody them in our own distinct communities offers us an invitation to Christian faith that is both grounded in historical practice and open to new and diverse forms of expression. This path comes with challenges and change as well as with a sense of possibility that together we will see and feel the presence of the risen Christ among us. May God give us the courage to explore and experience the gift of word and sacrament in hopes that the Spirit will lead us into the future.

Notes

Introduction

1. Christopher Elwood makes a similar observation in his reflection on the development of a Reformed understanding of the Eucharist. He notes that there were functionally two sets of eucharistic symbols, one that was "interpreted by the French Reformed" that contrasted with the approach of Roman Catholics. See Christopher Elwood, *The Body Broken: The Calvinist Doctrine of the Eucharist and the Symbolization of Power in Sixteenth-Century France* (New York: Oxford University Press, 1999), 10.

Chapter 1: Calvin's Influences: Scripture

1. See Peter Matheson, *The Imaginative World of the Reformation* (Minneapolis: Fortress Press, 2001). Also Christopher Elwood, *The Body Broken*, 4, 31 (note 23), and 33 (note 33).
2. It is important to acknowledge that Erasmus and others who remained in the Roman Catholic Church also advocated for a central role of Scripture in their efforts to reform the church.
3. John Calvin in Bard Thompson, *Liturgies of the Western Church* (Cleveland: Collins World, 1961), 197.
4. Calvin in Thompson, *Liturgies of the Western Church*, 198.
5. Calvin in Thompson, 198.
6. Calvin in Thompson, 191.
7. John Calvin, *Institutes of the Christian Religion*, 4.14.6, ed. John McNeill, trans. Ford Lewis Battles (Philadelphia: Westminster Press, 1960), 1281. "Augustine calls a sacrament 'a visible word' for the reason that it represents God's promises as painted in a picture and sets them before our sight, portrayed graphically and in the manner of images." See also Calvin (from the Geneva Catechism) in Elwood, *The Body Broken*, 61–62. "A sacrament 'is an outward attestation of the grace of God which represents to us by a visible sign spiritual things in order to imprint the promises of God more firmly in our hearts and makes us more certain of them.'"
8. John Calvin, *Institutes of the Christian Religion*, 4.14.18, 1294–95. Calvin even explores what he calls secondary signs as sacraments, such as the fleece in Judges 6 or the sundial in 2 Kings 20. It is also important to note a point on which Calvin differs from Augustine. Augustine's definition of sacraments begins with a general description of sacraments as religious rites (including "pagan rituals"). The distinction here is related to Calvin's suspicion of any form of general revelation that is not tied to Scripture. For more on Augustine's interpretation, see K. W. Irwin,

"Sacramental Theology" in *New Catholic Encyclopedia*, 2nd ed. (Farmington Hills, MI: Thomson/Gale, 2003) 465–68.
9. Calvin, *Institutes of the Christian Religion*, 4.14.18, 1303.
10. Calvin in Thompson, 206. Elsewhere I point out the irony that the apostle Paul links the proper celebration of the Lord's Supper with equitable sharing of the food in the community. Worthiness is determined by one's willingness to provide food for those who are hungry. Paul's critique is based upon ethical action within the community, and it is the indifference to the needs of the poor in the community that leads to the charge that the actions of the wealthy in Corinth justify the charge that it fails to meet the standards of the Lord's Supper. See Paul Galbreath, *Leading from the Table* (Lanham, MD: Rowman & Littlefield Publishers, 2008), 20–26.
11. From Martin Bucer's liturgy in Strassburg in Thompson, 170.
12. See Calvin's commentary on Acts 2 where he proclaims that "the Church can be repaired by no other means, saving only by the giving of the Holy Spirit." John Calvin, *John 12–21/Acts 1–13*. Volume 1 of *Commentary upon the Acts of the Apostles*. Volume 18 of *Calvin's Commentaries*, ed. Henry Beveridge, trans. Christopher Fetherstone (Grand Rapids: Baker Book House, 1979, reprint), 84.
13. Daniel Migliore, *Faith Seeking Understanding*, 3rd ed. (Grand Rapids: William B. Eerdmans Publishing Co., 2014), 233.
14. As we will see in part 3 of this book, Jürgen Moltmann's theology makes a concerted effort to reclaim a primary role for the Holy Spirit. More recently, a body of work from Grace Ji-Sun Kim focuses on an expanded Reformed pneumatology. While I deeply appreciate the ways in which her work brings new attention to the role of the Spirit in Reformed theology, I have significant questions about whether her approach maintains a sufficient Trinitarian focus.
15. Christopher Elwood, *A Brief Introduction to John Calvin* (Louisville, KY: Westminster John Knox Press, 2017), 41.
16. Elwood, *The Body Broken*, 69. Calvin makes this point clearly in the Genevan Catechism: "For the spirit of God is the one who can touch our hearts, illumine our understanding and assure our consciences."
17. While support for each of these theological positions can be identified in the *Institutes*, Calvin's theology is framed by a focus on the sovereignty of God and grace in ways that avoid the scholastic attempts to provide detailed explanations for theological doctrines. Ironically, Calvin's followers moved toward forms of theology that relied on neo-scholastic arguments.
18. See John Calvin and Jacopo Sadoleto, *A Reformation Debate*, ed. John Olin (New York: Fordham University Press, 2000).
19. Calvin in Thompson, 209. As we will see in chapters 2 and 3, Calvin's theological interpretation of atonement drives his liturgical language in the Lord's Supper and baptism. It is interesting to note that these same tendencies are found in the mediating work of Christ depicted in this prayer.
20. Calvin in Thompson, 209.
21. Calvin in Thompson, 209.
22. Calvin in Thompson, 209.
23. Elwood, *A Brief Introduction to John Calvin*, 45.
24. Calvin in Thompson, 215. One could also point to Calvin's commitment to almsgiving as a Christian response to the needs of those within the community as a practice that reinforces this primary dimension of life within Christian communities.
25. Elwood, *The Body Broken*, 42–43. Elwood notes the influence of the French Reformed theologian Guillaume Farel on Calvin. Elwood concludes, "The unity

of believers in Christ creates a bond of mutual reliance among the faithful; participation in the Supper impels one to care for one's neighbor and to support the weak and the needy."
26. For more on the history and development of this prayer, see Paul Galbreath, "The Curious Case of the Collect: Between Form and Freedom," in *Re-Forming the Liturgy* (Eugene, OR: Cascade, 2019).
27. See the Scots Confession, chapter 18 in the *Book of Confessions, Study Edition*, revised (Louisville, KY: Westminster John Knox Press, 2017), 47.
28. John Calvin, *John Calvin: Writings on Pastoral Piety*, ed. and trans. by Elsie McKee (Mahwah, NJ: Paulist Press, 2002).
29. Thompson, 192.

Chapter 2: Calvin's Influences: The Lord's Supper

1. Elwood, *The Body Broken*, 32.
2. See the letters between Calvin and Sadoleto in *A Reformation Debate*.
3. Roman Catholic practice also included attention to self-examination as part of the practice of penance.
4. Thompson, 204.
5. Calvin in Thompson, 204.
6. For a helpful summary of historical approaches to atonement theory, see Paul Fiddes, *Past Event and Present Salvation: The Christian Idea of Atonement* (Louisville, KY: Westminster John Knox Press, 1989).
7. See the artistic depictions that linked the blood of Christ on the cross with the chalice on the altar. One famous example is the Ghent Altarpiece by Jan van Eyck in 1432.
8. Calvin in Elwood, *The Body Broken*, 83.
9. Calvin in Thompson, 205.
10. See also Elwood, *The Body Broken*, 87.
11. Calvin in Thompson, 205.
12. Calvin in Thompson, 206.
13. Calvin in Thompson, 206.
14. Ironically for a movement that seeks to reclaim the historical basis of the meal by locating it in the narrative of Jesus's actions in the upper room, there seems to be no recognition of the varied moral status of the "original disciples," including Judas.
15. Calvin in Thompson, 206.
16. Elwood, *The Body Broken*, 149.
17. Calvin in Thompson, 206.
18. Calvin in Thompson, 206. "If we have this witness in our hearts before God, never doubt that He claims us as His children, and that the Lord Jesus addresses His Word to us, to invite us to His Table and to give us this holy Sacrament which He imparted to His disciples."
19. Calvin in Thompson, 206.
20. Calvin in Thompson, 206.
21. Elwood, *The Body Broken*, 29. An emphasis on the spirituality of the sacrament as opposed to the materiality provides the primary and distinctive Reformed understanding that is carefully depicted throughout Elwood's presentation of the early history and theology of the Reformed movement. For example, the early Reformed writer Antoine Marcourt insisted on "a spiritual and symbolic interpretation of the eucharist: Christ's Supper is a memorial of his historic act of redemption rather

than a ritual that of itself has redemptive value." Marcourt in Elwood, *The Body Broken*, 41.
22. Calvin in Thompson, 207.
23. See Martha Moore-Keish, *Do This in Remembrance of Me: A Ritual Approach to Reformed Eucharistic Theology* (Grand Rapids: William B. Eerdmans Publishing Co., 2008).
24. Calvin in Thompson, 207. Christopher Elwood notes that this shift from the objective, external materiality to the subjective, internal spirituality became a focus of Roman Catholic critiques of Reformed eucharistic theology. Elwood, *The Body Broken*, 108–10.
25. Calvin in Thompson, 207.
26. Calvin in Thompson, 207.
27. As we saw in the opening chapter the debate on the role of grace and free will erupted in the controversy with Arminius, who was condemned by the Synod of Dort. Oddly enough, Arminius's teachings seem in many ways to be in line with this section in Calvin's liturgy.
28. Calvin in Thompson, 207.
29. Calvin in Thompson, 207.
30. Calvin in Thompson, 207.
31. Calvin in Thompson, 208.
32. Calvin in Thompson, 208.
33. Psalm 138:2.

Chapter 3: Calvin's Influences: Baptism

1. John Calvin, *Institutes of the Christian Religion*, 4.15.2, 1311. See also 1464 for Calvin's description of baptism as the sacrament of repentance.
2. Calvin, *Institutes*, 4.15.2, 1304. Notice the subtitle of this section: "Its [baptism's] virtue not in water without the Word."
3. The French Confession of 1559 was primarily written by Calvin. https://www.creeds.net/reformed/frconf.htm. Article 25 includes the following claim: "baptism, is given as a pledge of our adoption; for by it we are grafted into the body of Christ, so as to be washed and cleansed by his blood, and then renewed in purity of life by his Holy Spirit."
4. Calvin, *Institutes*, 4.15.6, 1307.
5. Mathew 3:17.
6. Calvin, *Institutes*, 4.15.7, 1308.
7. Theodore Beza in Elwood, *The Body Broken*, 106. Elwood notes that other prominent Reformed theologians including Antoine Marcourt, Huldrych Zwingli, and Johannes Oecolampadius. This figurative approach to hermeneutics contrasted to what was viewed as a literal interpretation by the Roman Catholic Church. Elwood notes that Calvin's approach to reading Old Testament texts through a reliance on "sacramental signification" was attacked as "a regression to the old dispensation to the Jews who lived before the birth of Jesus" (Elwood, 123). This led to the naming of Calvin as a "Judaizer" for not proclaiming the incarnation of Jesus as constituting a new era. From today's vantage point, we can only shake our heads at the anti-Semitic claims on either side of this debate.
8. Calvin, *Institutes*, 1310.
9. See the fascinating exploration in Karen Spierling, *Infant Baptism in Reformation Geneva: The Shaping of a Community, 1536–1564* (Louisville, KY: Westminster John Knox Press, 2009).
10. Calvin, *Institutes*, 1324–25.
11. Calvin, *Institutes*, 1327.

12. Calvin, *Institutes*, 1327.
13. Calvin, *Institutes*, 1327.
14. Spierling, *Infant Baptism in Reformation Geneva*, 41–42.
15. Calvin, *Institutes*, 1330.
16. Calvin, *Institutes*, 1339.
17. Calvin, *Institutes*, 1359.
18. Calvin, *Tracts and Treatises*, vol. 2 (Grand Rapids: William B. Eerdmans Publishing Co., 1958), 113.
19. Calvin, *Tracts and Treatises*, 113.
20. Calvin, *Tracts and Treatises*, 113. Calvin's liturgy directly addresses this claim with a repeated emphasis that we are "perverted and cursed" and our "first nature" of "perverseness and malediction" must be "abolished."
21. This may be Calvin's way of avoiding the understanding of baptism as a literal washing away of original sin.
22. Calvin, *Tracts and Treatises*, 114.
23. It is a curious and indirect way of using the Pauline images from Romans 6.
24. Calvin, *Tracts and Treatises*, 114.
25. Calvin, *Tracts and Treatises*, 115.
26. Calvin, *Tracts and Treatises*, 115.
27. Calvin, *Tracts and Treatises*, 116.
28. Calvin, *Tracts and Treatises*, and Matthew 22:37.
29. Calvin, *Tracts and Treatises*, 118.

Chapter 4: Modern Influences: Scripture

1. Jaroslov Pelikan, *The Christian Tradition: A History of the Development of Doctrine, Vol. 4, Reformation of Church and Dogma (1300-1700)* (Chicago: The University of Chicago Press, 1984) 185–86. Pelikan notes the change that Melanchton made to Article X on the Eucharist in the 1540 edition of the Augsburg Confession known as the Variata, which read: "that with the bread and wine the body and blood of Christ are truly presented [exhibeantur] to those who eat the Lord's Supper."
2. The French Confession of 1559, Article 4, https://www.ccel.org/ccel/schaff/creeds3.iv.vii.html
3. The Westminster Confession of Faith, *Book of Confessions*, 6.021, 217.
4. Edward A. Dowey in Jack Rogers, *Presbyterian Creeds: A Guide to the Book of Confessions* (Louisville, KY: Westminster John Knox Press, 1991) 211.
5. Claude Welch, *Protestant Thought in the Nineteenth Century*, vol. 1, *1799–1870* (New Haven, CT: Yale University Press, 1972), 59–60.
6. Schleiermacher in Welch, 60.
7. Friedrich Schleiermacher, *The Christian Faith*, vol. 2, trans. Terrence Tice, Catherine Kelsey, and Edwina Lawler (Louisville, KY: Westminster John Knox Press, 2016), xxx. See also Friedrich Schleiermacher, *On Religion: Speeches to Its Cultured Despisers*, trans. by John Oman (New York: Harper Torchbooks, 1958), 249: Scripture acts as a "logical mediator to open for the knowledge of God the finite and corrupt nature of the understanding, while the Holy Spirit . . . was an ethical mediator, whereby to draw near to the Deity in action."
8. Zwingli in Friedrich Schleiermacher, *The Christian Faith*, Vol. 2, 914, note 2.
9. Schleiermacher, *The Christian Faith*, vol. 2, 916.
10. Schleiermacher, *The Christian Faith*, vol. 2, 916.
11. Karl Barth, "The New World in the Bible" in *The Word of God and Theology*, trans. Amy Marga (London: T & T Clark, 2011). Previous translations of this essay titled the essay as "The Strange New World of the Bible."

12. Barth, "The New World in the Bible," 26.
13. "The Theological Declaration of Barmen" in *Book of Confessions, Study Edition*, revised (Louisville, KY: Westminster John Knox Press, 2017), 357.
14. *Book of Confessions*, 357.
15. "The Confession of 1967" in *Book of Confessions*, 369.
16. "The Confession of 1967" in *Book of Confessions*, 373.
17. "The Confession of 1967" in *Book of Confessions*, 373.
18. Barth, "The New World in the Bible," 26.
19. *Sacrosanctum Concilium*, no. 51, https://www.vatican.va/archive/hist_councils/ii_vatican_council/documents/vat-ii_const_19631204_sacrosanctum-concilium_en.html.
20. Horace Allen, a prominent Presbyterian liturgical scholar who served as one of the Reformed delegates to CCT, fought vigorously for this approach.
21. Harry E. Winter, "Presbyterians Pioneer the Vatican II Sunday Lectionary: Three Worship Models Converge" in *Call to Worship: Liturgy, Music, Preaching and the Arts*, vol. 38.1, 37.
22. Karl Barth in Jean-Jacques von Allmen, *Worship: Its Theology and Practice* (New York: Oxford University Press, 1965), 13.
23. Von Allmen, 21.
24. Von Allmen, 13.
25. Von Allmen, 21.
26. Von Allmen, 133.
27. Von Allmen, 135.
28. *The Worshipbook: Services* (Philadelphia: Westminster Press, 1970) 7.
29. Von Allmen, 156.
30. For example, see the liturgy "Order for the Celebration of the Sacrament of the Lord's Supper or Holy Communion" in the *Book of Common Worship* (Philadelphia: The Board of Christian Education of the Presbyterian Church in the United States of America, 1946), 155–65.

Chapter 5: Modern Influences: The Lord's Supper

1. Note the prevalence of bread, wine, and water imagery, particularly in the Old Testament readings throughout the liturgical year.
2. For more on Nevin, see Martha Moore-Keish, *Do This in Remembrance of Me* (Grand Rapids: Eerdmans, 2008).
3. John Knox, *The Liturgy of John Knox* (Glasgow: Thomas D. Morison, 1886), 140.
4. Knox, 140–41.
5. Knox, 141.
6. Knox, 142.
7. Knox, 142.
8. Knox, 146.
9. *Book of Confessions*, Scots Confession, 3.21, 50.
10. *Book of Confessions*, Scots Confession, 3.21, 50.
11. *Book of Confessions*, Scots Confession, 3.21, 50.
12. *Book of Confessions*, The Heidelberg Catechism, 4.075, 91.
13. *Book of Confessions*, Heidelberg, 4.076, 91.
14. *Book of Confessions*, 4.078, 93. Heidelberg distances itself from any form of literal language: "Just as the water of baptism is not changed into Christ's blood . . . so too the holy bread of the Lord's Supper does not become the actual body of Christ."

15. *Book of Confessions*, The Second Helvetic Confession, 5.180 and 5.183, 173–74.
16. *Book of Confessions*, Second Helvetic, 5.195, 176.
17. *Book of Confessions*, Second Helvetic, 5.202 and 5.203, 178.
18. *Book of Confessions*, Second Helvetic, 5.205, 179.
19. *Creeds and Confessions of Faith in the Christian Tradition*, vol. 1, part 4: *Creeds and Confessions of the Reformation Era*, ed. Jaroslav Pelikan and Valerie Hotchkiss (New Haven, CT: Yale University Press, 2003) 580–81.
20. *Book of Confessions*, 6.161, 246. It's worth noting that the Westminster Assembly provides the following biblical warrants for this defining paragraph: 1 Cor. 11:23–26; Matt. 26:26, 27; Luke 22:19, 20; 1 Cor. 10:16, 17, 21; 1 Cor. 12:13. This shows the way in which the Reformed tradition has augmented its use of 1 Cor. 11 with a conflated reading of the Last Supper narrative in the Synoptic Gospels. The citation of 1 Cor. 10 is particularly intriguing with its contrast between the cup of the Lord and the cup of the Gentiles/devil and the implication that the Reformed approach was the only proper one.
21. *Book of Confessions*, Westminster Confession, 6.162, 247.
22. *Book of Confessions*, Westminster, 6.163.
23. *Book of Confessions*, Westminster, 6.166.
24. *Book of Confessions*, Westminster, 6.167–68, 247–48.
25. The Westminster Standard, Directory for the Publick Worship of God, https://thewestminsterstandard.org/directory-for-the-publick-worship-of-god/.
26. Directory for the Publick Worship of God, https://thewestminsterstandard.org/directory-for-the-publick-worship-of-god/.
27. Joshua Ralston, "Rewriting Calvin: Schleiermacher on the Atonement and the Priestly Office of Christ," *Scottish Journal of Theology*, 75, no. 2, (May 2022): 89.
28. Ralston, "Rewriting Calvin," 93. Ralston cites the tension in the *Institutes* in book 2, chapters 12–17. "Calvin is aware that a singular focus on Christ's death jeopardizes God's freedom and might call into question the unmerited nature of grace." One can also point to the shift in Calvin's placement of the doctrine of election over the course of his rewriting the *Institutes* from its initial location in book 1 (doctrine of God) to book 3 (doctrine of the church).
29. Schleiermacher, *The Christian Faith*, vol. 2, 902.
30. Schleiermacher, vol. 2, 907.
31. Schleiermacher, vol. 2, 906. Schleiermacher describes the benefit of participation as "the consciousness of the forgiveness of sins . . . of a new influx of the power of spiritual life from the fullness of Christ" (908).
32. Ralston, 97.
33. Karl Barth, *Church Dogmatics*, vol. 4, *The Doctrine of Reconciliation*, ed. G. W. Bromiley and T. F. Torrance, trans. G. W. Bromiley (London: T & T Clark, 2009), 19. This work is abbreviated below as *CD*.
34. Barth, *CD*, vol. 4, 41.
35. Barth, *CD*, vol. 4, 45. Barth immediately contrasts this approach with Schleiermacher by insisting on the distinctive nature of Jesus Christ: ". . . everything is plainly topsy-turvy if we picture this relationship in such a way that the being of Jesus Christ is deduced and interpreted from the being of man and the world instead of the other way around, if we derive the atonement from creation instead of creation from the atonement . . . " (45–46).
36. Barth, *CD*, vol. 4, 67. Barth follows by referencing Question 64 of the Heidelberg Catechism that, without an emphasis on God's grace and our thanksgiving for God's action in Jesus Christ, the doctrine can lead to "wild and careless folk."

37. Barth, *CD*, vol. 4, 126.
38. Karl Barth in von Allmen, 115.
39. This is solely a descriptive claim. Whether or not one can legitimately defend a way of categorizing Christian rituals as essentially different than those of other traditions remains an important question for us to consider in part 3.
40. Von Allmen, 147.
41. Von Allmen, 147.
42. Von Allmen, 154.
43. Von Allmen, 155.
44. *The Book of Common Worship* (Philadelphia: The Board of Christian Education of the Presbyterian Church in United States of America, 1946), 162.
45. *The Book of Common Worship* (1946), 162.
46. *Book of Confessions*, Westminster Confession, 6.162, 247.
47. *Book of Confessions*, Confession of 1967, 9.09, 370.
48. *Book of Confessions*, Confession of 1967, 9.48, 377.
49. *Book of Confessions*, Confession of 1967, 9.52, 378.
50. *The Worshipbook*, 36.
51. *Book of Common Worship* (1993), 6–8.
52. *Book of Common Worship* (1993), 70.
53. Martha Moore-Keish, "Sacraments," in *The Oxford Handbook of Reformed Theology*, ed. Michael Allen and Scott R. Swain (Oxford: Oxford University Press, 2020), 542.

Chapter 6: Modern Influences: Baptism

1. *Book of Confessions*, The Scots Confession, 3.21, 49.
2. *Book of Confessions*, The Scots Confession, 3.21, 49.
3. Knox, 154. Knox's liturgy provides assurance that "fathers and mothers may take hereby moste singular comfort, to see your children thus received in to the bosome of Christes congregation" (156).
4. Knox, 157.
5. *Book of Confessions*, The Heidelberg Catechism, 4.074, 90. The confession cites Col. 2:11–13, which interprets baptism as a "spiritual" form of circumcision as its biblical warrant.
6. *Book of Confessions*, The Second Helvetic Confession, 5.169, 170.
7. *Book of Confessions*, Second Helvetic, 5.175, 171.
8. *Book of Confessions*, Second Helvetic, 5.171, 170–71. Confirmation and extreme unction are identified as "human inventions."
9. *Book of Confessions*, Second Helvetic, 5.177, 172.
10. *Book of Confessions*, Second Helvetic, 5.176, 171.
11. *Book of Confessions*, Second Helvetic, 5.178, 172.
12. *Book of Confessions*, Second Helvetic, 5.180 and 5.182, 173.
13. *Book of Confessions*, Second Helvetic, 5.187, 175.
14. *Book of Confessions*, Second Helvetic, 5.187, 175.
15. *Book of Confessions*, Second Helvetic, 5.192, 176.
16. *Book of Confessions*, The Westminster Confession of Faith, 6.149, 245.
17. There is an interesting variation in the Directory for Worship between the standard language that the sacraments were "instituted by Christ" and a change in 1989 to the language that the "sacraments were instituted by God and commended by Christ" that is more reminiscent of the language of Westminster. The revision of the Directory in 2017 reverts back to the previous language of "instituted by Christ."

18. *Book of Confessions*, Westminster, 6.154, 245.
19. A Puritan's Mind, The Directory of Public Worship, https://www.apuritansmind.com/westminster-standards/directory-of-publick-worship/.
20. The Directory of Public Worship, https://www.apuritansmind.com/westminster-standards/directory-of-publick-worship/.
21. The Directory of Public Worship, https://www.apuritansmind.com/westminster-standards/directory-of-publick-worship/.
22. Jack Rogers, *Presbyterian Creeds: A Guide to the Book of Confessions* (Louisville, KY: Westminster John Knox Press, 1991), 211. In particular, note this statement by theologian Edward Dowey Jr: "While Westminster is thus a post-Reformation statement, it is by no means a modern one. It derives from an age of scholastic theology, of preoccupation with authority and law, of churchly and political absolutism" (Dowey in Rogers, 211).
23. David F. Wright, "Baptism in Scotland," in *Infant Baptism in Historical Perspective* (Bletchley: Paternoster, 2007), 304.
24. In his essay "Baptism in Scotland," 301–7, Wright outlines the lack of theological inquiry and engagement around baptism. A similar conclusion was reached by the Sacraments Study Task Force of the PC(USA), which concluded that questions around the administration of the sacraments could not be answered until there was a more developed theology of baptism. See Office of Theology and Worship of the Presbyterian Church (U.S.A.), *Invitation to Christ: A Guide to Sacramental Practices*, (Louisville, KY: Presbyterian Church (U.S.A.), 2006), https://www.presbyterianmission.org/wp-content/uploads/Invitation-to-Christ.pdf.
25. Schleiermacher, *The Christian Faith*, vol. 2, 867.
26. Schleiermacher, vol. 2, 881.
27. Schleiermacher, vol. 2, 883.
28. Schleiermacher, vol. 2, 889.
29. Theodore Vial, *Liturgy Wars: Ritual Theory and Protestant Reform in Nineteenth-Century Zurich* (New York: Routledge, 2004), 117.
30. Vial, 118.
31. Vial, 119.
32. Vial, 120.
33. For an interesting parallel on the debates about the role of creeds in the Protestant Church in Germany, see my summary of the *Protestantenverein* and the *Apostolikumstreit* in Paul Galbreath, *Doxology and Theology* (New York: Peter Lang, 2008), 18–35.
34. Vial, 101–3. Vial depicts the question of language about atonement as growing out of the primary concern around whether the liturgical rite should be directed toward God. Here Vial shows the vital role that Christology plays in directing our liturgical language.
35. *Book of Confessions*, 207.
36. *The Book of Church Order of the Presbyterian Church in the United States* (Richmond: The General Assembly of the PCUS, 1964).
37. *The Constitution of The United Presbyterian Church in the United States of America*, Part II, *Book of Order* (Philadelphia: The Office of the General Assembly of the UPC in the USA, 1967), 18.03.
38. *Book of Order* (1967), 20.01.
39. For example, note the baptismal liturgies for the United Presbyterian Church in *The Book of Common Worship* (1946) 121–30. There are separate rites for infants and adults. Similar to the alternative liturgy in Zurich, the language of the prayers is

directed toward God. While the infant rite does include a reference to God "who has redeemed us by the sacrifice of Christ," it avoids explicit language of blood/atonement. The adult rite includes the use of the Apostles' Creed, unlike the infant rite.

40. Karl Barth, *The Teaching of the Church Regarding Baptism*, trans. Ernest Payne (London: SCM Press, 1948) 9.
41. Barth, *The Teaching of the Church*, 15.
42. Barth, *The Teaching of the Church*, 10.
43. Barth, *The Teaching of the Church*, 25.
44. Barth, *The Teaching of the Church*, 27.
45. Barth, *The Teaching of the Church*, 40.
46. Barth notes how Calvin portrays the place of decision and confession in baptism before observing, "How strange that Calvin seems to have forgotten this in his next chapter where he sets out his defence of infant-baptism, there commending a baptism which is without decision and confession." Then, Barth declares that Calvin "was visibly nervous, in a hopelessly confused train of thought, abusing where he ought to inform and when he wants to convince, seeking a way in the fog, which can lead him to no goal, because he has none." Barth, *The Teaching of the Church*, 48–49.
47. Barth, *The Teaching of the Church*, 49.
48. Jürgen Moltmann, *The Church in the Power of the Spirit*, trans. Margaret Kohl (New York: Harper & Row, Publishers, 1975), 227.
49. Moltmann, 228.
50. Moltmann, 232. "If we abide by the bourgeois religious form of the church in a 'Christian society', as we have described it, then if infant baptism is the general rule, the individual baptism of an adult on the basis of a personal profession of faith would only lead to baptism's becoming a matter of the inner, personal life, which would have to be lived in private; or it would lead to a life in the exclusive circle of the converted. In both cases baptism would love the character of a public, confessional sign of resistance and hope."
51. Moltmann, 235.
52. Moltmann stresses the role of liberation in contrast to Barth's emphasis on freedom.
53. My colleague, Martha Moore-Keish, pointed out that the *Book of Order* for the northern church recognized that either infant or adult baptism can serve as the norm.
54. Barth, 52.
55. *Book of Confessions*, 378.
56. *The Worshipbook*, 43.
57. *The Worshipbook*, 44.
58. *Book of Order*, 1983/85, S-3.0400.
59. Von Allmen does quote Barth in the introduction by noting that "all worship is bound by baptism," which makes it even more surprising that this significant contribution to Reformed liturgical vision lacks a robust baptismal theology. Barth in von Allmen, 14.
60. Von Allmen, 58.
61. Barth in von Allmen, 115.
62. Von Allmen, 187.
63. *Book of Common Worship*, 1993, 420–21.

Chapter 7: The Future of Reformed Worship: Scripture

1. To be clear, Scripture includes both the stories of the powerful (e.g., King David) as well as many unnamed marginalized people. Since much of Scripture involves the story of the liberation of people (whether held in slavery in Egypt or under the control of the Roman Empire), there is much to learn from these texts as we relocate ourselves on the underside of history.
2. Graham Hughes, *Worship as Meaning: A Liturgical Theology for Late Modernity* (Cambridge: Cambridge University Press, 2003), 48.
3. Stanley J. Grenz, *A Primer on Postmodernism* (Grand Rapids: William B. Eerdmans Publishing, 1996), 13–14.
4. These approaches follow different philosophical (but related) paths that include the work of Ludwig Wittgenstein, Jacques Lacan, and Jacques Derrida.
5. Graham R. Hughes, *Reformed Sacramentality*, ed. and introduced by Stephen Lösel (Collegeville, MN: Liturgical Press, 2017), 2.
6. Barth, "New World in the Bible," 20–25.
7. Hughes, *Reformed Sacramentality*, 127.
8. Hughes, *Worship as Meaning*, 70.
9. The Year D Project, http://theyeardproject.blogspot.com/p/start-here.html.
10. Working Preacher, https://www.workingpreacher.org/narrative-faq.
11. Season of Creation, https://seasonofcreation.org/about/.
12. Womanist Wading in the World (Wil Gafney), https://www.wilgafney.com/womenslectionary/.
13. The African American Lectionary, http://www.theafricanamericanlectionary.org/about.asp.
14. For example, I can imagine the value of following a continuous reading from focusing on a particular book of the Bible during ordinary time.
15. Calvin in Leanne Van Dyk, "The Gifts of God for the People of God," in *Feminist and Womanist Essays in Reformed Dogmatics* (Louisville, KY: Westminster John Knox Press, 2006), 204.
16. Mark I. Wallace, *When God Was a Bird: Christianity, Animism, and the Re-enchantment of the World* (New York: Fordham University Press, 2019), 73.
17. Proposals for engaging with earth-centered readings of Scripture include a proposal for a season of creation that focuses on elements of the earth. Lectionary readings are suggested to highlight thematic foci such as mountain or ocean Sunday. I have highlighted my concerns about this approach in *Leading into the World*, 7–8.
18. Wallace, 170. Wallace concludes that "all things would be viewed as bearers of the kenotic sacred; each and every fleshly creature and natural element would be seen as a portrait of the avian God; and everything that is would be cherished as holy and blessed and good" (172).
19. I often ask students to reflect on the process of reading biblical texts in different locations. For example, what are the hermeneutical consequences of reading the apostle Paul's sermon in Athens (Acts 17:16–34) in a public park?
20. Cláudio Carvalhaes, *Rituals at World's End: Essays on Eco-Liturgical Liberation Theology* (York, PA: Barber's Son Press, 2021), 81.
21. Carvalhaes, *Rituals*, 83. Carvalhaes draws on the practices of indigenous communities as providing models of ways to reconnect with the earth.
22. Carvalhaes links this with the preferential option for the poor, which we will explore later in this chapter. But note that the definition of the poor is expanded here to include any form of life that is marginalized.

23. Carvalhaes, *Rituals*, 86.
24. Carvalhaes, *Rituals*, 87.
25. Carvalhaes provides a model for this liturgical reorientation by outlining a revised liturgical calendar. It is not clear what role Scripture plays in this formulation (100–103). It is interesting to observe the places where Carvalhaes develops a theological position that is rooted in Calvin's primary concern about idolatry and where his theological position seems to diverge significantly from the Reformed commitment to the priority of Scripture as the primary basis for constructing worship.
26. See Paul Galbreath, *Elemental: A Journey through Lent with the Earth* (Cleveland, TN: Parsons's Porch Books, 2022).
27. For more on this research, see Paul Galbreath, *Leading into the World*.
28. See William P. Brown, *Deep Calls to Deep: The Psalms in Dialogue amid Disruption* (Nashville: Abingdon Press, 2021).
29. For example, see Lisa Dahill, "Lent, Lament, and the River: Interfaith Ritual in the Ashes of the Thomas Fire," in *Liturgy* 34 no. 4 (2019): 1–12.
30. Calvin in Thompson, 215.
31. Gustavo Gutiérrez in "Theology: An Ecclesial Function," in Gustavo Gutiérrez and Cardinal Gerhard Ludwig Müller, *On the Side of the Poor* (Maryknoll, NY: Orbis Books, 2015), 4.
32. James Cone, *A Black Theology of Liberation* (Maryknoll, NY: Orbis Books, 2014), xxiv.
33. Elsa Támez, "Poverty, the Poor, and the Option for the Poor," in *The Option for the Poor in Christian Theology*, ed. Daniel G. Groody (Notre Dame, IN: University of Notre Dame Press, 2007), 42.
34. Támez, 42.
35. Támez, 44.
36. Jon Sobrino, "Spirituality and the Following of Jesus," in *Mysterium Liberationis: Fundamental Concepts of Liberation Theology*, ed. Ignacio Ellacuria, S.J., and Jon Sobrino, S.J. (Maryknoll, NY: Orbis Books, 1993), 688.
37. For a fuller development of this theme, particularly in regard to a careful exegesis of Scripture, see Sobrino's classic work *Jesus the Liberator* (Maryknoll, NY: Orbis Books, 1993).
38. Sobrino, "Spirituality and the Following of Jesus," 688.
39. Gustavo Gutiérrez, "Option for the Poor" in *Mysterium Liberationis: Fundamental Concepts of Liberation Theology*, 241–44.
40. See Cone, *A Black Theology of Liberation*, 49–50.
41. Gilberto da Silva Gorgulho, "Biblical Hermeneutics" in *Mysterium Liberationis: Fundamental Concepts of Liberation Theology*, 124.
42. Martha Moore-Keish, "Sacraments" in *The Oxford Handbook of Reformed Theology*, ed. Michael Allen and Scott R. Swain (Oxford: Oxford University Press, 2020), 532.
43. In the mid-twentieth century, Anglican scholar Dom Gregory Dix popularized the notion of worship as the historical foundation and reducible core that has been preserved and passed down through the church's tradition. See Dom Gregory Dix, *The Shape of the Liturgy* (Glasgow: Dacre Press, 1945). More recently, Lutheran liturgical scholar Gordon Lathrop has argued that a fourfold pattern of worship (*ordo*), identified as gathering, word, thanksgiving, and sending, is grounded in Scripture. See Gordon Lathrop, *Holy People: A Liturgical Ecclesiology* (Minneapolis, MN: Fortress Press, 1999), 127. See Paul Galbreath, "Chasing the Sacramental Circle" in *Re-Forming the Liturgy*, 112–16.

44. Theodore Vial, "Toward a Reformed Theory of Ritual in Modernity," in *Semper Reformanda: John Calvin, Worship, and Reformed Traditions*, ed. Barbara Pitkin (Göttingen: Vandenhoeck and Ruprecht, 2018), 188.
45. Theodore Vial, "Toward a Reformed Theory," 188.
46. Vial, 195–96.
47. Vial, 196.
48. Cláudio Carvalhaes, *Liturgies from Below: 462 Acts of Worship* (Nashville: Abingdon Press, 2020). If one reads this book as offering models of engagement with the poor, then it serves an important purpose. On the other hand, if one appropriates the liturgical texts, then it runs the risk of exploiting the cries of the poor.

Chapter 8: The Future of Reformed Worship: The Lord's Supper

1. Paul Bradshaw, *Eucharistic Origins* (Oxford: Oxford University Press, 2004), 14.
2. *Book of Common Worship* (Louisville, KY: Westminster John Knox Press, 2018), 129–30. Eucharistic prayer 9 collapses the division between thanksgiving addressed to God the Creator and to Christ in a way that blurs the Trinitarian framework that can be seen in the other prayers.
3. *Book of Common Worship*, 2018, 27.
4. *Book of Common Worship*, 2018, 27.
5. Ralston, 97.
6. *Book of Common Worship*, 2018, 123.
7. *Book of Common Worship*, 2018, 126.
8. *Book of Common Worship*, 2018, 129.
9. See my analysis in "Reexamining our Sacramental Language and Practices," in *Re-Forming the Liturgy*, 84–87.
10. Charles Taylor in Hughes, *Reformed Sacramentality*, 26.
11. Hughes, *Reformed Sacramentality*, 30.
12. It is interesting to read this as an implicitly Barthian claim. See Barth, "The New World in the Bible," in the *Word of God and Theology*.
13. Hughes, *Reformed Sacramentality*, 1. Ironically, Hughes links this to widespread experiences of "sensing God's presence . . . most vividly through the natural environment" (Hughes, 1), which as we have seen remains a highly contested debate in Reformed theology in light of Barth's famous response of "Nein" to Brunner.
14. Hughes, 5.
15. Hughes, 33.
16. Hughes, 37.
17. Hughes, 57.
18. On this point, I would note the difference between sacraments as images and embodied acts.
19. Hughes, 109.
20. Hughes, 109–11.
21. Note the significance of the oft-repeated citation *ecclesia reformata, semper reformanda secundum verbum Dei*, the church reformed, always being reformed according to the word of God.
22. Anglican liturgical scholar Andrew McGowan, in his reflection on the centrality of bread and wine at Communion, notes that "supposed essential connections with the foods of the Passover Seder are often invoked; these however tend to over-read the historical connections with the Last Supper as a sole basis for eucharistic practice, connections that are in any case unconvincing as explanation for the use or significance of bread and wine, common rather than peculiar foods as they

are." Andrew McGowan, "'The Firstfruits of God's Creatures': Bread, Eucharist, and the Ancient Economy," in *Full of Your Glory: Liturgy, Cosmos, Creation*, ed. Teresa Berger (Collegeville, MN: Liturgical Press Academic, 2019), 70. There is wisdom for us on this point in terms of the temptation to appropriate rituals from other religious traditions. Note the inherent dangers in Christian worship services on Maundy Thursday that are based on pretending to celebrate a Jewish Seder. It is also disappointing to see a form of this practice included in the 2018 *Book of Common Worship* in Prayer 10, 130–32. We should reflect on how we would feel if members of another religious tradition pretended to celebrate a service of Holy Communion.
23. It is worth noting that in Zurich, Zwingli replaced the ornate Communion ware with wooden dishes and that in Scotland tables were set up in the church for the celebration of the Lord's Supper. In some way, there was a certain recognition of the importance of showing connections between the Lord's Supper and regular meals.
24. McGowan, "The Firstfruits of God's Creatures," 71.
25. McGowan, 78–79.
26. McGowan, 81.
27. McGowan, 83.
28. McGowan, 84.
29. McGowan, 86.
30. *Book of Order*, Directory for Worship, W-3.0401.
31. *Book of Common Worship*, 2018, 11 and 28.
32. Instead, the Directory for Worship draws primarily on covenant language for its description of the Lord's Supper. The result is that our attention is primarily focused on ourselves. The one exception is the generic language that by participating in the liturgy, we renew the vows taken at baptism; and "recommit ourselves to love and serve God, one another, and our neighbors in the world." Directory for Worship, W-3.0409. For more on the critical need to link Communion to hunger, see my article "Eucharist and Global Hunger" in *Call to Worship* (December 2022).
33. Sara Miles, *Take This Bread: A Radical Conversion* (New York: Ballantine Books, 2008).
34. Dennis Smith, *From Symposium to Eucharist: The Banquet in the Early Church* (Minneapolis: Fortress Press, 2003). Hal Taussig, *In the Beginning Was the Meal: Social Experimentation and Early Christian Identity* (Minneapolis: Fortress Press, 2009).
35. Andrea Bieler and Luise Schottroff, *The Eucharist: Bread, Bodies, and Resurrection* (Minneapolis: Fortress Press, 2007), 115. Note as well that the passing of a law does not mean that everyone will follow it.
36. One important example of this pattern is outlined in Justin Martyr's *Apology*, which describes the eucharistic service in terms of sharing the food, distributing it to those who are absent, and collecting contributions to provide for orphans, widows, the sick, those in prison, and visiting strangers. See Justin Martyr in Lucian Deiss, *Springtime of the Liturgy: Liturgical Texts of the First Four Centuries*, trans. Matthew O'Connell (Collegeville, MN: Liturgical Press, 1979), 94.
37. St. Lydia's, https://stlydias.org/about/.
38. Thomas O'Loughlin. *The Eucharist: Origins and Contemporary Understandings* (London: Bloomsbury Press, 2015), 88.
39. O'Loughlin, 93.
40. O'Loughlin, 97.
41. Justin Martyr, "Apologia I," in Deiss *Springtime of the Liturgy: Liturgical Texts of the First Four Centuries*, 94.

42. My initial attempt to describe this approach in terms of sacramental ethics: "Doing Justice with a Sacramental Heart," *Hungry Hearts*, 14, no. 3, (2005): 1–10. My trilogy of books grew out of this approach: *Leading from the Table, Leading through the Water,* and *Leading into the World.*
43. See the fascinating work by Richard Burridge, *Holy Communion in Contagious Times: Celebrating the Eucharist in the Everyday and Online Worlds* (Eugene, OR: Cascade Books, 2022).
44. Jon Sobrino, *Jesus the Liberator*, trans. Paul Burns and Francis McDonagh (Maryknoll, NY: Orbis Books, 1993), 204.
45. Victor Codina, "Sacraments," in *Mysterium Liberationis*, 661.
46. Codina, 666–67.
47. Clodovis Boff in Codina: "faced with the poor, human beings are called to love, service, solidarity, and justice. . . . The way to God goes necessarily, for everyone without exception, through human beings—human beings in need, whether their need is of bread or the word."

Chapter 9: The Future of Reformed Worship: Baptism

1. Presbyterian Church (U.S.A.), *Invitation to Christ*, https://www.presbyterianmission.org/wp-content/uploads/Invitation-to-Christ.pdf.
2. In Calvin's Strassburg liturgy, the Decalogue (Ten Commandments) were sung following the assurance of pardon as a way of providing shared guidance on the goal of Christian life.
3. See Galbreath, "Calvin's Use of the Law and Christian Formation," in *Re-Forming the Liturgy: Past, Present, and Future* (Eugene: Cascade Books, 2019), 18–29.
4. BCW, 2018, 21.
5. BCW, 2018, 62–63.
6. BCW, 2018, 404.
7. Only one of these alternative texts (Prayer 4) includes thanksgiving for the gift of water itself. BCW, 2018, 446.
8. BCW, 2018, 828.
9. BCW, 2018, 867.
10. John Hart, *Sacramental Commons: Christian Ecological Ethics* (Lanham, MD: Rowman and Littlefield, 2006), 91.
11. See *Re-Forming the Liturgy*, 13–33.
12. *Didache*, 7, http://www.thedidache.com.
13. Linda Gibler, *From the Beginning to Baptism* (Collegeville, MN: Liturgical Press, 2010), 24.
14. Gibler, *From the Beginning to Baptism*, 24.
15. Larry Rasmussen, *Earth-Honoring Faith: Religious Ethics in a New Key* (Oxford: Oxford University Press, 2013), 282.
16. Gibler, *From the Beginning to Baptism*, 33.
17. Wallace, *When God Was a Bird*, 9.
18. Christine Gudorf in Susan A. Ross, *Extravagant Affections: A Feminist Sacramental Theology* (New York: Continuum Press, 1998), 193.
19. *Book of Common Worship*, 2018, 447. My thanks to Westminster John Knox Press for permission to include this prayer.
20. Directory for Worship, W-3.0401.
21. Directory for Worship, W-3.0407.
22. The Anglican Church of Canada, *Covenant and Care*, https://www.anglican.ca/news/covenant-and-care-a-baptismal-promise-to-safeguard-creation/3006799/.

23. See the service outlined in "An Eco-Liturgical Experiment in Contextuality" in *Re-Forming the Liturgy*, 122–27.
24. Cordina, "Sacraments," in *Mysterium Liberationis*, 670.
25. Cordina, 670.
26. Cordina, 671. It is essential to note how the preferential option for the poor is not exclusionary in orientation. In Jesus Christ, God calls all people and all of creation to participate in the ongoing work of liberation and the in-breaking of the reign of God.
27. Cordina, 670.
28. Alan Kreider, *The Change of Conversion and the Origin of Christendom* (Harrisburg, PA: Trinity Press International, 1999), 5. Kreider highlights this contrast in both the teachings of Justin Martyr and Cyprian
29. Gutiérrez, "Where Will the Poor Sleep?," in *On the Side of the Poor*, 118.
30. Ignacio Ellacuría, "The Church of the Poor, Historical Sacrament of Liberation," in *Mysterium Liberationis*, 549.
31. Jürgen Moltmann, *The Church in the Power of the Holy Spirit: A Contribution to Messianic Ecclesiology*, trans. Margaret Kohl (New York: Harper & Row, Publishers, 1977), 197.
32. Moltmann, 204.
33. Moltmann, 241.
34. *Book of Common Worship*, 2018, 786.
35. Moltmann, *The Church in the Power of the Spirit*, 242.

Bibliography

Webpages are listed separately at the end of the bibliography.

Barth, Karl. *Church Dogmatics.* Vol. 4, *The Doctrine of Reconciliation.* Edited by G. W. Bromiley and T. F. Torrance. Translated by G. W. Bromiley. London: T & T Clark, 2009.
Barth, Karl. *The Teaching of the Church Regarding Baptism.* Translated by Ernest Payne. London: SCM Press, 1948.
Barth, Karl. *The Word of God and Theology.* Translated by Amy Marga. London: T & T Clark, 2011.
Bieler, Andrea, and Luise Schottroff. *The Eucharist: Bread, Bodies, and Resurrection.* Minneapolis: Fortress Press, 2007.
The Book of Church Order of the Presbyterian Church in the United States. Richmond: The General Assembly of the PCUS, 1964.
Book of Common Worship. Louisville, KY: Westminster John Knox Press, 2018.
Book of Common Worship. Philadelphia: The Board of Christian Education of the Presbyterian Church in the United States of America, 1946.
Book of Confessions, Study Edition. Rev. ed. Louisville, KY: Westminster John Knox Press, 2017.
Book of Order, part II of *The Constitution of The United Presbyterian Church in the United States of America.* Philadelphia: The Office of the General Assembly of the UPC in the USA, 1967.
Bradshaw, Paul. *Eucharistic Origins.* Oxford: Oxford University Press, 2004.
Brown, William P. *Deep Calls to Deep: The Psalms in Dialogue amid Disruption.* Nashville: Abingdon Press, 2021.
Burridge, Richard. *Holy Communion in Contagious Times: Celebrating the Eucharist in the Everyday and Online Worlds.* Eugene, OR: Cascade Books, 2022.
Calvin, John. *Institutes of the Christian Religion.* Edited by John McNeill. Translated by Ford Lewis Battles. Philadelphia: Westminster Press, 1960.
Calvin, John. *John 12–21/Acts1–13.* Vol. 1 of *Commentary upon the Acts of the Apostles.* Vol. 18 of *Calvin's Commentary's.* Edited by Henry Beveridge. Translated by Christopher Fetherstone. Grand Rapids: Baker Book House, 1979 (repr.).
Calvin, John. *John Calvin: Writings on Pastoral Piety.* Edited and translated by Elsie McKee. Mahwah, NJ: Paulist Press, 2002.
Calvin, John. *Tracts and Treatises.* Vol 2. Grand Rapids: William B. Eerdmans Publishing Co., 1958.

Calvin, John, and Jacopo Sadoleto. *A Reformation Debate*. Edited by John Olin. New York: Fordham University Press, 2000.

Carvalhaes, Cláudio. *Eucharist and Globalization: Redrawing the Borders of Eucharistic Hospitality*. Eugene, OR: Pickwick Publications, 2013.

Carvalhaes, Cláudio. *Liturgies from Below: 462 Acts of Worship*. Nashville: Abingdon Press, 2020.

Carvalhaes, Cláudio. *Rituals at World's End*. York, PA: Barber's Son Press, 2021.

Codina, Victor. "Sacraments" 654–76. In *Mysterium Liberationis: Fundamental Concepts of Liberation Theology*. Edited by Ignacio Ellacuria, S.J., and Jon Sobrino, S.J. Maryknoll, NY: Orbis Books, 1993.

Cone, James. *A Black Theology of Liberation*. Maryknoll, NY: Orbis Books, 2014.

The Constitution of The United Presbyterian Church in the United States of America. Part II, *Book of Order*. Philadelphia: The Office of the General Assembly of the UPC in the USA, 1967.

Dahill, Lisa. "Lent, Lament, and the River: Interfaith Ritual in the Ashes of the Thomas Fire," *Liturgy* 34, no. 4 (2019): 1–12.

Da Silva Gorgulho, Gilberto. "Biblical Hermeneutics." 123–49. In *Mysterium Liberationis: Fundamental Concepts of Liberation Theology*. Edited by Ignacio Ellacuria, S.J. and Jon Sobrino, S.J. Maryknoll, NY: Orbis Books, 1993.

Deiss, Lucian, C.S. Sr. *Springtime of the Liturgy: Liturgical Texts of the First Four Centuries*. Trans. by Matthew J. O'Connell. Collegeville, MN: The Liturgical Press, 1979.

Dix, Dom Gregory. *The Shape of the Liturgy*. Glasgow: Dacre Press, 1945.

Ellacuría, Ignacio. "The Church of the Poor, Historical Sacrament of Liberation," 543–64. In *Mysterium Liberationis: Fundamental Concepts of Liberation Theology*. Edited by Ignacio Ellacuria, S.J. and Jon Sobrino, S.J. Maryknoll, NY: Orbis Books, 1993.

Elwood, Christopher. *The Body Broken: The Calvinist Doctrine of the Eucharist and the Symbolization of Power in Sixteenth-Century France*. Oxford: Oxford University Press, 1999.

Elwood, Christopher. *A Brief Introduction to John Calvin*. Louisville, KY: Westminster John Knox Press, 2017.

Fiddes, Paul. *Past Event and Present Salvation: The Christian Idea of Atonement*. Louisville, KY: Westminster John Knox Press, 1989.

Galbreath, Paul. "Doing Justice with a Sacramental Heart." *Hungry Hearts* 14, no. 3 (2005): 1–10.

Galbreath, Paul. *Doxology and Theology*. New York: Peter Lang, 2008.

Galbreath, Paul. "An Eco-Liturgical Experiment in Contextuality." 110–27. In *Re-Forming the Liturgy: Past, Present, and Future*. Eugene, OR: Cascade Books, 2019.

Galbreath, Paul. *Elemental: A Journey through Lent with the Earth*. Cleveland, TN: Parsons's Porch Books, 2022.

Galbreath, Paul. "Eucharist and Hunger: Who Gets to Eat?." *Call to Worship* 56, no. 3 (December 2022).

Galbreath, Paul. *Leading from the Table*. Lanham, MD: Rowman and Littlefield Publishers, 2008.

Galbreath, Paul. *Leading through the Water*. Lanham, MD: Rowman and Littlefield Publishers, 2011.

Galbreath, Paul. *Leading into the World*. Lanham, MD: Rowman and Littlefield Publishers, 2015.

Galbreath, Paul. *Re-Forming the Liturgy*. Eugene, OR: Cascades Press, 2019.

Galbreath, Paul. "Tracing the Sacramental Circle." 99–109. In *Re-Forming the Liturgy: Past, Present, and Future*. Eugene, OR: Cascade Books, 2019.

Gerrish, B. A. *Grace and Gratitude: The Eucharistic Theology of John Calvin*. Minneapolis: Fortress Press, 1993.

Gibler, Linda. *From the Beginning to Baptism*. Collegeville, MN: Liturgical Press, 2010.

Grenz, Stanley J. *Primer on Postmodernism*. Grand Rapids, MI: William B. Eerdmans Publishing, 1996.

Gutiérrez, Gustavo. "Option for the Poor," 235–50. In *Mysterium Liberationis: Fundamental Concepts of Liberation Theology*. Edited by Ignacio Ellacuria, S.J., and Jon Sobrino, S.J. Maryknoll, NY: Orbis Books, 1993.

Gutiérrez, Gustavo. "Theology: An Ecclesial Function," 1–10. In Gutiérrez, Gustavo, and Gerhard Ludwig Müller. *On the Side of the Poor*. Maryknoll, NY: Orbis Books, 2015.

Gutiérrez, Gustavo. "Where Will the Poor Sleep?" In *On the Side of the Poor*. Gutiérrez, Gustavo, and Gerhard Ludwig Müller. Maryknoll, NY: Orbis Books, 2015.

Hair, Jesse. "Covenant and Care—a Baptismal Promise to Safeguard Creation." The Anglican Church of Canada, https://www.anglican.ca/news/covenant-and-care-a-baptismal-promise-to-safeguard-creation/3006799/.

Hart, John. *Sacramental Commons: Christian Ecological Ethics*. Lanham, MD: Rowman and Littlefield, 2006.

Hughes, Graham. *Reformed Sacramentality*. Edited and introduced by Stephen Lösel. Collegeville, MN: Liturgical Press, 2017.

Hughes, Graham. *Worship as Meaning: A Liturgical Theology for Late Modernity*. Cambridge: Cambridge University Press, 2003.

Irwin, K. W. "Sacramental Theology." In *New Catholic Encyclopedia*. 2nd ed. Farmington Hills, MI: Thomson/Gale, 2003.

Kim, Grace Ji-Sun. *Embracing the Other: The Transformative Spirit of Love*. Grand Rapids, MI: William B. Eerdmans Publishing Co., 2015.

Kim, Grace Ji-Sun. *Reimagining Spirit: Wind, Breath, and Vibration*. Eugene, OR: Cascade Books, 2019.

Knox, John. *The Liturgy of John Knox*. Glasgow: Thomas D. Morison, 1886.

Kreider, Alan. *The Change of Conversion and the Origin of Christendom*. Harrisburg, PA: Trinity Press International, 1999.

Lathrop, Gordon. *Holy People: A Liturgical Ecclesiology*. Minneapolis, MN: Fortress Press, 1999.

Martyr, Justin. "Apologia I," 89–94. In Deiss, Lucien. *Springtime of the Liturgy: Liturgical Texts of the First Four Centuries*. Translated by Matthew O'Connell. Collegeville, MN: Liturgical Press, 1979.

Matheson, Peter. *The Imaginative World of the Reformation*. Minneapolis: Fortress Press, 2001.

McGowan, Andrew. "'The Firstfruits of God's Creatures': Bread, Eucharist, and the Ancient Economy." In *Full of Your Glory: Liturgy, Cosmos, Creation*. Edited by Teresa Berger. Collegeville, MN: Liturgical Press Academic, 2019.

Migliore, Daniel. *Faith Seeking Understanding*, 3rd Edition. Grand Rapids: William B. Eerdmans Publishing Co., 2014.

Miles, Sara. *Take This Bread: A Radical Conversion*. New York: Ballantine Books, 2008.

Moltmann, Jürgen. *The Church in the Power of the Spirit*. Translated by Margaret Kohl. New York: Harper & Row, Publishers, 1975.

Moore-Keish, Martha. *Do This in Remembrance of Me: A Ritual Approach to Reformed Eucharistic Theology.* Grand Rapids: William B. Eerdmans Publishing Co., 2008.
Moore-Keish, Martha. "Sacraments." In *The Oxford Handbook of Reformed Theology.* Edited by Michael Allen and Scott R. Swain. Oxford: Oxford University Press, 2020.
Nevin, John Williamson. *The Mystical Presence: A Vindication of the Reformed or Calvinistic Doctrine of the Holy Eucharist.* Philadelphia: S. R. Fisher, 1867.
Office of Theology and Worship of the Presbyterian Church (U.S.A.). *Invitation to Christ: A Guide to Sacramental Practices.* Louisville, KY: Presbyterian Church (U.S.A.), 2006, https://www.presbyterianmission.org/wp-content/uploads/Invitation-to-Christ.pdf.
O'Loughlin, Thomas. *The Eucharist: Origins and Contemporary Understandings.* London: Bloomsbury Press, 2015.
Pelikan, Jaroslav. *The Christian Tradition: A History of the Development of Doctrine.* Vol. 4, *Reformation of Church and Dogma (1300–1700).* Chicago: The University of Chicago Press, 1984.
Pelikan, Jaroslav, and Valerie Hotchkiss. *Creeds and Confessions of Faith in the Christian Tradition.* Vol. 2, *Creeds and Confessions of the Reformation Era.* New Haven, CT: Yale University Press, 2003.
Ralston, Joshua. "Rewriting Calvin: Schleiermacher on the Atonement and the Priestly Office of Christ." *Scottish Journal of Theology* 75, no. 2 (May 2022): 89–103.
Rasmussen, Larry. *Earth-Honoring Faith: Religious Ethics in a New Key.* Oxford: Oxford University Press, 2013.
Rogers, Jack. *Presbyterian Creeds: A Guide to the Book of Confessions.* Louisville, KY: Westminster John Knox Press, 1991.
Ross, Susan A. *Extravagant Affections: A Feminist Sacramental Theology.* New York: Continuum Press, 1998.
Sacrosanctum Concilium, no. 51, https://www.vatican.va/archive/hist_councils/ii_vatican_council/documents/vat-ii_const_19631204_sacrosanctum-concilium_en.html.
Schleiermacher, Friedrich. *The Christian Faith.* Translated by Terrence Tice, Catherine Kelsey, and Edwina Lawler. Louisville, KY: Westminster John Knox Press, 2016.
Schleiermacher, Friedrich. *On Religion: Speeches to Its Cultured Despisers.* Translated by John Oman. New York: Harper Torchbooks, 1958.
Smith, Dennis. *From Symposium to Eucharist: The Banquet in the Early Church.* Minneapolis: Fortress Press, 2003.
Sobrino, Jon. *Jesus the Liberator.* Maryknoll, NY: Orbis Books, 1993.
Sobrino, Jon. "Spirituality and the Following of Jesus," 677–701. In *Mysterium Liberationis: Fundamental Concepts of Liberation Theology* Edited by Ignacio Ellacuria, S.J., and Jon Sobrino, S.J. Maryknoll, NY: Orbis Books, 1993.
Spierling, Karen. *Infant Baptism in Reformation Geneva: The Shaping of a Community, 1536–1564.* Louisville, KY: Westminster John Knox Press, 2009.
Támez, Elsa. "Poverty, the Poor, and the Option for the Poor." In *The Option for the Poor in Christian Theology.* Edited by Daniel G. Groody. Notre Dame, IN: University of Notre Dame Press, 2007.
Taussig, Hal. *In the Beginning Was the Meal: Social Experimentation and Early Christian Identity.* Minneapolis: Fortress Press, 2009.
Thompson, Bard. *Liturgies of the Western Church.* Cleveland: Collins World, 1961.

Van Dyk, Leanne. "The Gifts of God for the People of God," 204–20. In *Feminist and Womanist Essays in Reformed Dogmatics*. Louisville, KY: Westminster John Knox Press, 2006.

Vial, Theodore. *Liturgy Wars: Ritual Theory and Protestant Reform in Nineteenth-Century Zurich*. New York: Routledge, 2004.

Vial, Theodore. "Toward a Reformed Theory of Ritual in Modernity." In *Semper Reformanda: John Calvin, Worship, and Reformed Traditions*. Edited by Barbara Pitkin. Göttingen: Vandenhoeck and Ruprecht, 2018.

Von Allmen, Jean-Jacques. *Worship: Its Theology and Practice*. New York: Oxford University Press, 1965.

Wallace, Mark I. *When God Was a Bird: Christianity, Animism, and the Re-enchantment of the World*. New York: Fordham University Press, 2019.

Welch, Claude. *Protestant Thought in the Nineteenth Century*. Vol. 1, *1799–1870*. New Haven, CT: Yale University Press, 1972.

Winter, Harry E. "Presbyterians Pioneer the Vatican II Sunday Lectionary: Three Worship Models Converge." *Call to Worship: Liturgy, Music, Preaching and the Arts* 38 no. 1 (2004–2005): 37–54.

The Worshipbook: Services. Philadelphia: Westminster Press, 1970.

Wright, David F. "Baptism in Scotland." In *Infant Baptism in Historical Perspective*, 301–7. Bletchley: Paternoster, 2007.

The African American Lectionary, http://www.theafricanamericanlectionary.org/about.asp.

The *Didache*, http://www.thedidache.com.

The Directory for the Publick Worship of God, https://www.apuritansmind.com/westminster-standards/directory-of-publick-worship/.

Saint Lydia's, https://stlydias.org/about/.

Season of Creation, https://seasonofcreation.org/about/.

Womanist Wading in the World (Wil Gafney), https://www.wilgafney.com/womens lectionary/.

Working Preacher, https://www.workingpreacher.org/narrative-faq.

The Year D Project, http://theyeardproject.blogspot.com/p/start-here.html.

Printed in the USA
CPSIA information can be obtained
at www.ICGtesting.com
CBHW070758130824
12989CB00002B/4